EMERGENT EVOLUTION

EMERGENT EVOLUTION

THE GIFFORD LECTURES
DELIVERED IN THE UNIVERSITY OF ST. ANDREWS
IN THE YEAR 1922

BY

C. LLOYD MORGAN, F.R.S.

NEW YORK
HENRY HOLT AND COMPANY
LONDON: WILLIAMS AND NORGATE LTD.
1927

B
818
.M67
1927
c.2

83430

PREFACE

HALF a century ago, as years run, a student was called on to take the chair at a dinner in connection with the Royal School of Mines. Members of the staff were present. And the fortunate youth was honoured by the support of Professor Huxley.

"Which of the lines of science you have followed has chiefly engaged your interest?"

Following up the thread of my reply, he drew from me the confession that an interest in philosophy, and in the general scheme of things, lay deeper than my interest in the practical applications of science to what then purported to be my bread-and-butter training. With sympathetic kindliness that soon dispelled my fear of him he led me to speak more freely, to tell him how this came about, what I had read, and so on. That such a man should care to know what Berkeley and Hume had done for me; what I had got from Descartes' Discourse; how I was just then "embrangled in difficulties" over Spinoza; filled me with glad surprise. His comments were so ripe; and they were made to help *me*! "Whatever else you may do," he said, "keep that light burning. But remember that biology has supplied a new and powerful illuminant." Then speeches began. His parting words were: "When you have reached the goal of your course, why not come and spend a year with us at South Kensington ?"

So when I had gained the diploma of which so little direct use was to be made, and when my need of the illuminant, and my lack of intimate acquaintance with the facts on which the new lamp shed light, had been duly impressed on me during a visit to North America and Brazil, I followed his advice, attended his lectures, and worked in his laboratory.

On one of the memorable occasions when he beckoned me to come to his private room he spoke of St. George Mivart's *Genesis of Species*. I had asked him some questions thereon a few days before to which he was then too busy to reply ; and he gave me this opportunity of repeating them. Mivart had said : " If then such innate powers must be attributed to chemical atoms, to mineral species, to gemmules, and to physiological units, it is only reasonable to attribute such to each individual organism " (p. 260). I asked on what grounds this line of approach was unreasonable ; for even then there was lurking within me some touch of " Pelagian heresy " in matters evolutionary. Far from snubbing a youthful heretic he dealt kindly with him. The question, he said, was open to discussion ; but he thought Mivart's position was based on considerations other than scientific. Any analogy between the growth of a crystal and the development of an organism was of very doubtful validity. " Yes, Sir," I said, " save in this that both invite us to distinguish between an internal factor and the incidence of external conditions." He then asked what I understood by " innate powers," saying that for Mivart they were the "substantial forms" of scholastic tradition. I ventured to suggest that the Schoolmen and their modern disciples were trying to explain what men of science must perhaps just accept on the evidence. And I asked whether for "an innate power" in the organism one might substitute what he had taught us to call "an internal metamorphic tendency" which must be "as distinctly recognised as that of an internal conservative tendency" (H.E. ii. p. 116). "Of course you may so long as you regard this merely as an expression of certain facts at present unexplained." I then asked whether it was in this sense one should accept his statement that nature does make leaps (ii. pp. 77, 97) and, if this were so, whether the difference on which Mivart laid so much stress—that between the mental capacities of animals and of men—might not be regarded as a natural leap in evolutionary progress.

This was the point to which I was leading up. I do not clearly recollect all that Huxley said. My notes, written unfortunately not at the time but a year later, give: "Stress on speech and language: no evidence of *jump* either in laryngeal, mouth, or brain structure: child passes from animal stage to man stage *continuously*: neuroses and psychoses."

That which he was chiefly concerned to emphasise in dealing with Mivart was that—whether there were natural leaps or not—there was always a strict correlation of neuroses and psychoses (ii. pp. 158, 164), which must be accepted by science as the natural outcome of the evolution of brain and mind. Believing that he courted rather than resented a frank expression of that which one felt as a difficulty, I asked on what grounds he spoke of neurosis as *antecedent* (i. 238) to psychosis; and why, if they were correlated as concomitant, one might not follow Spinoza in regarding *each* as causal within its attribute, and therefore *both* as playing their parts in natural causation. He was doubtful whether Spinoza's metaphysical treatment was helpful in scientific interpretation, but gave him credit for trying to dig down *more suo* to fundamental issues.

In conclusion, as he answered a knock at the door, he dismissed a mere neophyte with the encouraging words: "You might well make all this a special field of enquiry."

This among other things I have since attempted to do. That the Senatus of the University of St. Andrews should have deemed me worthy to present, as Gifford Lecturer, the conclusions to which I have been led, is an honour of which I am deeply sensible.

The outcome is a constructive scheme which Huxley would not accept—and that upon more counts than one. He was not, however, intolerant of conclusions at variance with his own (though he might feel called on to combat them), if they were honestly come by. And so, bearing tribute to what he did for me fifty years ago and after, I say of him what Professor Alexander has finely said of Spinoza: "A great man does not exist to be followed slavishly, and may be more honoured by divergence than by obedience."

C. LLOYD MORGAN.

BRISTOL, *February* 1923.

CONTENTS

LECTURE	PAGE
I. Emergence	1
II. Mental and Non-Mental	35
III. Relatedness	64
IV. Reference	90
V. Memory	117
VI. Images	143
VII. Towards Reality	173
VIII. Vision and Contact	210
IX. Relativity	243
X. Causation and Causality	274
Appendix: Evolutionary Naturalism	302

WORKS QUOTED, WITH REFERENCE LETTERS

ALEXANDER, S.	Space Time and Deity. 1920	S.T.D.
,,	Spinoza and Time. 1921	Sp.T.
BERGSON, H.	Matter and Memory (Eng. Tr.). 1911	M.M.
,,	Creative Evolution (E. Tr.). 1911	C.E.
,,	Introduction to Metaphysics (E. Tr.). 1913	I.M.
,,	Mind Energy (E. Tr.). 1920	M.E.
BERKELEY, G.	Principles of Human Knowledge. 1710. (2nd Ed., 1734)	P.H.K.
BROAD, C. D.	Perception Physics and Reality. 1914	P.P.R.
CAIRD, E.	Critical Philosophy of Kant. 1889. (2nd Ed., 1909)	C.P.K.
CARR, H. W.	Philosophy of Change. 1914	P.C.
CLIFFORD, W. K.	Lectures and Essays. 1879.	L.E.
DEWEY, J.	How we Think. 1909	H.T.
EINSTEIN, A.	Relativity: the Special and the General Theory (E. Tr.). 1920	T.R.
HALDANE, LORD	Reign of Relativity. 1921	R.R.
HAMILTON, SIR WM.	Lectures on Metaphysics. 1859	L.M.
HUME, D.	Treatise on Human Nature. 1739	T.H.N.
HUXLEY, T.H.	Essays (in nine volumes). 1893-4	H.E.

WORKS QUOTED

JAMES, W.	Meaning of Truth. 1909	M.T.
LAIRD, J.	Study in Realism. 1920	S.R.
LEWES, G. H.	Problems of Life and Mind. 1875	P.L.M.
LOCKE, J.	Essay concerning Human Understanding. 1690	E.H.U.
MACH, E.	Popular Scientific Lectures (E. Tr.). 1893	P.S.L.
MILL, J. S.	System of Logic. 1843	S.L.
POINCARÉ, H.	Science and Hypothesis (E. Tr.). 1905	S.H.
RUSSELL, B.	Principles of Mathematics, 1903	P.M.
,,	Philosophical Essays. 1910	P.E.
,,	Analysis of Mind. 1921	A.M.
,,	Philosophy of Leibniz. 1900	P.L.
,,	Mysticism and Logic. 1918	M.L.
SELLARS, R. W.	Evolutionary Naturalism. 1922.	E.N.
SHERRINGTON, SIR CH.	Integrative Action of the Nervous System. 1906	I.N.S.
SHINN, M.	Biography of a Baby. 1900	B.B.
SPINOZA, B.	Ethics (Elwes Tr. 1884)	Eth.
STOUT, G. F.	Manual of Psychology, 3rd Ed. 1913	M.
WHITEHEAD, A. N.	Concept of Nature. 1920	C.N.
WUNDT, W.	Introduction to Psychology (E. Tr.). 1912	I.P.
	Proceedings of the Aristotelian Society	P.A.S.

LECTURE I. EMERGENCE

I. Emergents and Resultants. II. A Pyramidal Scheme. III. Involution and Dependence. IV. Towards Space-Time. V. Deity.

§ I. *Emergents and Resultants.*

WE live in a world in which there seems to be an orderly sequence of events. It is the business of science, and of a philosophy which keeps in touch with science, to describe the course of events in this or that instance of their occurrence, and to discover the plan on which they proceed. Evolution, in the broad sense of the word, is the name we give to the comprehensive plan of sequence in all natural events.

But the orderly sequence, historically viewed, appears to present, from time to time, something genuinely new. Under what I here call emergent evolution stress is laid on this incoming of the new. Salient examples are afforded in the advent of life, in the advent of mind, and in the advent of reflective thought. But in the physical world emergence is no less exemplified in the advent of each new kind of atom, and of each new kind of molecule. It is beyond the wit of man to number the instances of emergence. But if nothing new emerge—if there be only regrouping of pre-existing events *and nothing more*—then there is no emergent evolution.

The naturalistic contention is that, on the evidence, not only atoms and molecules, but organisms and minds are susceptible of treatment by scientific methods fundamentally of like kind; that all belong to one tissue of events; and that all exemplify one foundational plan. In other words the position is that, in a philosophy based on the procedure sanctioned by progress in scientific research and thought, the advent of novelty of any kind is loyally to be accepted wherever it is found, without invoking any extra-natural Power (Force, Entelechy, Elan, or God) through the efficient Activity of which the observed facts may be explained. The question then arises whether such scientific or naturalistic interpretation suffices, or whether some further supra-naturalistic explanation is admissible at the bar of philosophy, not as superseding but as supplementing the outcome of scientific enquiry. I shall claim that it is admissible, and that there is nothing in emergent evolution, which purports to be strictly naturalistic, that precludes an acknowledgment of God. This implies (1) that a constructive philosophy is more than science, and (2) that such acknowledgment is here to be founded on philosophic considerations only.

The concept of emergence was dealt with (to go no further back) by J. S. Mill in his *Logic* (Bk. III. ch. vi. §2) under the discussion of " heteropathic laws " in causation. The word " emergent," as contrasted with " resultant," was suggested by

G. H. Lewes in his *Problems of Life and Mind* (Vol. II. Prob. V. ch. iii. p. 412). Both adduce examples from chemistry and from physiology; both deal with properties; both distinguish those properties (*a*) which are additive and subtractive only, and predictable, from those (*b*) which are new and unpredictable; both insist on the claim that the latter no less than the former fall under the rubric of uniform causation. A simple and familiar illustration must suffice. When carbon having certain properties combines with sulphur having other properties there is formed, not a mere mixture but a new compound, some of the properties of which are quite different from those of either component. Now the weight of the compound is an additive resultant, the sum of the weights of the components; and this could be predicted before any molecule of carbon-bisulphide had been formed. One could say in advance that if carbon and sulphur shall be found to combine in any ascertainable proportions there will be such and such weight as resultant. But sundry other properties are constitutive emergents which (it is claimed) could not be foretold in advance of any instance of such combination. Of course when one has learnt what emerges in *this* particular instance one may predict what will emerge in *that* like instance under similar circumstances. One has learnt something of the natural plan of emergent evolution.

[Such emergence of the new is now widely accepted where life and mind are concerned. It is a doctrine untiringly advocated by Professor Bergson. Wundt pressed its acceptance under his

" principle of creative resultants " (*i.e.* what we distinguish as emergents) which, he says, " attempts to state the fact that in all psychical combinations the product is not a mere sum of the separate elements . . . but that it represents a new creation." (I.P. p. 164). Browning in *Abt Vogler*, poetically emphasised it in reference to our appreciation of a musical chord.

> And I know not if, save in this, such gift be allowed to man
> That out of three sounds he frame, not a fourth sound, but a star.

By " star " he lays poetic stress on the emergent character of " chordiness " which is something more than the additive resultant of the constituent tones—something genuinely new. If it be given in, or for, our hearing, all we can say is : " Consider and bow the head." That, in some sense, should be our loyal attitude towards all emergents. As Professor Alexander puts it, we must accept them, one and all, " with natural piety."

Professor M'Dougall has analytically distinguished what one may call the constituent notes in the chord of *reverence*. There is an element of tender emotion or love, of fear, suitably defined, of wonder ; there is an attitude of upward regard to some being at a higher level ; and so on. These and the like are the additive notes which are summed up in reverence. But is there not also something more ; something which gives to the additive result its distinctive character of reverence ; something of which we may say : " Consider and bow the head "? If this be so, that which gives to the combination of these several notes its character as a chord is, in our interpretation, an emergent quality.

Browning, be it noted, does not deny the summation of constituent notes in the chord; he asserts that there is more in the chord than can be interpreted as the outcome of summation only. Additive characters, as resultants, may be—I shall accept the hypothesis that they always are—co-existent with constitutive characters, as emergents. There may often be resultants without emergence; but there are no emergents that do not involve resultant effects also. Resultants give quantitative continuity which underlies new constitutive steps in emergence. And the emergent step, though it may seem more or less saltatory, is best regarded as a qualitative change of direction, or critical turning-point, in the course of events. In that sense there is not the discontinuous break of a gap or hiatus. It may be said, then, that through resultants there is continuity in progress; through emergence there is progress in continuity.

Lewes says that the nature of emergent characters can only be learnt by experience of their occurrence; hence they are unpredictable before the event. But it may be urged that this is true of all characters, whether resultant or emergent. Only as the outcome of experience can they be foretold. That, in a sense, is so. The point of emphasis, however, is this. Let there be three successive levels of natural events, A, B, and C. Let there be in B a *kind of relation* which is not present in A; and in C a kind of relation, not yet present in B or in A. If then one lived and gained experience on the B-level, one could not predict the emergent characters of the C-level, because the relations, of which they are the expression, are not yet in being. Nor if one lived on the A-level could one predict the emergent character of *b*-events, because *ex hypothesi*, there are *no such events* as yet in existence. What, it is claimed, one cannot predict, then, is the emergent expression of some new kind of relatedness among pre-existent events. One could not foretell the emergent character of vital events from the fullest possible knowledge of physico-chemical events only, if life be an emergent chord and not merely due to the summation, however complex, of constituent *a*-notes. Such is the hypothesis accepted under emergent evolution.

One does not either deny or ignore the evidence that some additive or resultant characters are, so to speak, discretely incremental. Nor does one deny that only through experience can one learn the incremental order. It seems not improbable that the so-called elements differ by the successive addition of an electron. Up to eight they may be pictured as forming an inner planetary electron, or set of electrons, whirling round a solar nucleus. Further additions are on a wider orbital sphere again up to eight. Beyond that we have a third and yet wider orbital course of the added electrons; and so on. But it seems also that there are certain constitutive or qualitative characters which distinguish instances of $+1, +2, +3, \ldots$ increments in successive orbits. They have certain features in common and form family groups. May one say that in each such family group there is not only an incremental resultant, but also a specific kind of integral relatedness of which the constitutive characters of each member of the group is an emergent expression? If so, we have here an illustration of what is meant by emergent evolution.

In a different field of scientific research much has lately been done to render probable resultant continuity between the not-living and the living. No evolutionist is likely to under-estimate its value. But one may still ask whether there is not at some stage of this process a new emergent character of life, the supervenience of which must be accepted with natural piety and described in suitable terms of vital integration or otherwise. There does seem to be something genuinely new at some stage of the resultant continuity.

And if we follow up the story further, with Dr. E. J. Allen's Presidential Address (Brit. Assoc. Sec. D. 1922), on *The Progression of Life in the Sea* as our guide, while the stress is perhaps on resultant continuity, one asks again and again whether there be not emergence also.

There is one more preliminary matter on which a few words must be said. It is pretty certain that the interpretation of nature I put forward will, in some quarters, be characterised as mechanical and vitiated throughout by an uncritical acceptance of what is sometimes spoken of as " the mechanistic dogma." The odd thing here is that the whole doctrine of emergence is a continued protest against mechanical interpretation, and the very antithesis to one that is mechanistic. It does not interpret life in terms of physics and chemistry. It does not interpret mind in terms of receptor-patterns and neurone-routes. Those who suppose that it does so, wholly misapprehend its purport.

One must, however, in some way characterise what is here to be regarded as the key-note of mechanism. I should characterise it thus: The essential feature of a mechanical—or, if it be preferred, a mechanistic—interpretation is that it is in terms of resultant effects only, calculable by algebraical summation. It ignores the something more that must be accepted as emergent. It regards a chemical compound as only a more complex mechanical mixture, without any new kind of relatedness of its constituents. It regards life as a regrouping of physico-chemical events with no new kind of relatedness expressed in an integration which seems, on the evidence, to mark a new departure in the passage of natural events. Against *such* a mechanical interpretation—*such* a mechanistic dogma—emergent evolution rises in protest. The gist of its contention is that such an interpretation is quite inadequate. Resultants there are; but there is emergence also. Under naturalistic treatment, however, the emergence, in all its ascending grades, is loyally accepted, on the evidence, with natural piety. That it cannot be mechanically interpreted in terms of resultants only, is just that for which it is our aim to contend with reiterated emphasis. But that it can only be explained by invoking some chemical force, some vital élan, some entelechy, in some sense extra-natural, appears to us to be questionable metaphysics. It may be that we have just to accept the newly given facts—*all* the facts as we find them—in the frankly agnostic attitude proper to science. Or it may be that in the acknowledgment of God an ultimate philosophical explanation, supplementary to scientific interpretation, is to be found. That will be the position I shall try to maintain.

§ II. *A Pyramidal Scheme.*

The most resolute attempt to give a philosophic interpretation of nature as a whole, with adequate stress on the concept of emergence, is that of Professor S. Alexander in *Space, Time, and Deity.* In order to get at the very foundation of nature as it now is, he bids us think out of it all that has emerged in the course of evolutionary progress—all that can possibly be excluded short of annihilation. That gives us, as an inexpugnable remainder, a ground plan of ultimate basal events (pure motions) with naught beyond spatio-temporal terms (point-instants) in fluent relations of like order. This he calls space-time, ubiquitous, all-pervasive, and inseparably hyphened. From this first emerged " matter " with its primary, and, at a later stage, its secondary qualities. Here new relations, other than those which are spatio-temporal only, supervene. So far, thus supervenient on spatio-temporal events, we have also physical and chemical events in progressively ascending grades. Later in evolutionary sequence life emerges—a new " quality " of certain material or physico-chemical systems with supervenient vital relations hitherto not in being. Here again there are progressively ascending grades. Then within this organic matrix, or some highly differentiated part thereof, already " qualitied," as he says, by life, there emerges the higher quality of consciousness or mind. Here, once more, there are progressively ascending grades. As mental evolution runs its course, there emerge, at the reflective stage of mind, the " tertiary qualities "—ideals of truth, of beauty, and of the ethically right—having relations of " value." And beyond this, at or near the apex of the evolutionary pyramid of which space-time is the base, the quality of deity—the highest of all—emerges in us the latest products of evolution up to date.

This thumb-nail sketch does scant justice to a picture worked out in elaborate detail on a large canvas. The treatment purports to formulate the whole natural plan of evolution. From all-pervasive space-time emerge in due historical order the inorganic, the organic, and the mental, in all their ascending grades, until the quality of deity is reached in some men.

May I give diagrammatic expression—the simpler and cruder the better—to such a pyramid of emergent evolution ? At its base space-time (S.T.) extends throughout all that is. At its apex, but within it no less than space-time, is deity (D), an emergent quality that characterises only certain persons at the highest and latest stage of evolution along a central line of advance. The narrowing which gives the pyramidal form expresses such a fact as that the range of occurrence of material events as such is more extensive than that of events which are also vital, but is not, in Mr. Alexander's view, co-extensive with the range of space-time. The vertical arrow above N stands for what Mr. Alexander calls *nisus*. He speaks of it as the nisus towards deity.

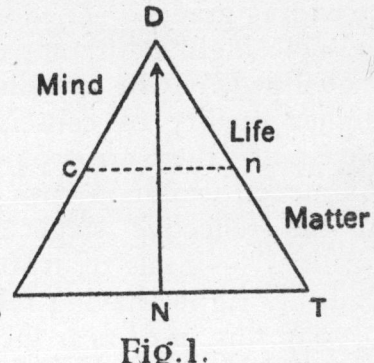

Fig. 1.

Such a diagram—for which Mr. Alexander is nowise responsible—is, so to speak, a synoptic expression, or composite graph, of a vast multitude of individual pyramids—atom-pyramids near the base, molecules a little higher up, yet higher, "things" (*e.g.* crystals), higher still, plants (in which mind is not yet emergent), then animals (with consciousness), and, near the top, our human selves. Classify how you will; but let every individual entity have its appropriate place in the synoptic pyramid. It is intended to embrace all natural entities from atoms—or, for Mr. Alexander, from "point-instants," upwards.

We are not to suppose that this means that an atom develops into a molecule, this into a plastidule (or whatever it may be called at the level of life), and so on. Each higher entity in the ascending series is an emergent "complex" of many entities of lower grades, within which a new kind of relatedness gives integral unity. May one say that each higher com-*plex* takes on the rôle of a *com*-plex in virtue of its integral unity ; and that the higher the status of any given entity along the line of advance, the more do both limbs of the compound word, and the concept it names, get the emphasis indicated by italics.

Since it is pretty sure to be said that to speak of an emergent quality of life savours of vitalism, one should here parenthetically say, with due emphasis, that if vitalism connote anything of the nature of Entelechy or Elan—any insertion into physico-chemical evolution of an alien influence which must be invoked to explain the phenomena of life—then, so far from this being implied, it is explicitly rejected under the concept of emergent evolution. One starts, let us say, with electrons and the like ; one sees in the atom a higher complex ; one sees in the molecule a yet higher complex ; one sees in a quartz-crystal, along its line of advance, a still more complex entity ; and one sees in an organism, along *its* line of advance, an entity with the different kind of complexity spoken of as vital integration. If one talks of vitalism, why not also of crystalism, of moleculism, of atomism ? May it not be better, in this regard, to drop overboard all these *-isms*, and lighten the ship of such encumbrances ; or, at any rate, only to retain " vitalism " to earmark a doctrine which invokes (as emergent evolution does not invoke) the supplementary concept of Entelechy or Elan from some disparate order of being ?

Here, discarding all such *-isms*, we seek to indicate purely naturalistic lines of advance, accepting such new kinds of relatedness as supervene, with natural piety. But assuredly, we are not to suppose that progress along the lines of advance implies that there is in detail no retrogression—no resolution of higher entities into others of a lower status—no degradation or descent within the pyramid. Disintegration or devolution, no less than integration with emergent evolution, has to be reckoned with in the history of natural systems.

One more preliminary question may be put in terms of the diagram—the good of which (such as it is) lies in the questions it provokes. If we acknowledge some Activity of which all pyramidal events are the manifestation, does the diagram suggest that, at this, that, or the other level—this of matter, that of life, the other of mind, and perhaps above all when rational self-consciousness is emergent—there is a special insertion *Ab Extra*? Does it suggest that emergent supervenience is to be explained by Divine (or other) intervention? This is just what the diagram is intended, for, better or worse, to preclude. From the strictly emergent point of view any notion of a so-called " alien influx into nature " is barred. And if we acknowledge Divine Activity, of which for my constructive philosophy emergent evolution is the expression, it is to be conceived as *omnipresent and manifested in every one of the multitudinous entities within the pyramid*. God, if in any, is in all, without distinction of entities.

And if there be no Divine insertion at sporadic points—say at the level of life, of mind in its inception, or of reflective consciousness—there is, assuredly, for us no other kind of insertion. All qualities are emergent *within the pyramid*. Life and mind in no sense act into it, or any part of it, from without—from some disparate order of being.

So far as it expresses, however inadequately, Mr. Alexander's philosophic scheme, the chief difficulties suggested by the diagram arise in connection with the base and the apex of the pyramid, and with regard to the concept of nisus which I have introduced into the diagram because it is, I think, for him a cardinal feature. How he grapples with these difficulties may be learnt from his book, from his subsequent statements in *Mind* (Vol. XXX. N.S. p. 409), and from his recent lecture on *Spinoza and Time*.

A further difficulty centres in the relation of mind to life, and hence in descending order to matter. For mind on the one hand and matter on the other hand, seem to be in some special sense heterogeneous in the very nature of their being. How then, it will certainly be asked, can the one " emerge " from the other?

Yet another difficulty arises when we remember that the diagram purports to be the synoptic expression of a vast number of individual pyramids. Take some two of them—one in which mind is emergent, another, say a quartz-crystal, in which the apex does not rise above the level of matter. How can the former in some sense know (perceive) the latter? As Mr. Alexander might put it: How can the mental as a quality of the one, apprehend the non-mental by which the other is " qualitied " in accordance with its lower evolutionary status? This cognitive problem is central for any philosophy. It will engage much of our attention in all that follows.

§ III. *Involution and Dependence.*

I have so far used the words "higher" and "lower," taking it for granted that their signification would be understood in a general way. On this understanding we might agree that natural events at the level of mind are higher than those at the level of life, and these higher than events at the level of matter. But we must now ask: Higher in what sense? They may be higher in more senses than one. What I here mean, however—as that on which the pyramidal concept is in large measure founded—is higher in a special sense on which a good deal of my treatment will hinge.

When two or more kinds of events, such as I spoke of before as A, B and C, co-exist on one complex system in such wise that the C kind involves the co-existence of B, and B in like manner involves A, whereas the A-kind does not involve the co-existence of B, nor B that of C, we may speak of C, as, in this sense, higher than B, and B than A. Thus, for emergent evolution, conscious events at level C (mind) involve specific physiological events at level B (life), and these involve specific physico-chemical events at level A (matter). No C without B, and no B without A. No mind without life; and no life without "a physical basis."

Note that I use the word "involve." I speak of events at any given level in the pyramid of emergent evolution as "involving" concurrent events at lower levels. Now what emerges at any given level affords an instance of what I speak of as a new kind of relatedness of which there are no instances at lower levels. The world has been successively enriched through the advent of vital and of conscious relations. This we must accept " with natural piety," as Mr. Alexander puts it. If it be found as somehow given, it is to be taken just as we find it.

But when some new kind of relatedness is supervenient (say at the level of life), the way in which the physical events which are involved run their course is different in virtue of its presence—different from what it would have been if life had been absent. If this be so, on the evidence, it too must be accepted with natural piety. It appears to me that, on the evidence, it is so. How, then, shall we give expression to it? I shall say that this new manner in which lower events happen—this touch of novelty in evolutionary advance—*depends on* the new kind of relatedness which is expressed in that which Mr. Alexander speaks of as an emergent quality.

The position then is this: Events of the kind we labelled C *involve* events of the kind we labelled B; and these in turn involve a-events. But in any given concrete case the specific way in which the a-events run their course, then and there, *depends on* the specific presence of some phase of vital B-relatedness; and similarly the specific way in which these b-events run their course—in behaviour for example —depends on such conscious C-relatedness as may be present.

I must beg that this specialised signification attaching to the words " involve " and " depend on," respectively, be steadily borne in mind. I am nowise wedded to this mode of verbal expression;

but I believe that what I seek thus to express is of much importance. At any rate a good deal of that which I shall hereafter say will turn upon it.

Emphasis on " dependence " is no less essential than that on " involution." In a physical system wherein life has emerged, the way things happen is raised to a higher plane. In an organism within which consciousness is emergent a new course of events depends on its presence. In a person in whom reflective thought is emergent behaviour is sustained at a higher level. If the quality of deity be supervenient, the plane of conduct is yet higher. Strike out deity, and conduct is no longer sustained at that level. Strike out reflective consciousness and action is of a lower impulsive order. Strike out all guiding consciousness and behaviour is that appropriate to the level of life. Strike out life and the course of events drops down to the physical level. The new relations emergent at each higher level guide and sustain the course of events distinctive of that level, which in the phraseology I suggest depends on its continued presence. In its absence disintegration ensues.

Let me further illustrate by taking progressive steps in mental evolution on its cognitive side. I shall presently distinguish (c) contemplative thought, (b) naïve perception, and (a) sensory presentation. The evolutionary genesis of contemplative thought involves that which has already been developed at the lower level of naïve perception ; and the genesis of such perception involves, as historically prior, sensory presentation. One cannot have thought unless perception has supplied some of the requisite data; one cannot have perception unless the re-presentative factors thereof have been derived from precedent presentation to sense. So far involution. But, at the level of contemplative thought, *how* perception runs its course depends on the guidance of reflective consciousness, so far as co-existent; and *how* what is given in sensory presentation takes form depends on the guidance of perception, if that level have been reached. One cannot, therefore, accept the old adage: *Nihil in intellectu quod non prius in sensu*; if this means that there is nothing *more* in thought than there is in naïve perception, and nothing *more* in this than is primarily given to sense. Nay, rather, those who may be led to accept emergent evolution will regard this old adage as radically false, just because it takes no account of that emergence on which so much natural progress depends. Leibniz's pregnant rider, *sive intellectus ipse*, receives evolutionary justification though perhaps not in the sense he intended.

§ IV. *Towards Space-time.*

We have now to follow Mr. Alexander downwards towards the space-time base of the pyramid. But we must first clearly grasp his use of the word "quality." He speaks of the emergence of new qualities. He would say that at some stage of inorganic evolution this or that so-called secondary quality, such as colour, emerged; that at some later stage of evolutionary process the quality of life emerged; and yet later the quality of consciousness. I shall often use the word "quality" in this sense.

But my own interpretation runs rather on lines of what I call relatedness. The discussion of relatedness, to which I shall devote the third chapter, requires the consideration of the terms in relation within any given field of relatedness, and of the relations of these terms. Relatedness, in my sense of the word, includes both ; not the terms only ; not the relations only ; for they can never be divorced if my usage of the word " term " be provisionally accepted. I shall speak of the relatedness which obtains wholly within any given system as *intrinsic* ; and I shall distinguish the relatedness of this system to some other system, or systems, as *extrinsic*. A system of intrinsic relatedness I shall provisionally call an entity. In so far as the character of a natural entity is determined by intrinsic relatedness I shall speak of it as a quality which is an expression of that intrinsic relatedness. In so far as the character of a natural entity is determined by extrinsic relatedness to other such entities, I shall speak of it as a property which expresses that extrinsic relatedness (cf. § XXXIII).

On this understanding what is supervenient at any emergent stage of evolutionary progress is a new kind of relatedness—new terms in new relations—hitherto not in being. In virtue of such new kinds of relatedness, not only have natural entities new qualities within their own proper being, but new properties in relation to other entities. The higher entities are not only different in themselves ; but they act and react differently in presence of others. At any given stage of emergent evolution the questions, then, are : What is the new kind of relatedness that supervenes? What are the new terms and what the relations? What intrinsic difference is there in the entity which reaches this higher level, and what difference is there in its extrinsic relatedness to other entities? When, for example, an entity becomes an organism, however lowly in status, what intrinsic difference is supervenient, and what extrinsic difference is there in relation to its " world "? Should it become a higher entity in which conscious relatedness is present in addition to all else that is involved—what difference does this make?

Now in order that there shall be a difference in the course of events the relatedness in question must be what I shall call *effective*. By this I mean that when it is present some change in the existing go of events occurs, which would not occur if it were absent.

I shall have occasion hereafter to urge, as against radical behaviourists, that mental guidance of events counts for progress and betokens a kind of relatedness that is effective. When it is present changes occur which do not occur in its absence. The manner of go in the enriched system is different. That is what I mean by speaking of guidance as dependent on the supervenient kind of relatedness at the level of mind. Passing down a stage I accept with natural piety the evidence that there is more in the events that occur in the living organism than can adequately be interpreted in terms of physics and chemistry, though physico-chemical events are always involved. Changes occur in the organism when vital relatedness is present the like of which

do not occur when life is absent. This relatedness
is therefore effective. Descending from the level
of life to that of matter, no one is likely to deny that
kinds of relatedness of the chemical and physical
orders are severally effective in the sense that the
go of events is different when they are present from
that which obtains in their absence.

Here someone may intervene and ask : Why this
cumbrous and pedantic phraseology ? Why relatedness ? Why not this or that force as the cause of
such and such change in what you call the manner
of go of events ? We are all quite familiar with the
forces of inorganic nature. And we used to be
told by materialists that these are the only forces
and that life, to go no higher, is merely a subtle
re-combination of purely physico-chemical events.
You seemingly have to confess that they were
mistaken ; none the less you shirk the admission
that life is a new and different kind of force.

I seek only to avoid ambiguity. I know well
that physicists speak of the force of cohesion—to
take but one example. But what do they mean ?
Do they mean more, in this or any other example,
than that, given such and such entities that function
as terms in certain describable relations, this or that
change does occur. This, I conceive, and nothing
more than this, is what most modern physicists
mean. But what many who *read about* science
take them to mean is that there is some agency that
makes the entities cohere. This agency it is that
they understand by the force of cohesion. And
then they ask why one presumes to deny that life,
too, is an agency—the vital force which makes

C

organisms live. There is, then, some ambiguity in the word " force." And this I seek to avoid by using the word " relatedness," which is meant to exclude the concept of " agency," or " activity," from any place in scientific interpretation.

On this understanding we distinguish mind, life, and matter. Within each, of course, there are many emergent sub-orders of relatedness. It is for science to work out the details—for psychology, for biology, for chemistry and physics. A constructive philosophy, in dealing with net results only, must accept nothing discrepant with the findings of these departmental branches of science. Nor must it accept anything contradictory to the outcome of modern philosophical criticism of the foundational concepts on which the departmental sciences severally build their superstructures.

The position we have reached, then, is that there are different natural systems to be reckoned with—mind-life-matter systems ; life-matter systems ; and matter systems. At the top-level there are modes of effective relatedness which are not present at the mid-level ; at the mid-level there are modes of relatedness which are not present at the bottom-level.

But is it the bottom-level? Mr. Alexander bids us descend a step lower to space-time. An integral system without mind is life-matter only ; an integral system without life is material only. But lower still is that which, in the absence of matter, is space-time only. In the ascending order of evolutionary progress, space-time has as yet no effective physical relatedness ; matter emerges but has as yet no vital relatedness; life emerges and has this but as yet no mind-relatedness. What then has space-time? It has spatio-temporal relatedness only in a continuum within which point-instants are terms in ever-changing partnership giving pure motion.

One must here ask: (1) Is spatio-temporal relatedness capable of existence apart from any physical events? (2) When it does co-exist with physical events which then become spatial-temporal-and-physical is the spatio-temporal factor as such effective? To the latter question one can give no reply on the basis of *our* criterion. For since spatio-temporal relatedness is ubiquitous and universally present, that criterion of presence or absence ceases to be applicable. Mr. Alexander would, I think, reply to both questions in the affirmative. Space-time is, for him, the primordial base of the pyramid and was existent prior to the emergence of any physical events. And spatio-temporal relatedness is effective at any rate in the sense that it affords the foundational go of the universe through the ceaseless flow of time. The metaphysical grounds of his constructive scheme and its multifarious metaphysical implications are set forth in *Space, Time, and Deity*.

Much more modest is the constructive scheme which the more limited range and penetration of my speculative insight permits me to entertain. I seek in vain for evidence that spatio-temporal relatedness does exist apart from physical events. I can pierce no deeper than events which, in their primordial form are not only spatio-temporal, but physical also. Furthermore, while I acknowledge the flow of physical events, subject always to spatio-temporal relatedness, I doubt whether the concept of the fluency of time, on which so much turns, will stand the test of philosophical criticism. That intrinsic to every minimal physical event, and extrinsic as between such events, there is (*a*) spatial here-there relatedness and that there is (*b*) temporal now-then relatedness—always co-related as inseparably (*ab*)—appears to me to be undeniable; but for the belief that here-there-ness or now-then-ness, severally and *as such*, is effective in determining the course of physical events I find no satisfactory evidence. Fluency there is; but it is the fluency of events in that which is methodologically conceived as a space-time frame.

Metaphysically my modest scheme will not bear comparison with that elaborated with admirable skill by Mr. Alexander, but it is all I have to offer.

How far then can I go towards a basal level of space-time? Only so far as to acknowledge a physical world in which spatio-temporal relatedness is ubiquitous, but as such non-effective. In other words I accept as a going concern such a physical world as may afford a basis for that which has been disclosed in the course of scientific research. But, as I shall have occasion to confess, I regard the independent existence of such a physical world in its own right as not susceptible of proof under rigid philosophical criticism. Hence I accept it under what I speak of as acknowledgment. I accept it, in brief, as part of a constructive scheme of emergent evolution.

Otherwise phrased, a physical world nowise inconsistent with the positive outcome of departmental researches in the several branches of science, on the one hand, and that of a critical philosophy which deals with the foundational concepts in these branches of science, on the other hand—this seems to lie at the base of our pyramid. And if it cannot be established on positive evidence I am content to acknowledge its existence as part of what purports to be a constructive philosophy of emergent evolution. Mr. Alexander goes further.

§ V. *Deity*.

In trying to work up towards deity which, it must be remembered, is an emergent quality of the highest natural systems that we know, *i.e.* some human persons—let us start from Mr. Alexander's space-time. Even at this basal level he speaks of time as the mind of space. He warns us, however, that he does not " mean that time is mind or any lowest degree of mind " (S.T.D. II. p. 44). What then does he mean? He means, I think, that throughout the universe, from base to apex of the pyramid, there are two diverse " attributes," as Spinoza called them, or " aspects," sometimes spoken of as " inner " and " outer." All these words, for lack of better, name a quite unique kind of diversity or duality, which, it is claimed, is inherent in the nature of all events. I shall speak of their inseparable union as " correlation " (cf. Huxley, ii. p. 163) in a sense of the word which includes what Mr. Alexander speaks of as identity (S.T.D. II. p. 5).

Without subscribing to Mr. Alexander's doctrine of time as, in any sense, the mind of space—this my attitude towards spatio-temporal relatedness precludes—I fully accept unrestricted and universal correlation as an acknowledgment—avowedly speculative, and admittedly beyond positive proof (or disproof), but essential to my constructive philosophy of evolution. This means, for me, that there are no physical systems, of integral status, that are not also psychical systems; and no psychical systems that are not also physical systems. All systems of events are in their degree psycho-physical. Both attributes, inseparable in essence, are pervasive throughout the universe of natural entities. This is crudely represented by the dotted line $c\ldots\ldots n$ crossing the diagram on page 11. Every natural entity, say from atom to man, expresses both attributes while still preserving its substantial identity, in some sense of this phrase. The concept is familiar to students of Spinoza, who says in effect that the physical aspect of the correlate constituting the human mind is the body (*Eth.* Pt. ii. Prop. 13), and is careful to add in the *scholium* that this applies " not more to men than to other individual things, all of which, though in different degrees, are animated," *i.e.* " enjoy " in their own fashion the psychical correlate.

I repeat that this is from the nature of things not susceptible of positive proof; but it is also, I urge, beyond disproof.

However we may phrase it, there are two quite different ways in which we human folk are acquainted with psycho-physical events. In one way we are acquainted with their physical nature. In the other way, with their psychical nature. The latter way M. Bergson speaks of as intuition; Mr. Alexander as enjoyment. And this latter way is restricted to each several integral system—to you or me or another.

Now, when we are discussing mind, at its appropriate evolutionary level, we install ourselves in the psychical attribute; and then we acknowledge physical correlates of all mental events in that psychical system. But when we are discussing physical systems, as such, then we acknowledge psychical correlates of the go of events in those systems. We name the level of mind from the point of view of psychical approach, acknowledging (in brackets, so to speak) physical correlates. We name the level of life from the physical approach, acknowledging (in brackets) psychical correlates. And so, too, at the level of matter. Hence our comprehensive scheme runs thus:

C, Mind (with physical correlates).
B, Life (with psychical correlates).
A, Matter (with psychical correlates).

It is at level C that there seems to be positive evidence of *some* correlation. But even here we must confess that there is no positive proof that *all* mental events have such correlates. We therefore accept this under acknowledgment which goes beyond the evidence but is not, we think, contradictory thereto—thus taking up a quite familiar philosophical position. We urge that from the nature of the case we can only " enjoy " such psychical correlates of life and matter as are involved in the whole integral psychical system at our level of mind. With psychical correlates of life at level B only, and of matter at level A only, we can have no direct acquaintance; for we cannot *be* an amoeba at the one level, or a molecule at the other level, so as to be *thus* acquainted with the psychical attribute which it alone can "enjoy."

It need hardly be added that there is no causal relation of the one attribute to the other. To modernise Spinoza : The orderly plan of advance in the psychical attribute is strictly correlated with that in the physical attribute. We have " one and the same thing [evolution], though expressed in different ways " (*Eth.* Pt. II. Prop. vii. cf. *scholium*).

I have departed from my text—Mr. Alexander's treatment—to put the position in my own way and not his. I now return to the text to raise some questions—partly verbal but surely also something more.

Starting with time as, in the sense intended, the mind of space, Mr. Alexander regards each quality in the ascending hierarchy as a higher mind-aspect supervenient in the course of evolutionary progress ; and that which lies below it—that which I speak of as involved—as playing to this mind the part of its body. Thus a secondary quality is, he says, the mind of its primary substrate (S.T.D. II. p. 60) ; life is the mind of physico-chemical events ; consciousness is the mind of the living organism in which it emerges. Furthermore, if I mistake not, each higher quality plays also the part of deity to that which lies below it.

I cannot here follow his lead. At any rate I should put the position differently. The word "mind" seems to be used in at least two senses; (1) as the name of a quality at a distinctively emergent level; (2) to signify the correlate of that which is also a bodily or physical process—such correlate implying substantial identity. If it be used in the former sense it seems inadvisable to apply it to anything other than that distinctive quality. The most that can be said is that life stands to matter in the same kind of relation as mind stands to life. And this, I submit, can be better expressed by saying that life involves a basis of matter just as mind involves a basis of life. The relation common to both is that which I call involution.

And if the word "mind" be used in the latter sense, I should urge that, *qua* correlate, it stands *on the same level* as that with which it is correlated—not above it.

I think, however, that the disagreement here is, at bottom, rather in modes of statement than in principles of interpretation. In any case, what is common to both of us is that hyphening of the two attributes which I speak of as correlation and he as substantial identity.

There is another reason why I think it undesirable to use the word "mind" in the two senses, (1) as a quality that emerges at an assignable level in our hierarchy, and (2) as correlated attribute at *all* levels. It will be urged by many critics of our thesis that *mind does not emerge*. That *is* true of mind (2) as correlate; *that* mind does not emerge. But there are emergent levels of such mind, as correlate ; and it is at an assignable level that mind (2) *does* emerge. It is an emergent quality of the correlated psychical order at an approximately definable stage of evolutionary advance. Hence if we say that mind emerges at this stage, whereas others affirm that mind does not emerge and cannot be treated as emergent, this *may* be because the word " mind " is used in these two different senses.

With regard to deity, towards which we are working up, we must revert to the *nisus*. We have seen that out of one level in the hierarchy of levels a new kind of existence emerges. This fact of progressive emergence is nisus which is, therefore, something more than the *conatus* of Spinoza (cf. § xxiv.). " Thus the nisus of the world is reflected in the transformation of types which takes place, as attested by observation and theory, out of lower to higher levels." And it is shared by everything. Within our reflective consciousness, within the minds of lowly organisms, and even of material things, it " is felt as a nisus towards something unattained " (Sp. T. pp. 72-77).

Here again I have difficulties. First I should say that the nisus towards deity—if deity be a quality supervenient on reflective consciousness—is along *one* quite specific line of advance. Otherwise I fail to see what answer can be given to the question : How do you propose to characterise this quality of deity ? Should it not be susceptible at least of indication if not of definition ? If so we can say : deity is that which is exemplified in this or that person, or group of persons, who attain this emergent level. If *all* lines of advance exemplify a nisus towards deity—then deity must be characterised in some different way—say, that which is higher on any line of advance.

Now I want to lay stress on *one* line of advance and take it quite literally ; and I want to emphasise what it may imply. It seems, as I think on the evidence, that the higher we ascend in the hierarchy —and especially when we reach human persons— the emergent complexity is such that it appears justifiable to say that no two persons are quite alike. Each person is an uniquely individual product along one of very many lines of advance—say Shakespeare, Goethe, Newton, and Darwin. If this be so, the nisus towards deity on its strictly central line should culminate in one unique person, at the very apex of the pyramid. If an impartial historical survey should lead to the conclusion that the nisus towards deity has culminated in one unique individual, there is, so far as I can see, nothing in the naturalistic interpretation of emergent evolution which precludes the acceptance of this conclusion.

Take, however, the view that *all* lines of advance exemplify in some sense a nisus towards deity, and that deity should be defined in such wise as will accord with this view—let us say " something higher as yet unattained "—even so the unattained, as such, seems to imply that which is not yet ; and this, as I think, can only be foreseen, however dimly and vaguely, when the level of conscious mind is attained.

But apart from some matters in which I am led to disagree I fully agree that, along multifarious lines of advance—all no doubt interconnected by branch lines into one system of nature—there is throughout, as net result, an upward and onward progress (notwithstanding many a backslide), which is that which I seek to emphasise under emergent evolution.

We come then finally to the concept of Activity.

An age-long question—not in science but in philosophy—takes on for us a new form. What makes emergents emerge? What directs the course of events in which a salient line is the nisus towards deity? Some may say we know not and cannot know. Others may ask what need there is for a directive Source of emergence. Why should it not proceed without one? Yet others may urge that it is idle to put into an active Source just what is said to come out of it. For if there be less, something remains to be accounted for; and if there be more (*eminenter*, as the Schoolmen said), what evidence thereof is as yet forthcoming?

On the other hand it may be urged that what at the outset I spoke of as the comprehensive plan of sequence in all natural events, is surely of itself sufficient evidence of Purpose; and this implies, it is said, some Mind through whose Activity (I use initial capital letters for concepts of this type), the course of events is directed. We have, however, in this concept of Mind, (3) something different from mind (1) as an emergent quality, as this is different from mind (2) as universal correlate. It is difficult to avoid the use of the word "Mind" in this sense. Perhaps the initial capital may suffice to indicate that it comprises indefinitely more than mind in sense (1); or it may be differentiated as Spirit.

Now apart from correlation, which I accept under what I speak of as acknowledgment, I accept, also under acknowledgment, a physical world existent in its own right quite independently of any human or sub-human mind. Why do I accept this *under acknowledgment*? Because I am not satisfied that its existence can irrefragably be established subject to the search-light of modern philosophical criticism. I admit then that in accepting it I go beyond the positive evidence. But I claim that it embodies nothing that is discrepant with, or contradictory to, that evidence. How, then, do I reach this acknowledged physical world? By following downwards the line of " involution " till I reach what is, for my constructive philosophy, the limiting concept. But if, in like manner, I follow upwards the line of " dependence " I again reach (for my constructive philosophy) a limiting concept—that of ultimate dependence in terms of which the whole course of emergent evolution is explained (not merely interpreted) within one consistent and balanced scheme. This, too, I accept under acknowledgment. It too lies, as I think, beyond proof by the positive evidence that philosophical criticism demands and, within its province, is right in demanding. But is it discrepant with, or contradictory to, any positive evidence that we are bound to accept with natural piety? I think not. And I feel therefore free to urge its legitimacy under acknowledgment. This, for me, leads upwards towards God, as directive Activity within a scheme which aims at constructive consistency.

Much more of course lies behind the scene in this manner disclosed. We must seek the relation of the God thus barely acknowledged to those persons in whom there is some measure of the quality of deity. For Mr. Alexander deity no less than mind (in sense 1) is an emergent quality. He distinguishes between " deity as a quality and God as a being." And he says that " God as actually possessing deity does not exist but is an ideal, is always becoming ; but God as the whole universe tending towards deity does exist " (*Mind*, XXX. p. 428). According to the second part of this statement, with its ring of Spinoza, God, as being, is the nisus of the universe pressing onwards to levels as yet unattained ; or, as I should prefer to say, is the Nisus directive of the course of events. With regard to the first part, the crucial question arises whether, and if so in what sense, such an ideal is veritably Real.

LECTURE II. MENTAL AND NON-MENTAL

VI. Minding and that which is Minded. VII. Presentation, Perception and Contemplation. VIII. Projicient Reference. IX. Phenomenalism. X. Acknowledgment.

§ VI. *Minding and that which is Minded.*

IN the foregoing lecture the notion of a pyramid with ascending levels was put forward. Near its base is a swarm of atoms with relational structure and the quality we may call atomicity. Above this level, atoms combine to form new units, the distinguishing quality of which is molecularity ; higher up, on one line of advance, are, let us say, crystals wherein atoms and molecules are grouped in new relations of which the expression is crystalline form ; on another line of advance are organisms with a different kind of natural relations which give the quality of vitality ; yet higher, a new kind of natural relatedness supervenes and to its expression the word " mentality " may, under safeguard from journalistic abuse, be applied. Vital*ism* and anim*ism* are excluded if they imply the insertion of Entelechy.

Now, Mr. Alexander says that the new quality at each ascending level must be loyally accepted "with natural piety." I accept the phrase. It is softer and less repellent than agnosticism.

For better or worse, while I hold that the proper attitude of naturalism is strictly agnostic, therewith I, for one, cannot rest content. For better or worse, I acknowledge God as the Nisus through whose Activity emergents emerge, and the whole course of emergent evolution is directed. Such is my philosophic creed, supplementary to my scientific policy of interpretation. Beyond philosophy it is not my business to go. I shall have, however, to give some grounds for my creed. But that must come a little later when I have in some measure prepared the way thereto. We have first to tackle the vexed problem of knowledge.

One cannot discuss emergent evolution as a claimant for serious consideration at the bar of philosophy without facing this problem of knowledge—the relation of knowing to that which is thereby known. It is obvious that if we regard knowledge as a practical business transaction, it can have no being in the absence of either contracting party. But does it follow that neither party can have being in other relations than this within the complex business transactions of the world? There is here a parting of the ways. Some say that it does follow—that being and being known are equivalent. This path leads up to objective idealism. "Excepting for knowledge," says Lord Haldane, "nothing has any meaning, and to have no meaning is to be non-existent" (R.R. p. 30). Others say that it does not follow—that being and being known are equivalent only in respect of this special business transaction, and that, important as this is, there are many others. This path leads up to some form of realism—let us say, of current new realism. The issue is cardinal for philosophy. Both idealists and realists—Edward Caird on the one hand and Mr. Alexander on the other hand—may claim the support of evolution as they severally interpret it. What, then, is to be our attitude? It is clear that the issue turns on the status of mind in the progress of events.

We have seen that the word "mind" may be used in three senses: first, as Mind or Spirit in reference to some Activity, for us God; secondly, as a quality emergent at a high level of evolutionary advance; and thirdly, as a psychical attribute that pervades all natural events in universal correlation. In what here follows I use the word in the second of these senses, *i.e.* as an emergent quality of correlates. I must here repeat that only in this sense is the word "emergent" in place or applicable; for Mind as directive of emergent evolution does not emerge; and mind as unrestricted and universal correlate is, in Spinoza's terminology, that "attribute" of the world from which the mind we are now to consider emerges at its level in the hierarchical order. What the criteria of mind in this sense are must be reserved for later discussion.

Let me lead up to the position for emergent evolution. Given a thing on the plane of matter. It may be interpreted as a group of events affording terms in intrinsic relations which give it its own proper qualities—let us say, as a coherent physical entity. It is also in extrinsic relations to other such things which give it its physical properties—its weight, for example. Similarly at a higher level an organism, in virtue of a new kind of intrinsic relatedness, hitherto not emergent, has the quality of life ; its life is within it and extends not beyond the confines of the group of events that it is. But, having this quality, it acts and re-acts differently in its extrinsic relations to other things. I speak of the outcome of this action and re-action to other things which function as terms in extrinsic relations to it, as affording evidence of new properties. Pass now to a yet higher level. Human persons and some animals, in virtue of a supervenient kind of intrinsic relatedness, have, under correlation, the quality of consciousness. This consciousness is within the person or the animal and extends not beyond the confines of the entity thus " qualitied." But that which has this quality acts and re-acts differently to other entities with which it is in extrinsic relations.

Thus far there is likeness in principle with regard to what goes on at these three ascending levels. But at the upper level there seems to be a quite new kind of extrinsic relation—that which we speak of as cognitive—that which we regard as one of the distinguishing features of mind. The situation seems to be unique. Consciousness as supervenient is a late product of emergent evolution. But when it comes—at any rate, when it reaches the reflective level in us—we can contemplate what goes on at all lower levels. We can have " in mind," as we say, chemical and physical events at the base of our pyramid. And unless they be in some fashion " in mind " how can we have knowledge of them as precedent stages of emergent evolution?

Now I take it that from the emergent standpoint, with which we are concerned, we must accept this situation with natural piety. Cognitive relatedness just emerges, as something genuinely new, at a critical stage of evolutionary advance. That, however, does not preclude—nay, rather, it imperatively demands from us as evolutionists a resolute attempt to analyse the situation and to trace, if possible, subsidiary stages of emergence, on the understanding that, in evolutionary progress, there is never any breach of continuity in the sense of a gap or hiatus.

It is part of the business of analysis to distinguish factors which are inseparable. In a well-known passage (P.H.K. § 49), Berkeley distinguished that which is in mind " by way of attribute " from that which is in mind " by way of idea." The former I shall speak of as mind*ing*; the latter as that which is mind*ed*. That which is minded always implies minding; and the more highly differentiated forms of minding imply something that is definitely minded. Thus perceiving implies something perceived; remembering, something remembered; thinking, something thought of; believing, something believed; and so on through a long list.

I spoke of the more highly differentiated forms of minding. I must add, parenthetically, that this differentiation is subject to the fluency of mental process within which there are no hard-and-fast lines of division or partition. As will be seen in its due place, I fully subscribe to M. Bergson's doctrine of mergency and interpenetration as applicable to mental process as such.

The distinction between what I call the *-ing* and the *-ed* may be put in another way. One may be said to be conscious *in* perceiving, remembering, and at large, minding; that which is perceived, remembered, believed or minded, is what we are conscious *of*. One is conscious *in* attending to the rhythm or the thought of a poem; one is conscious *of* that to which one so attends. I am well aware that the expression " conscious of " has not always this signification. It suffices to make clear the usage I accept.

Mr. Alexander emphasises the distinction by naming that which is, or may be, correlative to minding, " non-mental," or, at any rate, as including a non-mental factor. I cannot here follow his lead, because I shall need the word " non-mental " for use in what is for me a different sense. His meaning, however, is clear. When one sees a ruby, seeing is a mental process in which one is conscious; the ruby that one sees is obviously not in like fashion a mental process. Mr. Alexander names it the non-mental thing of which, as I put it, one is then and there conscious in the business transaction of knowing. But if I picture the Corcovado rising steeply beyond the waters of Rio bay, is that mental? The picturing in the mind's eye is a mental process, but that which is pictured in imagery is not mental in the same sense. What is not mental in this sense he calls non-mental. I speak of it as *objective*.

A wider issue is thus raised. Are we to include

" in mind " processes of minding only, or also that which is objectively minded ? So long as we are careful to distinguish the *-ed* from the *-ing* it is better, I think, to include both. This I shall do. On these terms, what is given even in naïve perception is, *qua* minded, no less mental than is the process of minding. We have, therefore, at present, no concern with anything non-mental if we take this to signify " having existence or subsistence independently of minding," on the part of some person.

§ VII. *Presentation, Perception and Contemplation.*

Thus far we have distinguished minding and that which is objectively minded in the most comprehensive sense. We must now distinguish successive levels of that which is in mind, either by way of attribute or by way of idea. It will be convenient to take the former for granted so as to lay stress on the latter, *i.e.* the minded.

At or near the foundations of mental life in its cognitive regard is that which I shall speak of as " given in presentation." By this I mean sensory presentation, *i.e.* a pattern of sensory data. We are to take the expression " given in presentation " as naming what seems to be a distinguishable class of data. We are not considering what function a presentation performs in the mental life. And we are not as yet asking by what these data are given. Berkeley said that they are directly given by God. Mr. Alexander says that they are given by a non-mental world in which colours, and scents, and sounds too, I suppose, are emergent qualities. I may believe that all that is here given is so given by some purely physical influence advenient from some external material source. We are not yet concerned with any of these views. I am, however, concerned to state distinctly that a sense-datum is not, for my interpretation, a gift *until it is received*, and that the person, as recipient, only has it when it reaches him.

A second class of data which we can often distinguish from the first—though, perhaps, not always, and sometimes with difficulty—comprises those which are " revived in memory " as we say. Of these again we do not now ask by what they are given, though it may be, as Mr. Bertrand Russell urges, that they owe their distinctive character to the special manner of their causation (cf. § XLVII.). They seem to be somehow copies of those that are members of the first class. In crude analogy they are gifts which have been banked, the equivalent value of which may be drawn on occasion. I shall speak of them as " given in re-presentation." All imagery, as such, is re-presentative. These second-hand data come too in patterns. That which is given in re-presentation, no less than that which is given in presentation, is particular in the sense that it is given in some form or pattern then and there existent as actually minded.

But data of both classes may so combine as to constitute one pattern in which the constituents are some of them given in presentation and others given in re-presentation. I shall speak of such a pattern as " given in perception."

MENTAL AND NON-MENTAL

Thus far, then, we have in analytic distinction :

(i) What is given in presentation ;
(ii) What is given in re-presentation ; and
(iii) What is given in perception,

where presentative and re-presentative data are combined in some particular and existent pattern.

But, in us, at any rate, universal plans no less than particular instances are sometimes minded and thus become objectively mental. How they come to be so minded is another question, and one of considerable difficulty. I seek at present only to name and to classify what seems to be there and not to ask how it got there. I submit that plans of events of which particular events are conceived as instances are there, and are frankly objective as minded. It seems that a pattern may acquire a new character as minded—that of being an instance of a plan that is universal in the sense that it is one of which there are (were and will be) other such instances. One may speak of that which is thus minded as " given in conception," and of the data as thereby conceptualised. Or one may speak of that which is thus minded as " given in contemplation." I here use the word " contemplation " in a restricted sense as tacitly qualified by the word " reflective," and not in the much wider sense in which Mr. Alexander uses it.

Now with us human folk there is probably little that is cognitively minded which is not in some measure conceptualised. Any given presentation is not only incorporated in a partly re-presentative pattern and thus has meaning (perceptual), but is interpreted as an instance of some plan of which there are other instances, and thus has significance (conceptual) for our thought—thus comes to be *known* in the reflective sense of the word. This is commonly so in daily life where nearly everything that we see is taken as an instance of a class, built to a plan, and commonly bearing a name. Hence, for us, in so far as we are reflective persons, what we call an object is generally a conceptualised object.

I cannot stay to consider how far this is accordant with Professor Whitehead's very interesting and valuable doctrine of " objects " (C.N. ch. vii.). For him " objects are elements in Nature which do not pass " (p. 143)—instances of which can be " again " and hence can be " recognised " on their recurrence. Such recognition (recognising) is clearly on the plane of mind. Mr. Whitehead uses the word " ingression " to denote the relation of " objects " which do not pass to events which are in passage. He speaks, however, of " ingression into nature "—nature being for him, as I understand, distinctively non-mental. I confess that I do not clearly understand what this " into " implies on Mr. Whitehead's scheme of interpretation, or whence the object is ingredient into nature as he defines nature. But this may be my fault. May I be allowed to use the word " ingredient " for the plan, as such, which is in my sense objective to contemplation as universal and timeless, as contrasted with timeful events in passage ; and to use it thus without prejudice to its being also constitutive of non-mental nature in its own right, *i.e.* independently of contemplation ?

MENTAL AND NON-MENTAL

To our data under (*a*) presentation, and (*b*) perception, we have now to add those afforded in (*c*) contemplation. It is unnecessary again to advert (cf. § III.) to the involution and dependence exemplified in these ascending stages of evolutionary progress. In what follows reflective contemplation (*c*) will be, for the most part, taken for granted so as to concentrate attention on (*a*) and (*b*).

§ VIII. *Projicient Reference.*

It is open to question whether what is given in presentation or gotten through bare sensory acquaintance, should, in strictness, be regarded as cognitive, or whether it does not only afford the requisite data on which subsequent cognition is founded. I take the latter view.

More to the purpose just now is the prior enquiry whether, even in sensory presentation, there are not distinguishable levels. Those who, in their interpretation, follow lines of emergent evolution, urge that we must approach such an enquiry through a preliminary consideration of the processes that are involved at the level of life, having regard also to the events which these processes involve on the plane of matter.

At the level of life, in multicellular organisms where differentiation and integration have reached a fairly advanced stage, sensory presentation involves the stimulation of a pattern of *receptors*. In relation to what we call the external world, presumably the earliest receptor-patterns were those of relatively passive touch gotten (long prior to what we speak of as manipulation) through direct contact with the surface on which the organism rested or moved. I do not suggest that there was, even then, no stimulation through radiant influence. But as yet it gave only a vague and diffused presentation. Far later in evolutionary progress was there such differentiation of retinal receptors and of the requisite ancillary structures—the dioptric or instrumental parts of the eye—as to give rise to the definite receptor-patterns involved in vision—in us binocular. Visual presentation, and the elaborate structural provision for its occurrence is, from the evolutionary point of view, very late in development. It involves what Sir Charles Sherrington names " distance-receptors," and a very complex " mechanism " for focussing an " image " of that physical thing which lies at a distance.

One can well understand how, in pre-evolutionary days, what seems to be so directly given in vision was taken as primary and typical. But an evolutionist finds it difficult to understand how some new-realists can, as it seems, regard as the chief exemplar of " direct apprehension " in the sense in which Dr. G. E. Moore uses this expression (P.A.S. 1913-4, p. 360), that which, so late in time, comes through vision, the most highly elaborated of all our senses, involving the most complex physiological and chemical changes, giving to the world (or, as they say, taking from it) its wealth of colour and much else, and yet, perhaps, of all avenues of perception, the most liable to the illusions of appearance, the very last whose delivery is safely to be taken at its face value.

This may seem to be a severe indictment of vision

MENTAL AND NON-MENTAL

which, if it be of all senses the most liable to illusion, is also of all senses the richest, the most delicate and the most refined. But may it not be both? The evolutionist must take the facts as he finds them. He finds that the objective world in which we live is, *qua* minded, the outcome of a prolonged evolutionary process in which vision has come to play the leading rôle. He finds that, for all its richness, delicacy and refinement, it is conspicuously subject to error if it be not co-related with other modes of sensory experience, especially that of contact-treatment founded on the more primitive data of touch supplemented by manipulation. He seeks to interpret what he finds. There is surely here no indictment of vision. If indictment there be it is that of the hypothesis that, from the evolutionary point of view, vision can adequately be interpreted in terms of " direct apprehension."

Of course, we adult folk have acquired, quite unreflectively, a serviceable acquaintance with objects of vision which common-sense may wisely take *as if* it were the outcome of an " intuitive act " of direct apprehension. But part of the business of philosophy is to criticise such naïve acceptance. And, as I read the story, a criticism based on detailed scientific research has conclusively shown that acquaintance with objects of vision, so far from being something quite simple—something to be naïvely taken at its face value,—is prodigiously complex, the outcome of a prolonged evolutionary process, and only attained in our own period of infancy by gradual steps of which, as such, no detailed trace remains in our personal memory.

It will, however, be said that no one questions the evolutionary history of the complex mechanism of vision. But this is wholly instrumental. It is analogous to some elaborate apparatus which enables us to apprehend ; the apprehension itself is simple and direct. If this be said, I must reply that this does not take the evolution of mind seriously. Nor as I think does it accord with the outcome of laboratory research. It comes pretty much to this : What is minded in vision can only be so minded when the bodily instrument reaches a certain stage of evolution. But the minding in direct apprehension has not been subject to a like evolutionary process. *That* I speak of as not taking the evolution of mind seriously. My contention is that what is objectively minded in vision is a product of mental evolution no less complex than—nay, only the correlated aspect of—that which is involved in the bodily organs which are concerned in and subserve vision—including, of course, the whole retino-cerebral system. And this applies just as much to seeing as to that which is seen. In no sense is the mind merely a spectator, viewing things as they are in themselves through a highly evolved instrument. It is a participator, in accordance with its evolutionary status, in making the objective world what it is. Here I am at one with idealists, though my line of approach is different from theirs.

I have taken the contact-pattern of touch, on the one hand, and the distance-receptor-pattern of vision, on the other hand, as in their origin, *qua* patterns, exemplifying perhaps the lowest and perhaps the highest evolutionary provision on the

MENTAL AND NON-MENTAL

plane of life for sensory presentations as correlates of certain physiological processes which are entailed by their stimulation. The biologist has taught us how much more is entailed under vision than under direct contact. Reference to an external world, as common-sense folk are wont to regard it, can hardly be said to have begun, at any rate, must have been at quite an incipient stage—before the differentiation of distance-receptors—those concerned in the reception of radiant influence (light and heat), of sound, and of odours—had reached a comparatively high level ; and the highest level attained is that in the life-processes concerned in vision. Sir Charles Sherrington has shown how, around these distance-receptors the brain has been evolved (I.N.S. p. 325). And, turning to the psychical aspect where, as I put it, consciousness is supervenient on life, he urges that perceptual reference is always, where distance-receptors are involved, *projicient*.

In adopting Sir Charles Sherrington's word " projicience," I take leave in some measure to adapt it to the purpose of my own interpretation, and, so far as that is concerned, I have no right to claim the support of his authority. It should be distinctly understood, therefore, that I make no such claim.

The word " projection " is commonly used for outward reference of objects to positions along the line of vision. Such outward reference is implied in my use of the word " projicience." But it is to imply far more than this. All the objective characters with which a thing is clothed—including but nowise restricted to, its " out-thereness "—are projicient in so far as they are the outcome, however indirect or mediate, of the stimulation of the distance-receptors of the retina. The hardness, coldness, and slipperiness of a piece of ice; the taste and colour of a strawberry; the beauty of a landscape or of the rainbow which overarches part of it; these are projicient properties *referred to* the several objects of vision when we see them. Nay more; extravagant as it may seem, even the name of an object may, subject to suitable safeguards, be said to be projicient. It is assuredly used in reference to the object—attaches to it, as we say, and as the child naïvely believes—though it is nowise an intrinsic quality of the thing. And if the name be not so referred, our talk is in large measure aimless. All of these as minded are in mind. They are conscious correlates of what occurs, on the plane of life, *within the person*—within that entity which is both body and mind. But, as minded, they are projiciently referred to the objects of which we are conscious. Hence the importance of that " reference " which will be more fully considered in the fourth lecture.

My doctrine is that all that is minded is within us, and founded primarily on the correlated outcome of receptor-patterns; that there are physical things existent in their own right outside us in a non-mental world; and that the properties which render them objective in mind are projiciently referred to these things.

On my view the mind is captain in the conning-tower of the bodily ship. It knows only such messages as come in from the world of battle around the ship. And the mind never gets outside its conning-tower of vision save through projicience. The person, however, acts on the basis of messages received within the mind ; on such action—such practical behaviour—mental projicience is biologically founded. It works on the whole most admirably as the outcome of a long and searching discipline, through trial and error, where, in the course of evolutionary history the penalty of grave error has been elimination.

Such, in brief, is my doctrine. For long I accepted the widely current view that direct apprehension is an inalienable prerogative of mind—something to be postulated *ab initio*. By slow degrees I came to realise that the genesis of apprehension is a problem—and a very difficult problem—which has to be solved. I could no longer accept—as I was bidden to do—direct apprehension as something that we must assume to be part of the very nature of mind from the outset—something which if it were not there from the first could never get there at last—and I therefore felt bound to tackle, as best I could, an evolutionary problem bristling with subtle difficulties. The concept of projicience is the result—to be tried out like any other hypothesis of the genetic order.

I can, however, at present barely indicate a method of treatment to be more fully developed at a later stage of my discussion of emergent evolution. I may, perhaps, so far anticipate now what will then be said (§ xxxvi.) as to distinguish (i) *advenient* physical influence from (ii) *projicient* reference, and to add that between the one and the other there is (iii) a complexly integrated system of *intervenient* processes on the intermediate plane of life. These intervenient life-processes are involved in all projicient reference ; they occur within the organism ; they are the intrinsic physical and physiological attribute of events which in their psychical attribute have the quality of consciousness.

Within us (I repeat for the sake of emphasis) this consciousness is supervenient. It is a quality of the person as correlated mind and body. How then can it reach out spatially and "in time" to the world around ? Does it reach out to grasp what is already there ? Take colour, for example—colour as such. Is it there, in the strawberry or the ruby as a thing for our *taking* by " direct apprehension " ; or is it there in the object through our *giving* by projicient reference ? We are again at a parting of the ways. New realists take one way. I take the other. I shall try to maintain an old position, and to support it perhaps in a new way. Admittedly advenient to us is electro-magnetic influence ; but colour is referred to the thing through projicience.

Assuming that one may be able to make good this position, we have to combine in one synthesis the joint outcome of advenient physical influence from the thing, and projicient psychical reference to the object. In what we commonly call an object of vision, say a ruby, both are in some way thus subtly combined. There is a centre from which there is advenient physical influence ; but it is also for perceptual experience the centre to which there is projicient reference. I speak of the centre from which physical influence comes as the non-mental

MENTAL AND NON-MENTAL

thing ; and of the centre to which there is projicient reference as the object—meaning that which is objectively minded. In the daily life of animals and men, at the level of perception, the two centres normally coincide. On purely pragmatic grounds it is essential that they should approximately do so. For behaviour in large measure depends on projicient reference ; and if such reference be not normally focussed on the thing from which physical influence comes, action with regard thereto must go astray.

But the two centres may not coincide. Owing to atmospheric and other refraction, or owing to reflection from some mirror-surface, the place of projicient reference may differ more or less widely from that which is occupied by the physical thing. I shall call the place *at* which, as I acknowledge, a physical thing really is (its position in the non-mental world of such things) the *assigned place* ; and I shall speak of the place *to* which the object given in perception is projiciently referred, as the *place of location*. These two places need not, and often do not, coincide. Nor need the " real time " of occurrence be the same as the " apparent time " of projective reference (cf. § XLII.).

§ IX. *Phenomenalism.*

It is under the predominance of projicient reference that the object, as minded, takes form in the course of individual experience. Even contact-data, in their re-presentative form under revival in perception, are projiciently referred to the thing which, as we say, looks hard and rough. And since projicient reference, predominantly visual, is that on which the guidance of behaviour so largely depends, it is around the data afforded by these distance-receptors that (long before the stage of logical treatment is reached under reflection) all other sensory data cluster in the process by which objects are progressively constructed.

Of this process a seemingly paradoxical feature is, that what comes so late in evolutionary genesis in the animal kingdom, comes first in the perceptual development of the child. At any rate, what impressed Miss Milicent Shinn in the careful observations on which she founded " The Biography of a Baby " (and has no less impressed others), is that, at the outset of mental development, vision takes the lead. " Out of the new-born baby's dim life of passivity the first path was that of vision " (p. 58). " It is plain that the eyes led in the development of the psychic life " (p. 74). But it came in progressive stages indicated by Miss Shinn with, I think, substantial accuracy. Not till the child was eight weeks old was there presumptive evidence of adjustment of the mechanism of vision for binocular focussing of objects at different distances (p. 93). Whether we speak of " direct apprehension " or of " projicient reference " it is, for all its seeming simplicity in later life, a very complex business acquired piecemeal by successive steps which may analytically be distinguished, subject throughout to prior integration involved on the plane of life.

Paradoxical as this visual lead may appear—with its seeming inversion of the order of racial and

MENTAL AND NON-MENTAL

individual progress—should it on further consideration cause surprise? In what does vision take the lead? Not assuredly in sensory presentation as such. Retinal patterns certainly do not precede many other kinds of receptor-patterns—those of passive touch, for example. In what, then? In perception having reference to an external world. The lead of vision is a referential lead into a world of appearances to which behaviour must conform. And the provision for that lead is afforded by those distance-receptors which, in the course of evolution, have proved the fittest to subserve that end. If, as Sir Charles Sherrington teaches, the brain be moulded on the distance-receptors ; if in correlation with this brain-development, there be evolution of mind ; if it be through projicience that the external world is rendered objective as minded ; is it matter of surprise that the evolutionary outcome has been that the eye takes the lead in " the development of the psychic life " in the child—the psychic life of perception ; and that around visual nuclei the experience of an external world gained through other senses progressively clusters in the process of object-construction?

On this clustering of sensory data, primarily given piecemeal in presentation, much stress is laid, and as I think rightly laid, by new-realists of the phenomenalist school. That entity, they say, which we speak of as directly apprehended through our several channels of sense is, from the strictly logical point of view, a construct—a word I ventured to use in this connection more than thirty years ago. The whole set of appearances which go together to form what we call a ruby may be regarded as actually *being* the ruby (cf. Russell, A.M. p. 98). That is what the object is " known as," in Shadworth Hodgson's favourite phrase. What more do we require ? What need is there for a so-called " real ruby " which is supposed to present the appearances, if the set of appearances, taken together as logical construct, give us all that we want. We live in a world of phenomena, and if we are to regard, as they say we should, the philosophy which deals comprehensively with that world, as a branch of scientific enquiry, we must steadily and consistently refuse to go beyond the evidence. Of physical things which our forefathers invented to support, or present, or give, the appearances, there is no shadow of evidence ; and science can, with suitable ingenuity, get along perfectly well without them. " From the beginning," says Professor Nunn, " new-realists would have nothing to do with the notion that sensations are mental events caused by ' physical objects,' but (like Einstein) declared that physical objects are but syntheses of, or constructs from, sense-data ... or ' events ' belonging to a single historical series " (P.A.S. 1921-2, p. 128). The most that can be said for their independence is that these events, as appearances, do hang together in orderly ways. But that is just an inalienable character of these appearances ; it is a feature of the phenomenal world with which we must reckon, as we must reckon with all other features which are in the evidence.

The gist of the contention is that the physical thing as an independent entity with its own space-time-event relatedness is an unwarrantable assumption, not susceptible of proof, and unnecessary, since science can get along without it. The logical construct gives us all we want. A crucial question then is: "Does it give us all we want?" On purely pragmatic grounds, Mr. Russell, avowedly "yielding to prejudice," wants something more, and accepts a belief in the existence of things outside his own biography (A.M. p. 133).

Outside his own biography. An odd thing about certain phenomena with which, say, half-a-dozen people may be directly acquainted in sensory fashion, is that they are common to all of the half-dozen, though no doubt with some difference in each case. They are public. " Confining ourselves, for the present, to sensations, we find," says Mr. Russell, " that there are different degrees of publicity attaching to different sorts of sensations. If you feel a toothache when other people in the room do not, you are in no way surprised; but if you hear a clap of thunder when they do not, you begin to be alarmed as to your mental condition. Sight and hearing are the most public of the senses; smell only a trifle less so; touch again a trifle less. . . . But when we pass to bodily sensations—headache, hunger, fatigue, and so on—we get quite away from publicity " (A.M. p. 118). Much here turns on definition. I think, however, that Mr. Russell might agree that, in this context, all the sensations belong (though they may not belong only) to a personal biography. They are his, or mine, or someone's. It is in what I speak of as their objective reference that they are differentiated as he suggests.

This *reference* may be public, or common to a number of persons, as in vision ; it may be private, *i.e.* to one's own body, as in toothache ; it may be either, or both, in touch. The evolutionary difference for the biologist lies in the kind of receptor-pattern involved in different kinds of sensory experience. Broadly speaking, publicity is a function of projicient reference, and involves distance receptors.

§ X. *Acknowledgment.*

David Hume, prince of phenomenalists, roundly asserted that " we never really advance a step beyond ourselves, nor can conceive any kind of existence but those perceptions which have appeared in that narrow compass (T.H.N. Bk. I. Part ii. § 6). Translate this into terms of personal biography. It may mean the history of events which Hume's predecessor spoke of as " in mind by way of attribute," *i.e.* it may in my usage be restricted to minding. Let us, however, include in the personal biography that *of* which, as minded, the person in question has experience—much of it in some way stored if you will. Let us include, in other words, all appearances given in sensory acquaintance with our external world. As I have insisted with perhaps wearisome reiteration, all this is within the person ; and what is involved on the plane of life is no less within the organism. They exist only within " that narrow compass." That is where Hume was right.

Now, Mr. Russell urges that " whatever lies outside my personal biography must be regarded, theoretically, as hypothesis. . . . Belief in the exist-

MENTAL AND NON-MENTAL

ence of things outside my own biography exists antecedently to evidence, and can only be destroyed, if at all, by a long course of philosophical doubt. For purposes of science, it is justified practically by the simplification it introduces into the laws of physics. But from the standpoint of theoretical logic it must be regarded as a prejudice, not as a well-grounded theory" (pp. 132-3).

Now for better or worse my notion of philosophy is that, while it involves the contributions of science in all departments, it should seek to express a constructive scheme of the world—a consistent scheme which is conceived at a level of reflective thought that supplements, though it does not supersede, science. There must be nothing in this scheme which is discrepant with science; but, on this understanding, there may be constitutive features which complete the otherwise incomplete delivery of strictly scientific thought. That, I think, has always been the aim of philosophy. It will, I feel sure, continue to be its aim. It seeks to develop a constructive creed and not only a working policy.

In any case, I want to nail my colours to the mast. In credal terms, I believe in a physical world and in systems of events from which there is what I have called advenient influence. But, with Mr. Russell and Mr. Nunn, I question whether the existence of such a physical world is susceptible of proof. I use, therefore, the word "acknowledgment" for the credal acceptance of a physical world, existent in its own right, independently of any sensory acquaintance therewith. This world, or any "thing" therein, is beyond appearance; it is that to which appearances are projiciently referred. It is the skeleton which we clothe with the flesh of objective experience. This clothing with which I endue it is part of my personal biography, within me ; but the skeleton is there to be clothed. That is not to be found " in this narrow compass."

Working downwards, then, in our pyramid of emergent evolution, the ultimate basis under such acknowledgment is a world of purely physical events (and their correlates) in changing spatial and temporal relatedness. On this all the emergent part of the pyramid is built up in an order of ascending levels, each one of which involves those that lie below it. Here, therefore, the physical world that is acknowledged is frankly materialistic.

But, as I contend, the concept of involution must, on the evidence, be supplemented by a concept of dependence. At any given level the manner in which natural events run their course depends on the kind of relatedness supervenient at that level. Thus the way in which the constituents of that complex physical entity we call a crystal glide to their places without gain or loss of energy, depends on that specific kind of relatedness which obtains in the specific kind of crystal. The changes which occur during karyokinesis, while they involve physico-chemical processes, depend on the presence of vital relatedness. In what is now called the " conditioned response " we seem to have the critical turning-point where the advent of the most primitive form of conscious guidance appears in the evidence. Where fully reflective consciousness is supervenient, at a far higher emergent level, we have the guidance of mind in human events. The development of the University of St. Andrews has been dependent on, and still depends on, those higher kinds of relatedness which are the outcome of mental evolution. If deity be an emergent quality, how a man lives depends on its presence or its absence.

The question, then, arises : If we acknowledge a physical basis of so-called matter and energy as ultimately involved in all natural events, may we not also acknowledge God, as the directive Activity on whom the manner of going in all natural events ultimately depends? May we, without taking it at the foot of the letter, paraphrase Mr. Russell's statement and say that belief in the existence of God outside my own biography exists antecedently to evidence and can only be destroyed by a long course of philosophical doubt? May we say that for purposes of religion this is justified practically by its outcome in the conduct of life?

Again I want to nail my colours to the mast. This is part of the philosophic creed I seek to render acceptable. Within the pyramid of emergent evolution involution without dependence gives an incomplete account of the observed phenomena from what I hold to be a strictly scientific point of view. From the philosophic point of view, I carry both to their ideal limits. I acknowledge a physical world which, I admit, is beyond proof. I acknowledge also God Who is, I contend, beyond disproof. And so far as I can judge, both acknowledgments work. There is pragmatic endorsement of that which is offered for credal acceptance. Of the former, Mr.

Russell says that it is justified practically by the simplification it introduces into the laws for physics. Can it be denied that acknowledgment of God, which is the heart and soul of Christianity, has been profoundly influential in the practical guidance of conduct?

Universal correlation is also part of my creed—assuredly beyond proof. And here my cry is: Back to Spinoza. Should this also be accepted it annuls the " fatal gulf " between the material and the immaterial aspects of the world. But I must leave this for more detailed consideration in my second course of lectures.

Subject to correlation emergent evolution interprets from below, accepting with natural piety the *de facto* nisus which, according to Mr. Alexander, is expressed in the supervenience of qualities in hierarchical order. For him, as I understand, it is the inherent go of time that pushes events onwards. A doctrine that acknowledges a directive Activity in evolution explains also from above, accepting, with its fitting form of piety, God who draws all things and all men upwards.

If one may claim that acknowledgment of God, on whom all natural events in their ascent, notwithstanding lapses to lower levels, are ultimately dependent, is no less permissible at the bar of philosophy than that other acknowledgment of a physical world, our current experience, so largely infected by the relativity of appearance, swings between the infra-vital beyond of materialism and the suprapersonal Beyond of Immaterialism. Both, as beyond, are strictly speaking, outside the realm of appearances in the body of our pyramid. But both are required for a constructive philosophy which purports to explain all occurrences therein. Spatio-temporal relatedness is carried up from below and is involved in all that happens within the pyramid. May one say that from above descend the logically timeless and spaceless universals which give "form" to the "matter of empirical knowledge"? May one say that those ideals that are of supreme value in the conduct of human life, are not only "emergent" but also in some sense "ingredient"? May we say that material reality, within us under involution, is *sub specie temporis*, and that Immateriality, no less within us under ultimate Dependence, is also subsistent *sub specie aeternitatis*? If so, emphasis must, I think, be laid on the *also*. There should be no disjunctive antithesis between the timeful and the timeless. They are not to be regarded as incompatible contradictories. Difficult as the task may be they must, in some way, be combined in a higher synthesis.

LECTURE III. RELATEDNESS

XI. Relation and Relatedness. XII. Terms in Relation. XIII. External and Internal Relations. XIV. Logical Sense and Natural Direction. XV. Three-entity Situations.

§ XI. *Relation and Relatedness.*

IF it be asked : What is it that you claim to be emergent ?—the brief reply is : Some new kind of relation. Revert to the atom, the molecule, the thing (*e.g.* a crystal), the organism, the person. At each ascending step there is a new entity in virtue of some new kind of relation, or set of relations, within it, or, as I phrase it, intrinsic to it. Each exhibits also new ways of acting on, and reacting to, other entities. There are new kinds of extrinsic relatedness. As an expression of its new intrinsic relations the higher entity has new qualities ; as expressing its new extrinsic relations it has new properties. Its own qualities and its acquired properties, as I use these words (cf. § xxxiii.), are distinguishable though they co-exist inseparably in concrete fact.

It may still be asked in what distinctive sense the relations are new. The reply is that their specific nature could not be predicted before they appear in the evidence, or prior to their occurrence. But what exactly does this mean ? Give some comprehensible example. Well, picture a state of matters in which, say at a high temperature, there is a system of molecules, such system being in the vapour condition ; this system gradually cools ; a stage is reached when liquid drops are formed ; there is further cooling ; and a stage is reached when solids appear. Conceive the molecules in the vapour-system to have reflective experience. It would be that of the kind of relatedness which therein obtains. Could such a molecule foretell the relations which will obtain in liquids or in solids ? We think not. And why ? Because there are as yet no instances of these kinds of relatedness of which to have experience ; and they are quite different from those in the vapour. Liquidity and solidity are what we speak of as emergently new and unpredictable before the event. When they come we accept them, and formulate their " law," saying : Such is the constitution of nature. In like manner we think that, on the level of physico-chemical events, there could be no knowledge on the basis of which vital relatedness could be foreseen before it came. And so, too, at a later stage with mind as an emergent quality which expresses new relatedness of the conscious order.

Let us here pause to note, parenthetically, that we should not nowadays dream of saying that liquidity makes things liquid, or that solidity renders them solid. But some do say that life gives to organisms the vital relatedness which obtains within them ; and that it is mind that renders some higher organism conscious. On our view liquidity, solidity, life, and mind are, one and all, names that we give to the specific kind of relatedness that obtains in this or that entity under consideration. We should hypostatise none of them or give to any one of them the status of an entity separable from the drop, the solid thing, the organism, or the person.

To resume the more direct thread ; it is, of course, open to a critic to say that, given sufficient knowledge, liquidity and solidity—to leave life and mind on one side—*could* be predicted ; nay more, that physicists, working backwards and forwards through the series, have bevelled off, under suitable conditions, the sharp angles of new departure. We are, I trust, not wholly ignorant of the facts which may be adduced. But we are still of opinion that the supposed prediction, from the standpoint of molecules in a vapour, of the relatedness which obtains in a drop of liquid, implies a foreknowledge of a kind of relatedness among entities of which the denizens of the vapour could as yet have no experience. There we must leave the matter, having said enough to indicate the stress to be laid on the kind of relations that obtain in entities of differing status.

There is one more matter for emphasis before we pass on. The concrete world we seek to interpret is a going concern. We may of course, under quite legitimate device of method, take intellectual snapshots of the fluent course of events ; and we may thus consider immobility in abstraction. But in concrete fact there is no immobility. Events are always involved ; and events imply change in the relations of terms. Even an electron, I take it, is an event; and an atom, for all its seeming stability, is a rhythmic whirl of events; nay, rather it is the continuance of rhythmic change which gives it stability. We must bear in mind, then, that relatedness, in the world at large and in everything therein, is *au fond* fluent and ever changing.

On this understanding, emergent evolution seeks to interpret, on the one hand, the persistence and continuity of natural events, and, on the other hand, progressive advance with novelty. There is a carrying forward of old relations and the emergent advent of new relations. Hence there is perhaps no topic which is more cardinal to our interpretation —and indeed for philosophic thought—than that which centres round what I shall call relatedness. In this lecture some of its more general and salient features will be considered.

It has, however, been said that relation is the vaguest term in the philosophical vocabulary (S.T.D. I. p. 171). What then do we commonly mean when we use the word? Locke replies: " Relation is a way of comparing or considering two things together. . . . When the mind so considers one thing that it does as it were bring it to and set it by another, and carry its view from one to the other, this is, as the words import, relation and respect " (E.H.U. Bk. II. ch. xxv. §§ 1 and 7). The stress here is on the bringing of things together so as to compare them and, in doing so, to "establish," as some put it, a relation between them. When Tennyson says: " A doubtful throne is ice on summer seas," he discloses a relation between things which have seemingly little or nothing in common. But he does so on a like basis of instability. The prosaically expanded idea, I take it, is that the doubtful throne is undermined by disaffection just as an iceberg is undermined in a warm current. So, too, Shelley brings dead thoughts and withered leaves into relation through a " fertilising " concept. It requires poetic thought to bring such things together. Hence Locke can say of relations, in the sense he intended, that they " are not contained in the real existence of things but are something extraneous and superinduced " (§ 8).

Out of this view of the matter in certain cases, and by extending it to every case, may have arisen the contention that, in the absence of mental acts, there are no relations—all relations, as Berkeley put it, involving an act of the mind (P.H.K. § 142). This in due course led to the Kantian position, and onwards.

Now it is unquestionable that we often do " bring things together " in order that we may compare them in some enlightening way. There is no call to deny that such procedure depends on an act of the mind in some sense of these words. But the outcome, familiar enough, is not the more restricted sort of relation with which I here deal in such fashion as may serve my purpose in hand. Icebergs and thrones—withered leaves and dead thoughts—do not dwell together on the same level of emergence. Comparison of events at different levels is the basis of analogy and of metaphor. I seek at the outset to keep within the bounds of concrete situations, each considered on the same

RELATEDNESS

level, without prejudice to such further comparisons as may be fruitful.

Mr. Alexander lays stress on what he calls " the integral situation " ; and he says that " a relation may be described as the whole situation into which the terms enter, in virtue of that relation " (S.T.D. I. p. 240). I shall speak of the whole situation as the *relatedness* which comprises both terms-in-relation and the relation-of-terms. This is not quite the sense in which Mr. Stout uses this word in a valuable paper (P.A.S. 1901-2, p. 7). The meaning he attaches to it may there be seen.

I want to make quite clear what I shall always mean when I use the word. It has rather an abstract look. But what I call an instance of relatedness is through and through concrete. It includes not only the relation-of-terms but also the terms-in-relation. An atom is an instance of relatedness ; so, too, is an organism ; and a person. Any entity, as such, is an instance of relatedness. Any concrete situation in which entities play their part, each in respect of others, is an instance of relatedness. And it is as an integral whole of relatedness that any individual entity, or any concrete situation, is a bit of reality. May I beg that this usage be steadily borne in mind ?

Relatedness in this sense gives the stuff and substance of the integral whole in some given respect on which attention is fixed for the purpose of analysis. As has already been indicated, or implied, I distinguish relatedness within the system under contemplation as *intrinsic* ; and that of one system to another as *extrinsic*. I am well aware that these words are used by other writers with a different connotation. I use them in a sense which is, I hope, comprehensible, merely to render my own interpretation clear. Thus, in my usage, the relatedness of molecules within a drop of water is intrinsic to that drop regarded as a natural system; and the relatedness of the atoms within a molecule is intrinsic to that molecule. But the relatedness of atom to atom, or of molecule to molecule is extrinsic, for we are now regarding each molecule, or each atom, as itself an integral whole—*i.e.* as a system of subordinate status.

It may be objected that the same relatedness seems here to be taken first as intrinsic and then as extrinsic in a manner that is quite arbitrary. But is it the same, or are we considering supervenient kinds of relatedness? Let that pass. Can some such method of treatment be justified? Well, suppose we take man, wife, sons, and daughters, as units in that integral whole of relatedness we call a family. Within that family, as our unit for contemplation, their relations are intrinsic thereto. Thus is the family system constituted. But if we regard man, wife, and children, as distinguishable and subordinate units for contemplation, then they are severally in extrinsic relations to each other. Is it not permissible, in the interest of analytic thought, to change our centres of attentive regard? Is not this what we are actually doing all day long? Is it not part of normal procedure in science? We may surely deal first with the relations of atoms as intrinsic to the molecule; and then, for the purposes of further research regard the atoms as subordinate systems with extrinsic relations *inter se*; then perhaps distinguish sub-systems within a complex atom; and eventually seek to determine the intrinsic relation of nucleus and electron or electrons within each sub-system. If the legitimacy of some such method be granted, let us take extreme cases. In the universe as a natural system all relatedness is intrinsic. There being, *ex hypothesi*, nothing beyond it, the universe is just a gigantic whole of intrinsic relatedness with no opportunity of extrinsic relations. On the other hand for the electron as a physical unit—supposing it to be ultimate in this respect—all relatedness is extrinsic; for again, *ex hypothesi*, there are no subordinate systems of physical order within it. But if it be ultimately a little bit of physical motion or a pure event, then, even within it, there is at least the intrinsic spatio-temporal relatedness which constitutes it as such. Our thought, in so far as it is based on methods of science, takes its start somewhere between these extremes, and works upwards or downwards from the chosen platform. And the successively more complex and less complex systems are not arbitrarily chosen; they are given as stages in emergent evolution, and exhibit new modes of relatedness in an ascending order. In short, the distinction is so far methodological in that we must always name the system wherein intrinsic relatedness obtains.

I have already (§ iv.) distinguished *effective* from *non-effective* relatedness. When the former obtains there is some change in the manner in which events run their course. I think that effective relatedness is pervasive, and that non-effective relatedness is considered in abstraction therefrom.

§ XII. *Terms in Relation.*

Any whole of relatedness comprises terms in relation and the relation of terms. What are we to understand by the word "term"? Revert to atoms in a molecule. We may use the word for the atom which *can* come into this, that, or the other mode of relatedness. This is the current usage. I shall use the word in a more restricted sense, in which I come into touch with Mr. Stout's use of the word "relatedness." I shall use it for the part which an atom plays, or the function it has, in the actual instance of relatedness (in my sense) which is under consideration, and which is susceptible of analysis into its terms in relation and the relation of its terms. I do not, of course, urge that persons or things or entities may not be said to be in relation; but that they are in such and such relation only in so far as they are terms in the specific relatedness concerned.

We commonly say that a person enters or comes into relation to other persons. He becomes, for example, debtor to his tailor, husband of a wife, or tenant to his landlord. Now in each event he is clearly what we call the same man; and he is usually said to be the same term in three different relations. In the usage I adopt or suggest, though he is the same *man* in these different relations, he is a different term in each. And as term we give to him a different name. He becomes a debtor to his tailor, a husband when he marries, a tenant when he takes a house. He becomes a new term, and in salient cases acquires a new title, whenever he comes into some new field of extrinsic relatedness of the social order. On this understanding the terms, as such, spring into existence with the relations as such in the course of evolutionary progress. Both are given together in the sense that if you find the one you are bound to find the other. They have neither existence in fact, nor significance for our thought, as sundered. We thus avoid the error of supposing that there can be terms (as I use the word) in existence awaiting some relation to connect them, or relations in existence on the watch, so to speak, for some terms which they may connect.

It may, perhaps, be said that some plausibility for the point of view here taken is secured by emphasis on the relations of persons, but that the suggested usage is much less plausible when we deal with the relations of things. I submit, however, that the exact procedure of science justifies such a restricted usage. The earth and the moon are in gravitative relation ; and for scientific treatment they are just gravitative terms and nothing else within this universe of discourse. The earth may be made of green cheese and the moon of the best margarine, for aught the physicist cares so long as he is dealing with the instance of gravitative relatedness as such. What they are " made of " is another question and beyond the evidence. Just as a man in household relatedness plays the part of a butler, so does the earth function as a mass. It matters not, in this field of relatedness, whether the man is also a radical in politics, or a Wesleyan, or a flautist, or a golfer ; it matters not whether the earth, in that field of relatedness, is an oblate spheroid, or made of green cheese.

I must beg that this restricted use of the word "term" be steadily borne in mind. Under current usage Miss Dorothy Wrinch (Mrs. Nicholson), says that "identical terms can form part of different facts. Unless the same term arrested our attention in several distinct complexes of fact we could not build up science" (P.A.S. 1921-2, p. 134). I fully agree with the tenour of this statement. But I should, for better or worse, so modify it as to say: Unless the same entity arrested our attention as playing the part of a distinct term in several distinct fields of relatedness we could build up no scientific or philosophical system.

From the usage I venture to suggest it follows that within any given instance of relatedness the terms and their relation are homogeneous. By this I do not mean quite what James meant and, I think, Mr. Alexander advocates, namely that, in rectilinear space-relatedness, for example, the terms are spaces and the relation is resolvable into other intervening spaces of like nature (M.T. p. 138, cf. S.T.D. I. pp. 165-239).

For me, what intervenes between the minimal spatial positions we call end-points is not an indefinite series of such positions traversible in "ambulatory" fashion, but just the indivisible distance-relation that is given as such. On this view no relation is divisible. But under convention an indivisible spatial distance may be co-related (as Mr. Russell shows, P.M. p. 181) with a "stretch" which is divisible and may comprise as many terms as we choose to make therein. Similarly with time. The time-interval between any two moments is indivisible. It is just the temporal relation that it is. Only under some method of conventional treatment can it be co-related with that which is divisible. What I mean, then, by homogeneous is that the relatedness being spatial, or temporal, or gravitative, or electro-magnetic, and so on, the terms in relation and the relation of terms are likewise spatial or temporal, and so forth.

On this view of the distinction between terms and their relation we escape, I think, the dilemma with which Mr. Bradley has made us familiar. For if a relation be (i) indivisible, and (ii) not a term, there is no such infinite regress as affords one horn of the dilemma. There must, however, be something pretty definite on which Mr. Bradley bases his view that a relation is itself a term—from which all the rest follows. Can we find a clue in Mr. Russell's statement (A.M. p. 275), that as soon as we have *words* for relations, verbal propositions have, as such, necessarily more terms than the facts to which they refer? Thus if we say : Socrates precedes Plato : the fact which makes the proposition true consists of *two* terms with a relation between them, whereas (he says) the word-proposition consists of *three* terms with a relation of order between them. If this be so one may hazard the suggestion that the starting-point of Mr. Bradley's doctrine of infinite regress may be of verbal origin, since, on Mr. Russell's showing, a word that *means* a relation *is* (in the verbal proposition) a term. Of course, it is not only a verbal matter ; for the word that means a relation expresses a distinguishable pulse of thought.

§ XIII. *External and Internal Relations.*

If terms (as I use the word) be what they are in virtue of the part they play, intrinsically within some entity, or extrinsically in relation to other entities in a situation, each of them is functionally what it is in virtue of what one might call its official status. An atom of hydrogen holds an official status in the molecule of water. Every brick in a building has its official status; and that of no two bricks is quite the same. So, too, of any cell in a multicellular organism. So, too, of every citizen in a social community. What I suggest is that the word "term" may conveniently, and without undue violence to traditional usage, be applied to a thing, or a person, in virtue of what I here call its official status—in virtue of the unique office it holds in relation to other things or persons. Again I think I am in touch with Mr. Stout's view of relatedness.

This opens up the vexed question of so-called "internal" and "external" relations. What we have first to notice is that this distinction is not the same as that which I have drawn between intrinsic and extrinsic relations. Intrinsic relatedness is that which holds for some given system, under contemplation, within which subordinate terms are interrelated. Extrinsic relatedness obtains in regard to such a system and some other such system, or some environing context. Now extrinsic relations might be called external, and intrinsic relations internal. But that is not what is meant in current discussion. What is meant by "internal" is that the relation makes a difference in the terms that are related, whereas in " external " relations the fact of relatedness makes no manner of difference in the terms that are so related. Thus those who hold that terms, as such, are what they are quite independently of the relations into which they chance to enter, emphasise this by speaking of external relations. Whether a book be on the shelf or on the table makes, they say, no difference whatever to the book. Furthermore —and herein lies the central motive of the contention for new realists—whether anyone chances to perceive the book or not, leaves the book itself, as an external term, completely unaffected.

Now if " thing " and term are to be used interchangeably (as they are currently used), this position may be cheerfully accepted in the sense intended. But if, as I think, it may conduce to clearness of thought to differentiate between them, and if this differentiation be allowed, the whole controversy may seem forthwith to lapse. But there is a valid distinction, though I should express it differently.

First, in what sense may one say : *Cadit quaestio* ? It may freely be admitted that the book as a thing— *i.e.* as an orderly complex of intrinsic terms in relation—is just what it is *in this respect*, whether it be on the shelf or on my desk. None the less spatially regarded, as a place-term in homogeneous relatedness with other such terms, the position of the book between two others on the shelf is quite different from that which it holds when it lies on my desk. The gist of my contention is that, as a term in *this* field of relatedness, the position of the book is all that counts ; and that its place is what it is only in relation to the contextual positions of other surrounding things. Its positional status is of the so-called internal order ; and its character, as spatial term in this respect (not, of course, as thing), is thus determined. So, too, with perception. The book as thing—in its intrinsic nature—is nowise affected by my seeing it ; but in so far as it functions as, or takes on the office of, or acquires the status of, term (without losing aught of its intrinsic thinghood) in the cognitive relation—namely as percept —it is what it is (and so far more than it was), in virtue of that relation. As such a term it takes its status in internal relatedness. If there be no cognition on the *tapis*, there is no relatedness of this kind, and therefore (on my usage) no term. Under such relatedness, as term, its *esse* is *percipi* ; but only as term ; not coincidently as thing. On this showing an object perceived is *more than* a thing unperceived, and that because in the course of emergent evolution the world has been enriched through the advent of conscious cognition. But Berkeley said that a thing can never be *less than* an object perceived. There I think that, from the point of view of emergent evolution, he was wrong.

In what respect, then, is there a valid distinction between relations of the so-called internal and external kinds respectively ? I suggest that it lies in the difference between effective and non-effective relatedness. Under effective relations the thing itself is in some way changed in its intrinsic nature under causal influence. When the earth and the moon are set in a joint field of gravitative relatedness, not only is there the extrinsic change which we speak of as mutual attraction, each is intrinsically changed through the differential strain that results, with " tidal deformation " in some measure. Even the book on the shelf is different from that book on my desk through differential pressure distributed to all its constituent parts ; and both shelf and desk are in this respect different. But if, under analysis, we distinguish spatial or positional from physical relatedness, though both are co-existent, then the place-relations *as such* make no difference in the intrinsic nature of earth or moon ; of book, shelf, or desk ; for we are deliberately abstracting from the relatedness which is effective. Now there are plenty of kinds of relatedness which it is convenient analytically to distinguish as non-effective. If, then, spatial relations, and, as I hold, temporal relations, and certainly those of perceptual reference under cognition, are non-effective, they induce no change in the nature of the things which thus function as terms. In this effective sense, therefore, the intrinsic character of the things which stand in *such* relations remains quite unaffected. And I think that it is this which justifies the new realist claim that the book on the shelf is no different from that book on the table (save under the different strain of physical influence) and that it makes no difference whatever to that book whether it be perceived or not.

It is, or was, the doctrine of some logicians that any given A, when it is in extrinsic relation to B, acquires an added character (becoming, say, Ab) and is therefore no longer intrinsically what it was. For the new character, b, is within it, and may be related to any, or all, of the precedent qualities.

Let us grant that this is so in the sense intended. I revert, however, to the distinction between effective and non-effective relatedness. Under effective relatedness *b* does make a difference in the intrinsic nature of the thing. The thing is in some measure altered. There is some change in the go of events within it. But under non-effective relatedness, regarded in abstraction, *b* makes no difference. If A, B, and C be three things so arranged positionally that B stands between A and C, the character of these things, as billiard balls, let us say, remains quite unaffected by their spatial positions *only*, though physically each is affected in some way, however slight.

§ XIV. *Logical Sense and Natural Direction.*

" It is characteristic of a relation of two terms that it proceeds, so to speak, *from* one *to* the other. This is what may be called the *sense* of the relation. . . . The sense of a relation is a fundamental notion which is not capable of definition " (Russell, P.M. pp. 95-6).

May we not say, however, that whenever the logical sense is determinate, in a concrete field of relatedness, it is always determined by the actual direction of events ; and fundamentally by the direction of passage in physical events ? If so, this seems to reduce all direction to that which obtains within a space-time frame. But what about the direction of thought regarded as a process of contemplating ? There is, I suppose unquestionably, temporal relatedness of before and after. But when

I think first of the colour and then of the scent of roses, or first of my friend's generosity and then of his love of poetry, interpretation in terms of spatial direction appears to be somewhat strained. None the less there is, from the evolutionary point of view, even in the thought-process spatial direction *in the vital and the physical events which are correlated with it*.

To the objection that such a point of view is terribly abstract the evolutionary reply might be that it alone is sufficiently concrete. To ignore, when thought-processes are under consideration, all that is implied in their very being, is the kind of abstraction which the evolutionist regards as characteristically vicious. The analytic abstraction that is not vicious is that under which one seeks to distinguish this or that kind of relatedness within a concrete whole, fully realising that other kinds are also co-existent.

On this understanding we may quite legitimately deal with that which is objective to thought " in abstraction." Let us, then, take the space-time direction of the physical events involved in the process of contemplating for granted ; let us direct our attention to that which is contemplated ; let us consider very briefly sundry instances of relatedness thus contemplated ; and let us take verbal statements in the light of what Mr. Russell speaks of as their " meaning." Then, if we have in view some given analytic instance of spatial, or of temporal, or of quantitative relatedness, as such, there seems to be no *natural* direction to determine the logical sense of the relation under consideration. It is a

L.M.E.

matter of indifference whether we say that Croydon is S. of, and smaller than, London, or that London is N. of, and larger than, Croydon. So far as temporal relatedness *only* is concerned we may say that sunrise is before noon or that noon is after sunrise. This is because in each case we are abstracting from the passage of events. If we are dealing with sunrise and noon from that point of view the direction is determined through the natural passage of events, and this determines the logical sense. And if we are dealing with the run of a train from Croydon to London, there is an actual event the nature of which gives the direction of passage from the departure platform in Croydon, at a given time, to the arrival platform in London, at a subsequent time. Departure from London and arrival in Croydon is another event with an opposite direction.

But even where there is an onward flow of events in the space-time frame that we construct for their interpretation, we may *think* of them either downstream or upstream. For though events in their passage run only forwards, our interpretation of these events may run either forwards or backwards. If we regard causation historically the effect is subsequent to some at least of the events which are comprehensively called the cause. But one may think either from cause to effect or from effect to cause.

One has, therefore, to distinguish the natural direction in the relatedness of events in passage, independently of thought-process, from the direction of the acknowledged events with which thought deals. If we fail to do so we are liable to fall into

RELATEDNESS

error. One may think from A to B, or from B to A; but if one asserts (as a mark of acceptance) that the course of events, independently of thought-procedure, is from B to A, one may be wrong. Or, more generally: Given (i) a set of events to be considered in their relatedness independently of constructive thought, and (ii) a working thought-model which purports to refer thereto, the one may be in accord with the other, or it may not. If the working construct be accordant with that which is (in some sense) independent of such construction,—what we commonly call the facts—we name it true; if it be not—if it be discordant therewith—we characterise it as false.

From what has been said it is, I trust, clear that I seek only to look at the matter from a special angle. Logical treatment deals largely with kinds of relatedness which I should call non-effective. With the way in which experts define logical sense in such cases it is not my province to meddle. Already I run sufficient risk of burning my fingers. All I venture to suggest is that where we are dealing with some passage of events, in objective regard, the logical sense is accordant with the direction of such passage. One may, of course, consider the relation of brother to brother, or of brother to sister, as examples of what Mr. Russell calls a symmetrical or a non-symmetrical relation; but one may ask whether there is passage of events from one to the other. Is there any passage analogous to that which the biologist seeks to trace in the asymmetrical relatedness of parents and offspring? Here there is a natural passage irreversible in direction; there one considers collateral phases of events in two lines of passage only connected historically through their origin from a common source.

§ XV. *Three-entity Situations.*

In dealing with any integral whole of relatedness we must accept the legitimacy of analysis. Under analysis one distinguishes different kinds of relatedness—say conscious, vital, chemico-physical, spatial or temporal—which may all be inseparably co-existent though distinguishable. Each of these must be treated in accordance with the terms and relations appropriate to its kind. In other words the treatment should be homogeneous. And it seems permissible to deal with any given kind irrespective of co-existent kinds, so long as we do so in analytic abstraction. Even Berkeley admitted that this is legitimate under " consideration." " A man," he says, " may consider a figure merely as triangular. ... *So far he may abstract* " (P.H.K. Int. § 16). The passage in which these words occur was added in the 1734 edition. But it was not an afterthought; for in the Commonplace Book he has a note : " Mem. A great difference between *considering* length without breadth and having an *idea* of or imagining length without breadth " (Frazer's Ed. of Works, Vol. I. p. 78).

When such analysis is pressed home our aim is to select just two terms and their relation, *e.g.* the spatial positions of the opposite faces of a cube, the moments of start and finish of a pendulum-swing, buyer and seller in some business transaction, an organism and its environment, a word and its context, and so on. One or other or both of them may be complex. That does but afford an opportunity for deeper analysis of the complex entity which, on my view, functions as a term, until we can go no further.

On this showing one may always bring any given instance of relatedness under some such generalised formula as $T R T^1$ where T is one term, T^1 the other term, and R the relation—no matter how complex T and T^1 may be. Of course, this is to be regarded merely as a methodological device.

But we may now ask whether in all cases we can profitably deal with only two terms in so-called dyadic relatedness. " A sees B give x to C." Now here, at the start, we can bring this under a two-term rubric. " A, in cognitive relation to (B giving x to C)—*i.e.* $T R T^1$ where T^1 is obviously complex. So, too, of course, is T; but that just now is a different story. The formula can, I think, be made to hold good in any instance of cognitive relatedness, by regarding T^1 as a perceived situation, or a contemplated system, with which one has to deal. But, in the example given above, the situation represented by T^1 may be analysed. In so analysing it as to throw further light on its nature and constitution, can we proceed comfortably on the basis of two-term procedure ? There certainly seem to be three terms. At any rate there are two persons and a thing ; B, who gives : C, who receives ; and x, which is both given and received.

Now, if there be three terms, or any *odd* number of terms, dyadic analysis does not work. But I submit that one *can* analyse (and that not unprofitably) in such a manner as to preserve duality if, in accordance with the usage I suggest, the same thing x which is both given and received here functions as *two* terms, one in relation to giver and the other in relation to taker. An uncle gives his nephew half-a-crown. It is no doubt one coin that passes from the man's pocket to the boy's. In a sense, perhaps, it has one and the same value. But in a different, and as I think quite legitimate sense, the value is not the same. The gain for the boy is greater than the loss for his uncle. Yes, it may be said, but only relatively greater or less. It is, however, the relation that, on my view, makes the *term* what it is. On this showing it may be urged that triadic relatedness is susceptible of dyadic treatment under adequate analysis.

But there are plenty of three-*entity* situations, the distinguishing feature of which is that one of the entities plays a dual part and, in my view, so functions as two terms as to link the three into one integral whole of complex relatedness. This I take to be the heart of the matter, whether we express it in one way or another. The heart of the matter is that we have not merely the additive resultant of this duality *plus* that ; but something more in their combination to constitute an integral whole.

Of course the three entities need not be two persons and a thing ; they may be three things, or three persons, and so on. If Mrs. Jones be jealous in view of the way in which Mr. Jones carries on with Miss Brown, the situation is utterly incomplete without all three persons. No dyadic treatment will adequately evaluate it. I may call Miss

Brown one *term* in the eye of Mrs. Jones and quite a different *term* in the regard of Mr. Jones. But that does not so much matter as the integral relatedness of the whole situation in which the three persons play their parts. That is the essential feature.

Of course the principle on which such interpretation is dependent, is nowise limited to three entities and no more. It applies to just so many entities as there are in the whole integral situation. Consider some instance of geometrical progression, say . . . 4, 8, 16, 32 . . . . In this order—and in any "order" as such—one must have (at least) a three-entity situation. Now one may, profitably enough, analyse dyadically, step-fashion, taking first the relatedness of 4 and 8, then that of 8 and 16, and so on. Grant, if you will, that the entity 8 functions as one term in relation to 4, and another (different) *term* in relation to 16—which follows from my usage. Next, one might deal dyadically with the relatedness of $\frac{8}{4}$ and $\frac{16}{8}$, as more complex terms in relation ; and so forth. But in breaking up the serial order into analytic fragments, one may lose sight of the unity of plan. One may so analyse the series as to destroy it, unless one synthetically restores the inter-relatedness which is the essential vinculum of the integral whole.

It may seem to savour of perversity to contend that 8 is one term in relation to 4, and a different term in relation to 16. And if I say that this same 8, which, of course, is just what it is as an "entity" under suitable definition, somehow *feels* different to me according as I approach it from this or that direction ($7 + 1$; $9 - 1$; 4×2 ; $24 \div 3$; and so on), this may be regarded as a mere psychological whimsy. I prefer, therefore, to urge that quantitative relatedness, expressible through numbers, is *as such* wholly non-effective, and is thus regarded in abstract " consideration." Let the relatedness, in some concrete case, be not only quantitative but also physical—or let these two kinds of relatedness be inseparably co-existent—then it may perhaps seem less perverse to say that a body of mass 8, in a field of gravitative relatedness, plays different parts in respect to one of mass 4 on the one hand, and in respect to one of mass 16 on the other hand. As Lotze might say it " takes note of " the less in a way other than that in which it takes note of the greater ; and " behaves " accordingly.

We may deal in resolute abstraction with quantitative relatedness only, turning our backs on physical events. We may comprise in our less abstract view pure events which will then be considered kinematically in their space-time-quantity frame. We may go further and introduce into our picture the physico-chemical and the emergently sequent orders of effective relatedness, vital, and conscious, in ascending grades. There we may stop, accepting what we find with natural piety. Emergence comes into the picture with effectiveness. What lies below the level of effectiveness, or what lies outside its range, I hold to be always dealt with under abstract " consideration."

Now the rubric of effectiveness—or if it be preferred the rubric of causation—is just this : Given *a* and *b* as *ad hoc* terms in some field of effective relatedness E, something happens, in the sense that some change occurs which would not occur in the absence of E. This change in the manner of go in events, is, as I phrase it, dependent on the kind of relatedness emergent in E. Such dependence is accepted with natural piety.

But there may be something more in the heart of events than such effectiveness—namely that which one may speak of as Efficiency—something more than causation, which I shall call Causality—something more than dependence which I capitalise as Dependence. In virtue of this, should it be accepted, not only does something happen under effectiveness, but all that is emergent has being through Efficiency. This, which of course may be rejected, is, for those who take the risk of the higher acknowledgment, the Creative Source of evolution—this is God.

The relatedness we have dealt with has for its subject matter some integral whole within which terms-in-relation and relation-of-terms are analytically distinguished. Now this integral whole is something given for our contemplation; and it may be said that what is so given must be accepted with natural piety; there is no need to ask any further question. But there have always been those who do ask this further question: Of what relating Activity is the given relatedness a manifestation? Some may say there is none; others may take the agnostic position and say *ignoramus et ignorabimus*; yet others may take the risk of acknowledgment.

For those who take this risk new problems arise. Their consideration must, however, be postponed till concept of an all-embracing Activity, relating and directive, has been further developed.

LECTURE IV. REFERENCE

XVI. Reference a matter of Conscious Regard. XVII. Perceptual Reference. XVIII. Is there initial Reference in the Primitive Mind ? XIX. That which is involved in the Genesis of Reference. XX. Reference supplemented under Acknowledgment.

§XVI. *Reference a matter of Conscious Regard.*

LITTLE, save incidentally, was said in the foregoing lecture on relatedness at the level of consciousness. A good deal, no doubt, was necessarily implied or tacitly taken for granted. But before we can deal with consciousness explicitly, and so far as possible comprehensively—in the second course of lectures— much preparation, and some laying of foundations, will be necessary. From the point of view of emergent evolution, conscious relatedness, for all its seeming simplicity and immediacy, has a history of bewildering complexity. Enjoyed as the correlate of vital relatedness at a very advanced stage of its evolutionary progress ; requiring the effective go of life as that requires the primary go of physical events ; affording a salient example of that which we have called dependence—since so much of the direction and manner of go in events depends on conscious guidance ; linked thus with emergent qualities at so high a level, and thus involving so many kinds of relatedness of lower orders ; its adequate analysis is bound to be very difficult. Only step by step can we disentangle some of the threads in a meshwork of relations so intricate.

Throughout the whole range of consciousness in its cognitive regard there is a factor which seems to be of cardinal importance—that of *reference* in some sense of the word, and of the concept the word names. I have now to try to present points of view which may be helpful in assigning to it a place in our scheme of emergent evolution.

The way in which we commonly speak of reference may be illustrated in connection with Literature. Suppose we meet with the oft-quoted lines :

" His honour rooted in dishonour stood
And faith unfaithful kept him falsely true."

The question may be asked : What is the reference here ? Perhaps one may refer the passage to Tennyson, or to the *Idylls of the King*. But if it were asked to whom the word " him " here refers, the reply would be : To Lancelot. Next it might be asked : To what salient feature in Lancelot's life is there here special reference ? To his love of Guinevere. Further questions might follow with regard to the concluding words " falsely true." True to whom ? To Guinevere. But why falsely ? To whom was he false ? To his king, Arthur, as Guinevere's husband. Until this double reference in the three-person situation is adequately grasped, the passage as a whole, with its play on " honour," and " dishonour," and on " faith unfaithful," will not be understood. For one who recalls the context of the lines as they stand in *Lancelot and Elaine*, there is, perhaps, some further reference to Elaine's love for him with the passing thought that had he loved *her* there would have been no call to speak of him as " falsely true."

Take as a further example the familiar words : " The quality of mercy is not strained." Portia, *Merchant of Venice*, Shakespeare, shoot to mind. Perhaps there is a fleeting memory-image of the birth-room at Stratford, to be dismissed, it may be, as just now irrelevant. More to the point, the last emphatic word " strained " may call up Shylock's preceding question : " On what compulsion ? Tell me that." Antonio's admission of the bond may then come into view. One is led step by step through the trial scene ; this is referred to its setting in the play ; and so on. Of course, in the case of one who knows his *Merchant of Venice* (note here our common use of the word " his "), a tolerably comprehensive view may develop rapidly ; for, as Hobbes pithily said, " thought is quick." The net result of previous study is revived in vague but influential form. There is also a " can follow it up " background rather difficult to analyse. Probably in no two persons will just the same lines of possible reference be followed up.

What seems to be essential in such cases (the more familiar the better for illustration), is that something being given, something else having significant relation to that which is so given, must be also in mind. The something else may be very vague or indefinite ; or it may be a well-defined situation ;

or it may involve such a connection as is exemplified in " strained " and " compulsion." But, vague or clear-cut, the something else must be such as to function as a term in relation to the something given. And both terms must be " in mind " ; otherwise there is, then and there, no reference.

One should distinguish the mental process of referring *in* which we (who *are* the process and its -*ing*-context, whatever else we may be) are conscious, from the objective field of reference *of* which, as minded, we are conscious. This we may call " the field of conscious regard." Here and now we may take the process of minding for granted on the understanding that in its absence there is no field of conscious regard.

It may be asked, however, whether *both* the terms in this relation need be present in mind, as what we are conscious of, at the same time. May they not occur in succession, that which is given at one moment, the something else in a following moment ? Is not that the natural order ; first that which is in some way given, and then what is suggested thereby to which it is said to have reference ? Undoubtedly this is the natural order, and unquestionably this does imply succession in time, however rapidly one may follow the other. None the less *this* must be held in the field of conscious regard at the time when *that* enters the field. For before *that* comes there is no second term in the field to which the first can be related ; and unless *this* be carried forward under retention, there is no first term in the field to which the second stands in relation. In the one case the second term has not yet come ; in the other case the first term has gone. Hence in the absence of retention, which falls broadly speaking under the head of memory, conscious reference would seem to be impossible.

But surely (it may be said) what is suggested is often past or future. If one refer a man's impending death to an overdose of strychnine there is reference of a coming event to an event that happened some time ago. Even here, however, must not the course of events be then and there minded if there be any conscious reference thereto? What is here minded is a scheme or plan of events which, in some sense, corresponds to the actual course of events, some of which are gone, some still to come. Hence it is questionable whether it be advisable to speak of conscious reference to that which is not, at the time being, minded.

No doubt we do often speak of reference when we do not necessarily mean conscious reference. We say that iron filings scattered around a magnet take up positions in reference to " lines of force " in the electro-magnetic field. We say that the upward growth of a plant-stem must have some reference to an interpretation under gravitative attraction. We say that the behaviour of lowly heliotropic organisms, or that of plants in a cottager's window, has reference to the incidence of light-waves, and so on. And it may perhaps be urged that this kind of thing went on ages before there was any conscious reference on the scene. Yes. But surely that means that there was then no " true " (*i.e.* conscious) reference. What, I think, we commonly mean in all such cases, is that certain events are so connected in the world around us as to afford *a basis* for conscious reference when it does come on to the scene. Such events must, of course, be taken into account. In any relation, having " sense," that from which one starts may, with Mr. Russell, be called the *referent* and that to which one proceeds the *relatum* (P.M. pp. 24-96). And I take it that from the logical point of view they need not both be in the field of someone's conscious regard. It suffices that the one shall be *referable* to the other. If this sufficiently indicate the part played by the connection of events within the world to be interpreted in thus affording a basis for conscious reference (which is always a mental transaction), may it not be better *not* to use the word " reference " in those cases in which it is often elliptically used, since there are other words which will quite adequately express what we mean? We might, perhaps, use as above the word " referable " where there may be, or will be, actual reference, *if* the course of events be somehow represented in the field of someone's conscious regard.

§ XVII. *Perceptual Reference.*

Thus far we have taken one or two cases illustrative of reference as it obtains in a field of conscious regard on the reflective level. The relatedness here is that of something given (itself a complex term) to something else—a significant context, or some specific feature of that context. If I can trust my own inspection (or so-called introspection), the initial phase of such reference may be, and often is, very vague and indeterminate—to something somehow significant—what one may call significance in general. Specific or differentiated significance may come later. And in what has gone before emphasis has been laid on the necessary co-existence of the something given and the something else—also given, of course, but not given in quite the same way—in the field of conscious regard correlative to the process of minding then and there in being. Even significance in general, however vague, must be there if there be reference to it.

But if not given in quite the same way, how given? Shall we say given under revival? In all reference of the reflective order something of the nature of memory is a *sine qua non*. And this, as we shall see in the next lecture, has its emergent levels, with involution and dependence.

May we then provisionally accept the view that only if there be conscious revival can the something else come into the reflective field of conscious regard? The question then arises: Is there revival only, or may there be something more than revival? It should be clear that to this question the answer, for us, is that assuredly there may be something more. Revival, I take it, should mean re-presentation of old material—or that which is in imagery like unto it—with perhaps re-arrangement in resultant patterns, but with nothing genuinely, or, as it is said, constructively, new. That comes under emergence. And there is nothing in what has been said to preclude the advent of an emergent quality in the integral whole. All that is claimed is that revival is involved. There is no denial—nay, rather this, too, is claimed—that evolutionary advance in reflective thought depends on the emergence of new synthetic qualities.

We must now descend a stage to the level of unreflective consciousness—that on which the guidance of animal behaviour in large measure depends. I do not say wholly depends, though in some animals it may be so—probably is so under emergent evolution. Let us say, rather, that on which the behaviour of a being with unreflective or perceptual consciousness only would depend, and speak of it as " such an animal." To get at this level we must divest ourselves, so far as we can, of the garment of reflective thought. What then of reference remains to such an animal the field of whose conscious regard we now seek to interpret? I suppose something pretty similar to that which there is in us on many current occasions of daily life, if, again so far as we can, we regard that mental life in abstraction from the reflective reference which is in some measure also on the *tapis*. I take it that the something given is here, typically, the presentation of some situation, and the something else is, in general, the objective " meaning " begotten of prior behaviour along many lines, and, in more specific detail, the *ad hoc* meaning attaching to the kind of situation of which that which is presented affords an instance. Meaning in general, at the unreflective level, like significance in general, at the reflective level, is not wholly undifferentiated. It is always in some measure relevant; for it is a term (however complex), in relation to the something given ; and, under relatedness, each of the two terms in relation is what it is only in relation to the other.

Unreflective meaning, as distinguished from reflective significance, has immediate utility for practical behaviour, whereas significance has mediate value for conduct. Meaning involves revival of the net result of prior experience in such a behaviour-situation. It must co-exist with the something given in the field of conscious regard. But from the cognitive point of view we commonly say that both the something given, say in presentation, and the something else, present under revival, have reference to what we call an object. Through its relation to meaning the presentation is raised to the level of a percept, which, as I think, is not only a resultant but an emergent with a quality which is genuinely new. May we say, then : No meaning, no percept ; and no perception, no object thereof ?

That may seem to be sheer topsyturvydom. Place the statement right way up : No object, no perception thereof. Then it is in accordance with common-sense. The trouble here is that the word "object" is ambiguous. It may mean the thing as it is in its own right whether it be perceived or not—*i.e.* what I speak of as the physical thing the existence of which we acknowledge. Or it may mean this thing as clothed with certain acquired properties due to its relation to us in perception. It is in this latter sense that I speak of the object, meaning that which comprises all that accrues to a physical thing in and through our minding it. The statement as I put it comes to this : The thing plays no part in constituting an object of perception until it is thus minded or perceived. This few will deny. But new-realists may add : What it is as perceived object is just identically that which it was, and will continue to be, as unperceived thing. Nothing "accrues" to it. This, I submit, is not in accordance with those principles of emergent evolution which I seek to develop. When perception comes it enriches the world into which, in the course of evolutionary progress, it so comes. Hence, just here there is a parting of the ways of interpretation.

§ XVIII. *Is there Initial Reference in the Primitive Mind?*

However, we may interpret it, we seem here to have passed to a different phase, if not a different kind, of reference. We have not only the reference of something given in a field of conscious regard to something else within that field—the context of meaning or some differentiated feature therein—but further reference of what is within the field to something, in some sense, beyond it—let us say to the thing the existence of which we acknowledge to be independent of any conscious reference.

In the case of an animal that has already gained experience the like of which may be revived, there is, as we have seen, perceptual reference on the unreflective level. But what about the animal, or the human infant, at the outset of mental life? If we probe as near as we can get to the very beginning of conscious experience in the individual, is there, so far as we can judge, reference either to something else in the field of conscious regard or to anything beyond what is actually given to sense? Is there a stage of development at which there is as yet no reference? Unfortunately no one can reach back retrospectively, along the lines of personal reminiscence, anywhere near to the beginning of individual experience. We are forced, therefore, to draw rather hazardous inferences from such observations as we can make of the earliest modes of behaviour in infants and animals.

The question before us comes to this : Is there a stage in the individual development of an organism in which consciousness is eventually emergent, when there are sensory presentations that as yet carry no meaning? From the point of view of emergent evolution there is such a stage—one at which a behaviouristic interpretation of that which happens is adequate and sufficient even if we acknowledge psychical correlates.

May we surmise that when one sees a chick a few hours old peck for the first time at what *we* call a small object, say a rice-grain, we are as near to the beginning of its acquaintance with particular things as we are likely to get for the purpose of an answer to our question? There is a visual presentation in some sense. But in what sense? First we may agree that to be a presentation it must have, under correlation, an accompaniment or concomitant of the psychical order, whether we call it sentience, or enjoyment, or consciousness in the most comprehensive signification of this ambiguous word. Secondly, we may, with Mr. Stout, further define a presentation as that which always has what he speaks of as " a two-fold implication." On these terms it is, under correlation, a mode of immediate sensory experience; but, in its presentative *function*, it also " specifies and determines the direction of thought to what is not immediately experienced " (M. p. 210). I agree that this is so in *our* mental life. But I submit that even here we should analytically distinguish between what it primarily *is* and what it functionally (and perhaps only secondarily) *does*. For the purpose in hand, therefore, I characterise what a presentation primarily *is* as the correlate of the physiological outcome in the organism of the stimulation of a pattern of sensory (*e.g.* retinal) receptors.

In our chick, then, there is such a presentation, and may at first be no more. The pecking response in behaviour is coming but has not yet come; so this is out of court so far as that bird's experience is concerned. The question, now in focus, is this: Has the presentation, as something for the first time given, initial reference to something else or something beyond? My own reply is, that, in such a case, there is no such initial reference—that conscious reference only derivatively begins when there is revival of such experience as the little bird has already, and individually, gained in the course of pecking and other modes of behaviour on prior occasions.

That, then, is one answer to the question whether from the first there is reference of something given in presentation to something beyond that which is so given. There is at the outset no such reference. The presentative function is not yet. All such reference, when it comes, is derivative from previous

H

experience in the individual life. The alternative answer, ably advocated by Mr. Stout (P.A.S. 1913-4, pp. 381 *ff.*), is that the something given in sensory presentation (called by him a " primary sensible ") is at the outset, originally, and initially, referred to " a source " as something beyond. " The primitive mind," he says, " directly apprehends a primary sensible, and in doing so refers it to a source " (p. 395). This is spoken of as an " original unreflective act," through which there is " an immediate knowledge of primary sensibles as correlated with a source" (pp. 389-390). In other words, there is " immediate knowledge of the sensible as incomplete " ; and it is this knowledge of connection with source that " is original and immediate " (p. 392). It is, however, source in a vague and undiscriminated form, not a specific object, as differentiated through experience. It is source in general, not a source in particular. This, I take it, means that even from the very outset, in the infant, let us say, the supposed existence of a sensory presentation which carries no reference to something beyond itself, is to be regarded as a vicious abstraction begotten of erroneous interpretation. Not only has such a presentation the function of leading on to something further, but it immediately introduces into the field of primitive conscious regard that which is really inseparable from it, namely (*a*) knowledge of its incompleteness, and (*b*) knowledge of source which completes it. Any given sensory presentation means initially, immediately, and directly, at least something from which it originates. But since this meaning is, *ex*

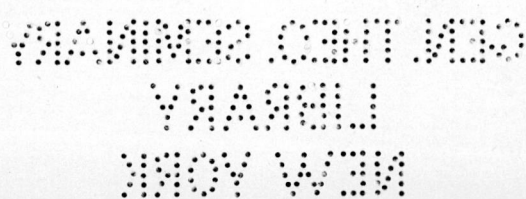

hypothesi, nowise the outcome of prior experience in the individual (for if so it would not be original), it must either be derived from experience inherited from ancestors, or must have its sufficient ground in the inherent nature of mind as initially intelligent. The former, Mr. Stout tells us, it is not safe to assume (M. p. 494) ; we seem, therefore, bound to accept the latter since we cannot get along without it. For if there were not from the very first some reference to source, such reference could not by any possibility come into being. " I cannot," says Mr. Stout, " stir a step without pre-supposing the reference of a primary sensible to a source, and without pre-supposing that the reference is initially to the whole source " (P.A.S. p. 396).

It goes without saying that, in the paper from which I have quoted, and elsewhere, Mr. Stout's discussion of the manner in which *specific objects* become differentiated as the experience of the individual develops, is admirable. It deals with that of which he elsewhere treats under the " category of thinghood." Such categories he speaks of as " ultimate principles of unity." And here again he says that we have " to determine whether the unity of the external world can be accounted for merely as due to acquired meaning, or whether on the contrary there is some apprehension of it, however rudimentary, from the outset " (M. p. 436). The question I take it is this : Is *the apprehension of* unity entirely derivative ; or is it in part at least original ? The reply is : " The mind starts with some general apprehension of the unity of the world, sufficient to enable it, when occasion arises, to expect and seek for connections not yet disclosed " (p. 437). Whether, in further detail, we take " spatial unity, temporal unity, causal unity, or the unity of different attributes as belonging to the same thing," in each several case, as I understand, what is given is initially apprehended—*e.g.* by our chick— as pointing beyond itself to a larger whole of which it is felt to be an incomplete part. " If we are not quite gratuitously to place an impassable gap between the earlier and the later stages of mental development, we must assume that it [some pre-notion of the unity we seek] is present in however indeterminate a way, from the beginning " (p. 444).

§ XIX. *That which is involved in the Genesis of Reference.*

I have given at some length Mr. Stout's philosophical thesis—I trust without serious misrepresentation—because the issue it raises appears to me to be of great importance. The cardinal issue, I think, is this : Does a few-hours old chick, a new-born infant, or any other sample of primitive mind one selects or posits—does such primitive mind start business with some apprehension of source to which there is initial reference ; or is reference to source quite a late product of reflective thought ?

It is clear that this issue is intimately connected with that which I have spoken of as projicience (cf. § VIII.). On my view, projicience is a process of very gradual development that begins when mind or consciousness is supervenient in the course of evolutionary progress, and takes definite form only when distance-receptors are differentiated on the plane of life. It presupposes the evolution of mind as an emergent quality of the psychical system correlated with the physical system of the organism. Until there is projicience there is as yet no external world envisaged in the primitive psychical system. On the alternative view mind has *ab initio* that which is one of its distinguishing features—that of apprehending an external world, in which things lie at a distance from the organism. Through bodily instruments, such as the eye, the mind gains definite and specific experience of the nature of the external world. But some apprehensive reference thereto *must* be present from the outset.

We are once more at a crucial parting of the ways. And I think at bottom it comes to this. One route leads to the view that mind is emergent in the course of evolutionary history. The other path leads to the view that mind is not emergent. It is not an evolutionary stage in the natural history of the psychical correlates of physical events. It enters the world endowed with an original capacity for apprehending that world, with its several categories, through the use of sense-organs and brains, evolved to that end in a manner which it is for biologists to disclose. This apprehension is part of the mind's inherent activity which, with the conduct it subserves, affords instances of a kind of causality elsewhere not to be found in nature (cf. M. p. 120). The two views are, I think, irreconcilable. If one be accepted the other must be rejected.

The citadel of projicience—the holding of which is essential to my strategic position—will thus be subject to attack from two sides, and must rebut the missiles of criticism directed against it from different besieging camps. Mr. Alexander, on the one hand, will seek to demolish it because it threatens the new-realist road that leads to the hill-top from which the independent status of secondary qualities comes clearly into sight—an outlook tower which must be maintained. Mr. Stout, on the other hand, will attack it because it bars the way to that shrine wherein dwells the mind, with its prerogative of initially apprehending the source from which our specific modes of objective experience have been differentiated.

If—to drop the citadel metaphor, which is only introduced parenthetically as perhaps throwing a side-light on the issue—if I be unable to accept initial reference to source in general ; if, as I have been led to believe, all conscious reference be secondary and derivative, it is clear that I must face the question : From what is it derived ? How can reference of something given, say in sensory presentation, to something else, or something beyond, which in some way enters the field of conscious regard—how can this genetically come into being if there be no reference in being at the outset ? What is its epigenetic origin ? From the standpoint of emergent evolution this question will take the form : What does such reference involve at a lower level of the ascending hierarchy ? Clearly the behaviouristic answer for us must be : There are on the plane of life kinds of relatedness which afford a basis for conscious reference preparatory to its advent. Life is the evolutionary precursor to mind.

REFERENCE

There is in any organism that has, under stimulation, something *physiologically* given, much else that is thereby excited as a further outcome of that stimulation. But this organic " something else," even if it be accompanied by consciousness in a wide sense of the word (I should say by enjoyment), affords only a physical basis on which there is founded the conscious reference that supervenes. Reference itself can only arise when the correlate of this something else is a revival which carries with it the undefinable quality or *quale* of " againness " (cf. § XXII.). We cannot, however, follow up this clue until we have traced the emergent stages which lead up to memory.

But we can draw attention to another clue in that which is biologically involved at the level of life. For one of the questions which is sure to arise is : How comes it that reference centres in that which progressively takes form as the object ? The answer to this question is that behaviour towards *this* or *that thing* is the natural progenitor, under emergent evolution, of conscious reference to *this* or *that object*. In so far as an acknowledged thing is a common centre on to which varied modes of behaviour are focussed at the level of life, it becomes also a common centre around which is grouped all that, in and through behaviour, is projicient at the level of consciousness. Contributory to the genesis of conscious reference behaviour is *involved* ; but behaviour does not initially *depend on* conscious reference. The infant or the animal does not initially and at the outset of active life behave towards a thing because it apprehends, however vaguely and indeterminately, that beyond the primary sensible there is something more as the source to which it is referable (still less actually referred) ; but we, at any rate, may come to learn in the course of reflective interpretation that the existence of such a source is based on an hypothesis worthy of serious consideration. We learn, too, eventually, what properties are referable to an object. In our infant days we become acquainted with certain salient ways in which sensory stimulation may come. But this is because behaviour, nowise consciously directed *ab initio* to seeking them, has led us, on the plane of life, to find them. One must invert Mr. Stout's dictum that the condition of finding is seeking. At the outset, in my interpretation, behaviour on the plane of life just finds ; only after having found does the animal, or an infant, seek in order to find *again*. It is in this felt " againness." that the psychical factor in conscious reference must be sought. Subject to retention and revival it affords the basis of what we commonly speak of as experience.

One cannot go into detail with regard to the progressive and, as I contend, genetically projicient, clustering of revived experience around some centre which thus becomes an object for reference. Nor is this necessary. It is a familiar story. Let it suffice then very briefly to illustrate the integrative coalescence by an example from the nursery. In the infant, random and unlearnt movements of head and eyes, or arms and hands, bring the little child into sensory commerce with things thus found but nowise initially sought. Now there appears to be a stage when acquaintance with such things through vision is not yet coalescent

REFERENCE

with acquaintance with them through manipulative touch. Visual exploration in seeking to find again seems to go on independently of what the hands are doing ; manipulation is apparently irrespective of that with which vision is concerned. Not until about the middle of the fourth month, according to Miss Milicent Shinn (B.B. p. 123), is there, in the child, reciprocal reference of both eye-data and hand-data to one and the same object. So far as one can draw safe inferences from what has been carefully observed, it is then, and not till then, that touching a thing suggests looking at it, and seeing it suggests what will come through grasping it. This must be a great moment. The centre of common reference becomes so far a perceptual object. The inverted (some will, I know, say perverted) view of the natural order in finding and seeking is, I think, near the heart of interpretation under emergent evolution. One has, of course, to distinguish between the primary behaviour that finds on the plane of life, and the secondary behaviour that seeks and finds again on the plane of consciousness. The former does not depend on consciousness either for its being or for the particular manner of its going. The way it goes is an expression of life at its appropriate level of emergence. The latter does depend on conscious relatedness, and on reference, for the effective guidance of the particular or specific manner of its going. If we are to render an evolutionary account of the emergence *of* mind, and not only of subsequent steps of emergence *in* mind, one must realise (1) that it is from behaviour, nowise dependent on conscious guidance, that the organism first finds on the plane of life, just as, on the plane of matter, a thing may be said to find another thing under some physical influence that we speak of as "attractive"; and (2) that only on the plane of mind is there even incipient seeking in order thereby to find again. Herein lies the evolutionary value of conscious reference when the level of mind is reached.

It is difficult to make my position clear in advance of the discussion of behaviour and consciousness which will follow in my second course. On a basis of correlation one has to distinguish a *primitive psychical system* before the quality of consciousness (which needs definition) emerges, from a *primitive mind* in which it *is* emergent. Mr. Stout will, I think, disallow this distinction.

My interpretation of the chick's status is frankly behaviouristic, if a correlated psychical system not yet effective in guidance be acknowledged. But *pari passu* with the evolution of its behaviour there is developed projicient reference to that towards which it behaves. And with this comes conscious guidance, which the behaviourist on his part will not allow.

In its inception, then, reference begins with the emergence of mind as effective in the guidance of natural events. But such reference finds its points of insertion in particular instances already given *for* reference under specific kinds of behaviour. It proceeds from individual cases to progressively universalised concepts. Quite late in mental development does there arise even the vaguest reference to "source in general." Acknowledgment of such a source is a *terminus ad quem* towards which the evolution of mind rises after prolonged perceptual preparation. It is doubtful whether the rabbit or the cow comes within sight of it in vaguest and least differentiated form or has even a dim inkling thereof. It is reached at the reflective stage only where we are very far removed from what I conceive to be the status of primitive mind.

§ XX. *Reference supplemented under Acknowledgment.*

Our discussion of reference has brought us into touch with a question which is one of the most central of all questions for philosophy. Is the concept of evolution applicable to mind?

There are two senses in which an affirmative reply may be given. In the first sense, it may be said that the concept of evolution is certainly applicable to mind. For what is evolution? As the word, properly understood, implies, it is the unfolding of that which is enfolded; the rendering explicit of that which is hitherto implicit. The evolution of mind in the history of events is the progressive coming to its own, in the fulness of time, of the intelligence or reason inherent always in the very nature of the world. In the beginning the end was enfolded; but only through unfolding do we learn what was, from first to last, the nature of this enfolded end. Apart from its teleological import the word " nisus " has neither explanatory nor etymological standing. Hence, it is said, for those who rightly grasp the philosophical meaning of evolution —whatever may have become the lax use of the word in science—any treatment which ignores the finalistic outcome stands condemned.

But it may be asked : What is evolved ? Is it the Activity manifested in natural events, or is it the expression of this Activity in the world which we seek to interpret ? The reply may be : Both, since neither is separable from the other in the integral whole of the universe. One may still, however, enquire whether the Activity should not be distinguished from its manifestation ; and, if so, whether it is not to the manifestation rather than to the Activity that the word " evolution " is properly applicable. It may be said in reply that since it is the Activity which is progressively unfolded in and through its manifestation—and which thus becomes explicit—one may justifiably speak of *its* evolution, *i.e.* its progressive unfolding. One more question must then be asked. This progressive unfolding is a process " in time." Does the Activity which is thus manifested subsist *sub specie temporis* or *sub specie aeternitatis* ; and if the latter, must we not take "*ab initio*" subject to a timeless Is ?

In the other sense of the word " evolution "—that which is nowadays accepted in science,—the emphasis is not on the unfolding of something already in being but on the outspringing of something that has hitherto not been in being. It is in this sense only that the noun may carry the adjective " emergent." The expression " the evolution of mind " has here a different implication. Nay more, the word " mind " itself is quite differently defined. It cannot connote Activity since the concept of Activity in any such rôle of efficiency is resolutely barred by those exponents of scientific thought whose teaching in the naturalistic domain we here accept (cf. § xlvii.). The evolution of mind, then, means for us the coming into being of a kind of relatedness which at preceding stages of evolutionary progress had as such no being at all.

Stress should again be laid on the supervenience of new kinds of *relatedness* (cf. § xi.), which are accepted, on the evidence, with natural piety. From the point of view of emergent evolution, we should not say that the relatedness observable in the crystal is implicit in the solution, but that there are lower kinds of relatedness therein which are involved as the physical basis of crystallisation. So, too, we should not say that mind is implicit in life, or life implicit in matter, but that vital relatedness is involved in the natural genesis of mind and physico-chemical relatedness is involved in the natural genesis of life.

Let us now briefly review and revise our position in the matter of reference.

(1) Objective reference is a kind of relatedness which obtains within a field of conscious regard, *i.e.* within the domain of the minded.

(2) In any given instance of reference, one at least of the terms in this relation is re-presentative in revival under memory—Mr. Russell would say is the " mnemic " factor in causation.

(3) At the perceptual level a typical instance of reference is that of some sensory presentation to the meaning (for behaviour) thereby revived in re-presentative form.

(4) Below the perceptual level there is as yet no

reference since no meaning is revived in a field of conscious regard.

(5) It is above the level of naïve perception, *i.e.* at the reflective level of consciousness, that reference is of so much importance. Here something given at a lower level of mind, say in naïve perception, has the relation of reference in a field of conscious regard that has become conceptualised for contemplation (cf. § VII.). What we speak of as an object, under such contemplation, is always in some measure a conceptualised object, commonly universalised through its name. The something else in mind, which is the complement of the something given, is, broadly speaking, the significant scheme for reflective contemplation.

(6) When this level is reached, therefore, schemes of interpretation—or frames for reference—are in the field of conscious regard. It is then realised that *any* kind of relatedness in natural events may afford *a basis for reference*, *i.e.* that which is involved in order that there may be conscious reference.

(7) Thus arises the concept of the *referable*. Under this concept " this " may be said to be referable to " that " (*a*) when " that " is regarded as part of the knowledge of the person under contemplation in some sense stored for such reference, though at the time being there is no actual process of referring " this " thereto ; or (*b*) when " that " is said to be part of the common knowledge of educated and adequately instructed persons ; or (*c*) when " that " is within the knowledge of some ideal all-knower. In either of these cases " this " (the something given), is referable to a scheme of

interpretation in some way retained in "knowledge."

But (8), by an extension of the concept, this knowledge, this scheme of interpretation, or some specific factor therein, may still be spoken of as referable to that which is thus interpreted—let us say to nature, as that with which knowledge deals.

On these terms (9) there is (*a*) knowledge, and (*b*) that to which such knowledge is referable. It may, however, be said that there is no valid separation of (*a*) from (*b*). For this makes knowledge a quite unnecessary and illegitimate *tertium quid*, intervening between the mind and nature. And here some (idealists and phenomenalists) say :

(i) That what we call nature is just the objectively mental—the minded as correlative to the process of minding—each inseparable from the other ; while others (radical new-realists) say :

(ii) That non-mental nature is directly apprehended as it veritably is, independently of chancing to be occasionally known.

Whether in view of "three-entity" situations a *tertium quid* may not after all be admissible I cannot here stay to consider.

(10) Emergent evolution takes a middle course. It urges that there is reference of the extended order to that which, in accordance with its constructive scheme of interpretation and explanation, must be *acknowledged* ; but that there is also projicient reference of that which is minded (*e.g.* in vision) to acknowledged centres for such reference.

Now, by acknowledgment I mean acceptance of that which is, as I think, not susceptible of logical proof or disproof, on the grounds that such acceptance gives consistency to a scheme otherwise incomplete. It is imperative, therefore, to state quite clearly and frankly what is posited under acknowledgment.

First, we acknowledge a system of physical events, intrinsically existent, as that which is basally involved in our completed scheme. Secondly, we acknowledge God as the ultimate Source on which emergent evolution is ultimately dependent. We ask: If the former of these be acknowledged, why not the latter within our completed scheme which aims at a synthesis of interpretation and explanation?

But thirdly, we also acknowledge unrestricted correlation of the kind Spinoza postulated under his doctrine of attributes. Within the domain of both attributes there is continuous development under progressive emergence. Each ascending stage in the one attribute is evolved *with* that of the other. Neither is evolved *from* the other.

It is within such an acknowledged frame of reference, with its three-fold relatedness of involution, dependence, and correlation, that world-events take their course " in space and time." But Dependence on God is *sub specie aeternitatis*. Widely as our conclusions differ from those to which M. Bergson has been led, we may still agree with him when he says: " Philosophy ought to follow science in order to superpose on scientific truth a knowledge of another kind which may be called metaphysical " (C.E. p. 208).

LECTURE V. MEMORY

XXI. A Tentative Scheme. XXII. Recognition and Againness. XXIII. Retention and Revival. XXIV. Restatement under Emergent Evolution. XXV. Secondary and Tertiary Retention.

§ XXI. *A Tentative Scheme.*

IT was said in the foregoing lecture that conscious reference always involves revival. It was also said that for "this" to be referable to "that," there is implied something of the nature of storage of knowledge. It is clear, therefore, that retention and revival, which fall under the general heading of memory, demand more detailed consideration from the point of view of our constructive scheme.

As a line of approach to an interpretation in accordance with emergent evolution, let us first take note of what the plain man may say about memory.

He commonly speaks of a retentive memory, and of retaining this or that in memory. And if we ask him wherein lies the advantage of having such a memory he may say that pretty obviously it enables us to recall that which is so retained. He may very likely add that we either remember such and such a fact without any effort, or may have to search for it among our store of memories. In the one case the remembrance just comes; in the other, we try to recollect with more or less effort and with more or less success. Let us ask him: What is the good of remembering or recollecting—what do we do with the fact recalled? He may reply that we place it where it is wanted for some purpose in hand. We refer it to some remembered time when as a fact it occurred; to some locality where it took place; to some episode in our life-history. I think he would include, under memory, reference to a place in a system of knowledge—chemistry, general history, geometry, and so forth—as well as to an episode in his own personal biography; but perhaps with a difference. And I think he would regard ready and rapid placing as a mark of a serviceable memory. If he were asked whether his personal biography, a system of geometry, or what not, must be in mind he might perhaps reply that the net result of what he knows about it must be so retained in memory as to be subject to recall, but that only what is immediately relevant need be actually recalled at the time. I suppose he would certainly attribute to a good memory the gift of recognising people, and to a yet better memory the rapid recall of the occasion where and when. And if he were asked why many old people who remember quite well what happened when they were young are so apt to forget the events of last week, he would perhaps interpret this by saying that the memory has lost the power of registering new facts, and perchance add that the senile brain no longer takes and keeps the impress of these facts.

Without pausing to dwell on some ambiguities in

the common use of the word " memory," *e.g.* now as a process or act of remembering or recollecting ; now as that which is revived or recalled ; and now that which is in some way so retained as to be revivable or within call—let us try to arrange such data as we have thus gleaned from the current usage of familiar speech, in something like systematic form in accordance with an order of involution and dependence, so as to get a scheme to which the facts connected with memory may themselves be referable. I say the facts connected with memory so as to make the scheme as comprehensive as possible. I tentatively suggest that, for our present purpose, they may conveniently be grouped in tabular form as under :

Reference,
Recognition,
Revival,
Retention,
Registration,
The Register.

Here the assigned order within the scheme means this : any item at any given level involves that which lies below it on the list, and cannot have being without it ; but it does not in the same sense involve that which lies above it. Retention, for example, involves what I set down as registration ("on the tablets of memory," as we say), in the absence of which, however it be registered, there would be nothing to retain. But it does not in like manner involve revival. A fact may be in some way retained ; but just now it may not be revived and we may strive in vain to recall it. Half an hour hence, however, it may come to mind unbidden; and this seems to show that something involved in its revival was in some way retained all the while. We often say, by the way, that we retain it *in* memory but cannot recall it *to* memory. Clearly the word " memory " is used with some difference of meaning in the two expressions. Is this because the word is used at different levels? Again, recognition involves revival; if there be nothing revived how, on seeing an acquaintance, can we recognise him?

This suffices for the present to indicate the principle on which the table is constructed. Let it stand just now on its own merits independently of emergent evolution. Read downwards the several items involve what lies below them; read upwards each item may be said proleptically to depend for its value or utility within the scheme on what lies above it. The good of retention is for revival and the good of revival is to subserve the ends of recognition and appropriate reference.

If we draw the distinction between remembering and what is remembered, each is in a broad sense correlative to the other. One cannot have " a memory," or a memory-image in objective regard— that *of* which one is conscious—without a process of remembering *in* which (I should say in the enjoyment of which) one is in some measure and in some sense conscious. But, reading down the list, the emphasis on minding, as a process which is distinctively psychical or mental in its nature, is more marked near the top than near the bottom. We cannot well use the word " recognizing " without any mental implication. But we can, and often do use the word "reviving" as applicable to the life of vegetation in the spring. And we can and do use the word "registering" of such things as thermometers and photographic plates. It may be said that these are metaphorical expressions. But take the table as expressing "facts connected with memory" in its purely mental aspect. Is there not more of the distinctive quality of consciousness in, say, recognizing than there is in just receiving an impress on the "tablets of memory"? In a sense memory is more active near the top than it is lower down in the scale. If we say that memory *is* the register; regarded as such, is it not relatively passive?

§ XXII. *Recognition and Againness.*

Passing now to some further detail, little need be added with respect to reference since I have already dealt with this at some length. In our own reflective life significant reference is a distinguishing feature of what many would regard as the upper reaches of memory. But *is* it memory? Or does it only, in my phrase, involve memory? The one or the other, I suppose, in accordance with the connotation accepted. Herein lies part of our trouble in interpretation. It is no doubt partly a matter of emphasis. Some writers lay stress on memory as register; others on retention; others on serviceable recognition and reference. Retentionists may say that reference of the reflective kind is a higher mental process which, of course, involves memory, but is more than memory properly so called. Others may urge that this excludes much in our mental life that memory is good for. Among those who include reflective reference there are some who restrict memory at this level to the field of that which is referred, or referable, to its place in one's personal life-experience. This is a widely accepted usage in psychology. I remember steaming into Reyjavik harbour; I do not remember, in like manner, the landing of William the Conqueror; I only remember that according to history he came to England. In a more liberal usage, however, the schoolmaster would include under memory a boy's assigning to the Reform Bill its proper place in the development of the British Constitution. Each, I take it, is right in accordance with that connotation of the word he accepts. In common speech the context generally shows the meaning that is intended. Within my present context I provisionally accept the most comprehensive usage, inclusive of all kinds of reference, so as to bring what we have to consider under one scheme, comprising what remembering and that which is remembered is good for and what it involves.

Take next recognition. Has it a distinguishable status between reference and revival? We often mean by recognition that which implies a deliberate process of comparison, bringing out points of similarity as contrasted with points of difference. Such reflective recognition so clearly depends on contemplative reference that a line of distinction between them is hard to draw. Let us, however, descend a step from the conceptual level. We commonly admit a lower perceptual form of recognition, belonging to an earlier stage of mental development than that which I have characterised as reflective. A puppy that has snapped at a toad and found it bitter, seems thereafter to " recognize " one when he sees it, and does not then snap at it as before. There is probably no reflective comparison here. There is, I think, no contemplative recognition of similarity ; there is only perceptual recognition of something to be avoided. Even this expression perhaps introduces by implication a psychological attitude higher than that which is present. The observed behaviour is much nearer what is now spoken of as a " conditioned response " where a visual stimulation (*a*) gives rise to behaviour appropriate to a taste-stimulation, (*b*) though there is no such actual stimulation. If there be here (as we may suppose) a lowly form of psychological recognition, it must be interpreted in connection with revived or re-presented taste-experience. It may be noticed, in passing, that what naturalists speak of as " recognition marks " afford data for such a process of recognition. That is what they are good for—to be recognized when again presented.

Now in so far as the nasty taste is referred to the toad which is avoided—generally at first with a pantomime act of snapping at it and rejection, though the toad is not touched, and with a conditioned flow of saliva—we have not yet got down to what I regard as the foundational note of recognition—that feature of recognition which underlies reference and justifies an analytical distinction of one from the other. I submit that this is given in that which may be called psychical " againness." By this I mean an indefinable character in experiencing, and of that which is experienced, which I think can only be described by saying that a feeling of " again " is superadded to that which comes again. Is there not, in our daily life, often a passing phase of conscious experience when there is just this felt againness, though *what* is again only comes to mind, if at all, under reflective recognition with reference? Of course, with our vigorous development of the higher reaches of memory, no sooner do we have this feeling of againness than we are apt to ask : If thus again, when before? And forthwith we try to recollect, and regard what is both now and before as referable to their due place as terms in that relational place-time scheme which is our conceptual frame for the setting of events. It so happens that I have seen pretty frequently for some months, in connection with an appeal for funds in support of the University of Bristol, Mr. Raemakers' striking picture of the kind of man to be benefited. Something rather specific about it has given me this feeling of againness. But what it was I could not say (and I troubled little to determine), till I was asked whether some likeness to Matthew Arnold was intentional. Then reference supervened on the vague feeling of againness ; then there was reflective recognition. I picked up a while since a novel that I had read some decades ago. Most of it felt quite new ; but here and there, in some salient episode or in some pithy remark, psychical againness was quite unmistakably there ;

and for the most part it just remained at that. I had, however, read it all before; and much of the experience in reading it a second time must have been substantially similar to that which I had when I read it before. There was for the most part what one may speak of as a *renewal* of experience, but without any feeling of againness.

A not uncommon experience is that of having lived through some episode before; and there has been much discussion of how it comes about. Some years ago, walking in the Lake District with a congenial companion, I had such an experience which may, or may not, be typical. The predominant feature at the moment was just a strange sense of againness. *When* before, was a subsequent and supplementary consideration. The whole episode just felt overwhelmingly again. There was renewal of previous cognition with this felt againness, and that was as far as it went. But ere it got further than this my companion broke the thread of our talk, and exclaimed: " How like this valley, with its rounded *roches moutonnées* and surrounding features, is to Borrowdale which we walked down last year—at Eastertide, too, and on just such a day as this. Then, as now, we were talking of the Lake poets "; and so on, in further detail. In his case there was not only re-cognition—renewal of like experience perceptual and reflective—but there was distinct recognition of similarity of factors on this occasion and that. The mere againness which is all that I had so far felt, was, in him swiftly supplemented by that which served as a clue to the interpretation of the occurrence. Whether this affords an interpretation which suffices for *all* such occurrences, is another matter.

It may no doubt be said that this foundational note (as I have called it), of againness ought not to be regarded as, or given the name of, recognition (or even re-cognition), which, it may be urged, is always something more than this. Let us not quarrel over the connotation of words. It is much more pertinent to ask whether it is a distinguishable phase in the memory-process. If this be granted, and if it be thought better to amend the wording of the tabular scheme, I raise no objection. Its upper part might then run : Conceptual and perceptual reference involving recognition ; and this in turn involving a feeling of againness. What I am concerned to emphasise is that this againness, felt only as such or felt as a factor in some higher synthesis, is *there* pretty nearly as low down as we can dig towards the base of a conscious system. It is quite distinctively of the mental order. There may be againness in the renewal of vital processes like those that have occurred in the organism before ; but *felt* againness in something supervenient. It is a mark, one of the most noteworthy marks, of the emergent quality of consciousness.

§ XXIII. *Retention and Revival.*

Our tentative scheme was to include not only the reference, reflective or perceptual, which remembering is good for, but all that remembrance involves. And in accordance with the arrangement of the items in our table, recognition (or, if it be preferred, the againness-factor in recognition) involves revival. Here again arises the question : Under what connotation do we use our words? It may be said that whenever we speak of revival in the memory-context we mean revival with a feeling of againness. For purposes of my treatment, however, I must ask that revival, as such, be distinguished from revival with againness.

To clear the ground we may press further the distinction of renewal from revival. All day long we have examples of the renewal of experience under stimulating influences substantially like those by which we have been stimulated before. There is againness of repetition with renewal of conscious enjoyment. But this againness in renewal *need* not carry with it the feeling of againness. One may tell a boy something connected with his studies a dozen times ; and on the twelfth occasion it seems to come to him with (one might almost say), beautiful and enviable freshness. Of any feeling of againness there seems to be hardly a trace. In the re-perusal of a novel there is much that is renewed without felt againness. But when the againness *is* felt then revival is involved. This revival, as such, is from within, and is supplementary to, or supervenient on, what I have called renewal which comes with external influence. But just as there may be renewal without any felt againness, so there may be revival from within which carries no such feeling.

Let us, for the present, deal with retention and revival—it will be convenient to take them together —in their distinctively mental regard ; and let us start again with quite familiar kinds of experience. We read a paragraph, and at the end (sometimes at any rate) we retain the gist of what has preceded. Recall is unnecessary ; the net result of what has gone before is still there and needs no revival. Following Mr. Stout we may speak of this as primary retention. But it is a not uncommon experience (I can at least vouch for one person) that the net result of the foregoing sentences in a difficult paragraph may not be thus retained. Certain important points may have dropped out ; they seem to be clean gone. And I suppose, on the principle : *De non apparentibus et non existentibus eadem est ratio* : we may say that they *are* clean gone so far as primary retention is concerned. It is not, however, always necessary to re-read the paragraph in order to recapture those salient points which have been lost for awhile. Let us suppose that with some effort one does recapture them without having to read the passage again. How can we recall that which is not in some way retained ? But it is not retained in primary fashion ; for in that case it would not have escaped us so as to need recapture. It must, therefore, be retained in some other fashion ; and this is what characterises that which Mr. Stout calls secondary retention. The question then is : What is thus retained ?

Here we reach a parting of the ways. Some take one route, and some another. And the view opened up is quite different. If there is one thing that M. Bergson and his disciples seek to impress on us by frequent reiteration, it is the utter absurdity of supposing that images are stored in the *brain*, and the sweet reasonableness of the hypothesis that they *are* stored in *mind*—that is in pure memory. Now if one speaks of storing goods one means that they are deposited in some safe place where they remain until they are needed and reclaimed. The wine in one's cellar was put away as wine, and as wine it remains until someone fetches it and brings it to table. So in Herbartian psychology ideas carry on their existence in a region of disembodied shades. Or shall we put it thus ? On the death of percepts and concepts they still survive as ghosts which may in due course reappear, bidden or unbidden, from the underworld of Hades, and bring back with them some of their ghostly associates. That is the view opened up by following one of the routes. It may be said that one can only describe what is then seen in language which is in some measure metaphorical. That may be true enough. But is this essential feature to be accepted as metaphor only : that what is preserved in memory still retains its spirit-form and is in this same form revived ?

For better or worse I take the other route. Let me put a bold face on it and roundly assert that for emergent evolution what is retained is not that which is mentally reproduced but some organic precondition (subject, of course, to correlation) of its so-called revival, such as is afforded by some neural " engram." There is, strictly speaking, no revival (in the etymological sense) of the memory image as from sleep or trance ; there is a new birth of an image-child like unto, but yet differing from, the parental percept. Secondary retention is of the same order as that which I shall speak of as tertiary retention in the plant, *e.g.* the capacity of flowering in the spring. Ghostly blossoms are not retained ; but new flowers are produced by the plant in due season and under appropriate conditions. So, too, images blossom forth to-day and reproduce with a difference the likeness of percepts of weeks, months, or years ago. Even the analogy of the gramophone record, if it be not pressed too far, is valid. It carries down retention to the physical world. Sounds, as such, are not retained therein ; not even physical vibrations are retained. What is retained is the complex harmonic form of a groove that has been duly registered. That is the kind of view opened up by following the other route.

§ XXIV. *Restatement under Emergent Evolution.*

In accordance with the general hypothesis I seek to develop reflective consciousness involves as natural basis a lower plane of consciousness which is unreflective and perceptual ; this involves a basis of life on which it is founded ; and this again involves a physico-chemical basis on which it, in turn, is founded. In descending order each emergent level cannot come into being save as " involving " (as I phrase it) the level or levels that lie below it. In ascending order there are at each higher level new and emergent kinds of relatedness which are there found, and which are to be accepted as we find them —accepted in an attitude of natural piety. But when they come—as we believe they do come—then the " particular go " of events at the level of their advent is altered. The go of physico-chemical events at the level of life is not the same as that which obtains at the level of materiality only ; the go of organic events at the level of effective consciousness is not the same as that which obtains at the level of vitality only. I speak of this alteration in the manner of go at any given level as " dependent on " the new and emergent kind of relatedness which there supervenes in the course of emergent evolution. So long as the words are used in a purely naturalistic sense, one may say that the higher kinds of relatedness guide or control the go of lower-level events.

In this lecture I seek to apply our general principles to the interpretation of memory, in the most comprehensive sense of that word. Given the person or mind-body system (cf. S.T.D. I. p. 103) which a human being *is* (for emergent evolution), there are concurrent many events at all the levels of reality. There are physico-chemical events, as such ; there are vital or organic events, as such ; there are conscious events, as such. All are integrated in the effective go of the system as a whole. Only under the distinguishing analysis of thought can the several sets of events be regarded as even quasi-independent. But in view of such analysis one may ask : Is such and such a factor common, in some form, to all these distinguishable levels ? Is it found in a natural system in which the upper-level kinds of relatedness are not in being ?

Let us now restate and rearrange our tabular scheme and express it thus :

> C. Reference and recognition with psychical againness.
> B. Revival with no such feeling of againness.
> A. Retention and registration.

A. With regard to registration and retention there is nothing (save, of course, in grade of development at this level or that) which is not, so to speak, " common form " throughout nature wherever causation obtains. Any system (and such a system is the register) subject to external influence retains in some measure the effects of this influence. Indeed, the effect *is*, in this regard, just that which is so registered in the system. For it is some modification of the way in which that system is already intrinsically going ; and this modification is retained until it is itself in some way causally modified under extrinsic give and take. Retention is at bottom (and also at top) just such intrinsic persistence, on the assumption that there is no extrinsic modification. And it is just because there is in any system retention of the existing manner of its going that it " tends " to persist as a system and to resist in the degree of its goingness extraneous influence.

To such persistence of intrinsic go, as a distinguishable factor in a system of events, Spinoza applied the word *conatus*. Descartes had said that " each particular thing continues to exist in the same state, as far as it can, and never changes it except by collision with others " (*Cog. Met.* II. vi.). Spinoza said : " Everything, in so far as it is in itself, endeavours to persist in its own being " (*Eth*. III. 6). This endeavour, or tendency, is *conatus*. It expresses what Spinoza calls the " essence " of the thing ; and it is in this sense that he speaks of it as a " force " (II. 45, *Schol*.). All that we are here concerned with is the *de facto* go of a system. Descartes' " so far as it can," Spinoza's " endeavour " or *conatus* must be taken in a purely descriptive and naturalistic sense. A thing goes ; and so far as it is nowise interfered with *ab extra*, this go persists or is retained. As Descartes said, it never changes except by collision with others. And this holds for the go of an atom, that of a molecule, that of a complex inorganic system, that of an organism, and that, under correlation, of a mind—as Spinoza taught. It is *a* factor, whatever other factors may be compresent.

Under correlation, then, primary retention, which perhaps may be regarded as the pivotal concept in memory, is the persistent go of a psychical system and involves an equally persistent go of neural process on the plane of vitality. Thus registration and retention are pervasive world-characters ; and there is, in a discussion of memory, for the purpose of a constructive philosophy, nothing new in the fact of retention—only in the special form it assumes at this level or that.

B. When we pass to revival we have no longer a pervasive world-character in the same sense. Even among ultimate physical events there is retention of the effects of causal influence ; but there is here no place for revival. As I use the word it betokens, not only renewal of some change in a given system by the repetition of extrinsic influence thereon, but renewal of like change by something that happens *within* the system. It is as a secondary change, intrinsically determined, and not only as a primary change, repeated as before on repetition of extrinsic influence, that it gets its status as revival. For illustration therefore we must turn to the organism. Reduce the essential feature to diagrammatic form, which has obvious bearing on our topic.

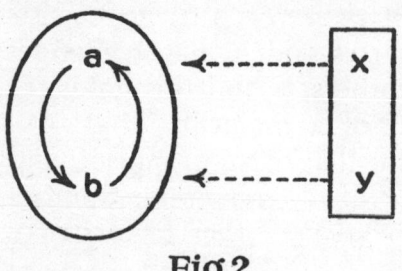

Fig. 2.

Let a and b be two related centres of change within an organism. Let x and y be extrinsic influences (from an external system) which take effect on a and b respectively. And let x and y so influence a and b in swift succession that changes in the latter are concurrent (owing to the retention of one of them) and connected within the system. One knows, of course, something of how such a-b connections are established, under "conditioned responses," in the nervous system. Finally, let x or y (not both) subsequently influence a or b. Then the changes in a (or in b) will induce secondary changes in b (or in a), and such induced change is a revival of that kind of change which was in the first instance due to direct influence from without. The good of revival at this stage on the life-plane lies in its connection with behaviour. For if x precedes y by five seconds, and intrinsic revival of b takes only one tenth of a second, renewal under revival forestalls renewal under extrinsic influence by 4.9 seconds; and this affords time for some adaptive behaviour. We have here a critical turning-point in the course of events.

Now, whether in physico-chemical systems, as such, there may be found the analogue of revival in the organism, we need not stay to enquire. There may be cases of which I am ignorant, or there may not. That does not much matter. What does matter is that revival is certainly a vital characteristic of the organism and plays no *such* distinctive rôle on the plane of materiality.

C. When we rise to the level of recognition, in however primitive a form, we find a character that is something more than organic or vital—that is an expression of the emergent quality of consciousness. I have suggested that the foundational note of recognition (or, if it be preferred, the note supervenient on organic revival) is the feeling of againness. And this may well be one of the criteria of conscious enjoyment. If this be so, not until there is enjoyment of againness, enriching revival, do we have one of the earliest signs of the emergent quality of consciousness. Here, therefore, we are at a level above that of revival only (for that need not carry any feeling of againness) as revival is at a level above retention.

Thus at the highest of our three emergent levels— that of consciousness—we have at least felt againness as well as revival and retention ; at the mid-level— that of life—we have no felt againness, no recognition, and no mental reference, but both revival and retention ; while at the lowest physico-chemical level we have neither recognition nor revival, but only registration and retention. None the less the mid-level involves retention; and the top-level involves both revival and retention. Furthermore, just how retention plays its part at the level of life depends on the vital relatedness that there obtains; and just how both retention and revival play their part at the level of consciousness depends on the new kinds of relatedness that supervene at that level.

§ XXV. *Secondary and Tertiary Retention.*

It may, I think, be said that although there is a sense, and perhaps a valid sense, in which retention may be called a pervasive character common to all levels of emergent evolution—that sense in which one may say that every system of events intrinsically conserves its existing go unless or until that go is causally altered by some extrinsic influence—still this has little practical bearing on what purports to be a discussion of memory. For here we are concerned with retention at the level of mind. This may mean that the concept of emergent evolution, and that of what I have called involution, are inapplicable to mind which belongs to a disparate order of being. Mind and consciousness, it may be said, simply do not emerge, as you call it, and there's an end on't! Nor does what you call life emerge. Life and mind alike belong to a different order of being which cannot arise out of—can only act into—the material order of being. That, of course, is an alternative hypothesis. I am here concerned with that of emergent evolution; must say what I can in support of it ; and, at any rate, must try to show what those who accept something of the sort are driving at.

Primary retention in consciousness involves, from our point of view, the continuance of a correlated set of vital processes in the central nervous system which, since they have not ceased going, stand in no need of revival. But when these processes are no longer going and there is therefore no conscious correlate in being (for when they *are* not it *is* not in being), they may be set going again, either

    (i) By renewal of extrinsic influence adequate to that end, or

    (ii) Under revival, by some other process within the organism.

Given (i) there is renewed presentation ; given (ii) there is re-presentation under revival. But such revival involves secondary retention. There must be some suitable physiological provision (nowadays spoken of as a " mechanism ") of means to this end of revival.

Now the point as I see it is this. If a set of, say, neural processes be not going, there is no conscious accompaniment of their go. It does not exist. If they be set agoing, one way or the other—let us say, loosely but comprehensibly, as percept or image—then, with the coming of neural go, the percept or the image comes also. Neither is, strictly speaking, retained when the physiological go has ceased. Let there be no mistake as to what is meant. What is definitely meant is frankly this.

Neither the percept nor the image is retained as a mental entity. Only the organic "mechanism" (the word is a misnomer, "organism" were it permissible would be much better) which provides for renewal as percept, or revival as image—only this is retained, and that on the plane of life. Conscious retention of the secondary order is a convenient metaphorical expression and should in strictness be replaced by some such phrase as the retention of those organic conditions which are involved in so-called revival.

The interpretation of what may be called tertiary retention is on similar lines. Here is a Blackcap. It has specific form and specific plumage ; it behaves in specific ways, secures a "territory," sings therein, mates, builds a nest, and so forth. We say that these specific traits in the adult are hereditary. But we cannot say that form, or plumage, or behaviour, is retained in the germinal disc of the recently fertilised egg. So far as the behaviour in singing, mating, and nest-building is concerned, we presumably believe that it is accompanied by conscious enjoyment which, under heredity, is similar to that of its parents under like circumstances. It is renewed in this generation in the likeness of that of the foregoing generation. But we cannot say that such specific kinds of enjoyment are retained in the egg. What, then, is retained ? Can one say more than that some "mechanism" is retained to provide for the individual development of the bird ? Such "mechanism" (whatever may be its nature as shown by genetic biology) is what is transmitted to afford the conditions of tertiary retention, if it be treated under the concept of epigenesis not of preformation. Even unit-characters which, as some think, lend colour to the latter interpretation, must be traced back to their epigenetic origin, subject to emergence. This is one of the crucial problems of modern biology.

Without here probing so deeply into the arcana of the germinal substance, let me put the matter thus. In the adult there are highly differentiated tissues, and cells, and their products. In the germ is the "mechanism" for their epigenetic development. Trace backwards as far as you can go along some hereditary line. Never again do you come to differentiated cells or tissues ; at most, as it seems, there may be some of their products (internal secretions) which circulate in the blood that bathes the germ and, in mammals, the developing embryo. But these secretions do not hold form, or plumage, or behaviour, in solution. Their influence, if it be admitted (a matter *sub judice*) is determining ; they supply certain requisite conditions. Apart from this, although the fertilised ovum is the mother of all the many differentiated cells incorporated in the body of the adult organism, it is the daughter of cells like unto itself, and its ancestry may be traced to others of similarly lowly status. Otherwise stated, there is germinal continuity in parents and offspring : but there is no such continuity of parental and daughter neurones ; for neurones die without issue. Nor is there continuity of parental and daughter consciousness. In each generation consciousness is a newly emergent quality. Continuity in mental development, as such, must be interpreted on the plane of life—nay, deeper still, on the plane of physico-chemical events.

Such is the materialism ultimately involved under emergent evolution. But my contention is that, though this is, as I think, a valid interpretation on naturalistic lines—though it is so far true, it is not the whole truth.

In the first place no allusion has been made—lest it should confuse the issue—to the hypothesis of universal correlation which I accept no less than the principle of involution. Does this invalidate what has been said above? It was said, for example, that there is no continuity of parental and daughter consciousness; nor even of cortical processes in the brains of father or mother and offspring. Nay more, it was said that continuity must be, *au fond*, interpreted on the plane of physico-chemical events.

What must now be added on the hypothesis of universal correlation? Clearly the rendering explicit of that which is implicit in the acceptance of this acknowledgment. We have to insist on the unrestricted presence of correlates from the base to the apex of our pyramid. There are correlates on the plane of matter and on the plane of life. Could we but trace them there are correlated qualities or "qualia" answering to those which we observe in the physical aspect all of entities in all ascending grades. But when we come to the level of mind the correlates take on *this* emergent form—that which is pre-eminently distinctive of this level and gives it its name (cf. § v.). That which is continuous with consciousness is the correlated aspect which is common to *all* events. If it be preferred we may say that on the plane of life's correlates is continuity to be sought. But consciousness is an emergent quality of the correlated aspect of nature supervenient at quite a late stage of evolutionary progress. Hence, when I say that there is no continuity of parental and daughter consciousness, I nowise deny continuity of correlation, *e.g.* in the life events that are involved. *That* there is, as part of the continuity of all psychophysical events. But there is no continuous existence of this emergent level of correlation, *e.g.* in the germ from which the daughter is developed.

But in addition to involution and correlation there is also dependence. And here I need only repeat that, on my philosophic creed, emergent evolution, from bottom to top, is ultimately dependent on an acknowledged directive Activity.

Seeing, however, that, under emergent treatment, the whole problem of memory and that which is involved in the ascending steps of its development, must necessarily be considered *sub specie temporis*, it might well seem that nothing of the nature of memory can subsist *sub specie aeternitatis*. It has indeed often been suggested that by extending our concept of the so-called " specious present " to its ideal limit there is afforded an avenue of approach to the annihilation of time-limitations. But can this goal be reached if the curve along which we travel towards it be asymptotic? Must one not accept the *saltum mortale* of acknowledgment?

Still, if some form of primary retention be regarded as central and salient, there may be a valid sense in which the universalised present tense may be acknowledged as properly applicable :

(*a*) To the physical go of events ;
(*b*) To a psychical aspect universally correlated therewith ;
(*c*) To nisus ; and
(*d*) To God on whom all is dependent.

In this sense the question : When ? (and also Where ?) is regarded as irrelevant. Of causation throughout the effective field of the universe we say that it *is* present at all times and in all places. I take it that the probability of this proposition is logically something less than 1. Hence the need of supplementary acknowledgment. *When* and *where* apply only to illustrative examples of its presence. So, too, the past or the future tense may be relevant only to this or that *instance* of go, of correlation, of nisus, or of dependence on God.

LECTURE VI. IMAGES

XXVI. The mark of the Past and of the Future. XXVII. Disparate Orders of being. XXVIII. Images at the level of Pure Perception. XXIX. Concrete Perception. XXX. Memory Images and Recollection.

§ XXVI. *The Mark of the Past and of the Future.*

IF there be any truth in the views to which I sought to give expression in the foregoing lecture there is no secondary, and *a fortiori* no tertiary, retention on the plane of consciousness. There is only such secondary or tertiary retention of the set of organic conditions, with their lower-level correlates, that are involved on the plane of life. Primary retention, however, *is* conscious retention under correlation, or, if it be preferred, persistence within some period of duration both of a process of minding and of that which is objectively minded. But this, too, involves not only a like persistence of vital events, but that of the physico-chemical events which are the basis of life. It is quite beside the point to say here that the facts may be interpreted on this or that very different hypothesis. Of course they may. But that with which I am just now concerned is *this* hypothesis, not any other. Is it not the business of a philosophical tribunal to give a full and patient hearing to every honest witness?

On this hypothesis, then, we must carry the matter a little further. The trouble is that, in us human folk, what we call our consciousness is terribly complex—so many psychical events are passing, many of them abreast, in so closely integrated a system, affording not only additive resultants through summation of constituent notes, but the emergent character that has been likened to a chord. We must try in analytic abstraction to fix attention on some one constituent note, without losing sight of the truth that it gets its harmonic value through its relations to other notes in the chord of consciousness. Each constituent note which we may call with Huxley a psychosis (in a sense of the word now rather out of fashion) involves some neural process or neurosis. The continuance of this neural process (the stress is on " process " as a specific manner of go at some given time and at some localisable place in the organism, say in the occipital cortex of the brain) is the physiological correlate of primary retention in consciousness. It begins and ends. Before it began it was not; after it ends it is not. But it may also wax; it need not suddenly begin full swing, though I think the waxing is for the most part negligible. Pretty certainly it wanes and fades away gradually into quiescence. I think I feel this waning as I listen to speech or to music. If conscious enjoyment be correlated with waning neurosis it must itself wane as the neural process passes towards quiescence. In other words, during its normal course through the field of primary retention any given psychosis, both in its aspect of minding and in that of what is minded, becomes attenuated, so to speak, ere it ceases to exist. Is this attenuation, this fading, this waning (however we name it) specifically experienced? I can only speak for myself, but I feel quite sure that it is. There is, I believe, a felt quality or *quale* of "passingawayness." This affords the primary mark of the past. Realise now that there are, in us, very many psychoses going on together at very many concurrent phases of waning; abstract, so far as you can, from all reflective reference to a scheme of the past much later in development; think yourself, if possible, into the level of development of a week-old infant or a year-old rabbit. I try to do this; and one must do something of the sort to interpret genetically. It is in some measure possible because the perceptual level is still involved when the conceptual level is reached. I can only speak as I find. That is just what my perceptual consciousness, so far as I can dig down to it, feels like.

Consider now psychical againness. This implies revival and not primary retention only. Now revival is reinstatement from within of some neurosis and psychosis, as process, similar to that which has occurred before, primarily under sensory presentation. Take some familiar episode: and take it perceptually, stripped of all reflective embroidery. There is practice-firing in the gunboat out at sea. Under rapid light transmission there is renewal of a visual process; there is revival of a re-presentative auditory process (say a^1): there follows renewal of a like auditory process (say a) when the more slowly transmitted sound-vibrations stimulate the ear some seconds later. If the psychosis a^1, re-presented, feel different from a in sensory stimulation (and to me it does feel different); and if a normally, in such episodes, is sequent on a^1; there arises, as I think, a specific qualification of the re-presentative a^1 which may be called a feeling of "comingness." Again I can only speak for myself. I'm pretty sure that on such an occasion it is there. I feel the boom of the gun, coming ere it actually comes. And this mark of the future seems to afford a genetic basis in naïve perception on which expectancy and anticipation are founded.

Thus in the concurrence, in varying phase and in close integration, of many unreflective psychoses there are, analytically distinguishable, specific qualifications or *qualia* of againness, of passingawayness, and of comingness. They attach to both mental aspects—to the *-ing* and to the *-ed*. Note that againness is a character of certain presentations in full swing; that passingawayness characterises the fading presentation; but that comingness attaches to a re-presentation which forestalls a like presentation and therefore implies prior experience of normal routine. They are quite distinctively characters within the emergent quality of consciousness and enter into composition only when this level of evolutionary advance is reached. But they involve physiological and physico-chemical processes on the planes of life and of matter; and they cannot adequately be interpreted, under emergent evolution, if these be not taken into consideration.

IMAGES

Mr. Alexander's interpretation is quite different. When we speak of memory we may mean remembering, just as when we speak of expectation we may mean expecting. This is universally admitted to be mental. But what is remembered (or expected) is not universally so regarded. Mr. Alexander says that it is non-mental. And when this or that is remembered or expected " experience declares the memory to have the mark of the past on its forehead, and the expected the mark of the future " (S.T.D. I. p. 117). I take this to mean that the event past or future, with which a mind may chance to be together or, as Mr. Alexander says, " compresent," bears this or that mark quite irrespectively of its being remembered or expected. We do not put the mark on its forehead; we find it there; and it is the non-mental mark that makes the difference between remembering and expecting the event which bears it.

Nay more. When I recall some episode of my past life there seems to be revival not only of what I then experienced objectively, but also of the experiencing. Recalling here and now the view from the Matterhorn I feel again how it impressed me. I am a young man in revival tingling with the climb. Is this experiencing now or then? Mr. Alexander says: Both. One is, of course, experiencing now in just that fashion in which one is now experiencing. That might go without saying. But that is not all. Within one's total enjoyment one is also experiencing *then*, not only in the time being but in the mental time which, as Mr. Alexander puts it, flows back to its former place. " A tract of brain may be occupied either by a present or a past enjoyment " (p. 130). This does not go, even with much persuasive saying. But it is Mr. Alexander's affair not mine. For me the past is no more ; the future is not yet ; and their marks characterise now-events, affording data for reference *to a conceptual scheme of the past and the future* no less present in mind. Then, and not till then, can one speak of a date. Mr. Alexander's interpretation and mine illustrate once more a crucial parting of the ways.

§ XXVII. *Disparate Orders of Being.*

It need hardly be said that the interpretation of memory that I accept differs *toto coelo* from that which is so brilliantly advocated by M. Bergson.

According to emergent evolution, as I seek to develop its thesis, there is an ascending hierarchy of kinds or orders of relatedness ranging from those that obtain in the atom, in the molecule, in the crystal, and so on near the base of the pyramid, to that of an order of reflective consciousness near the apex. That is one hypothesis. But one must not be blind to others. It is quite open to the constructive philosopher to contend that each and all of these orders of relatedness should be explained by an insertion of a new order of directive Activity into the pre-existing course of events within the pyramid. If it be asked whence in each case it comes, the sufficient reply, on this constructive hypothesis, might well be : From the realm of being appropriate to the existence of the order in question.

I do not know that anyone has entertained this hypothesis in just this form. But those who speak of the forces which " operate " in determining the course of events seem to have something of this sort in mind. And it might be urged that each belongs to its own order of being—atomicity and molecularity, no less than vitality and mentality.

For M. Bergson there are just two orders of being —broadly speaking that of matter and that of memory. Subject to correction my reading of his method is briefly as follows. A survey of that which is given in and for our experience reveals a number of rather drastic antitheses in some way subtly combined. Starting from their " solidary " union as given in concrete fact, he follows each up to its ideal limit, and at this limit he hypostatises an order of being wherein this or that of the antitheses is, as he phrases it, *pure*.

Where there is concrete cognition, minding and what is minded unite in solidarity. *In* the former one is conscious under primary intuition ; *of* the latter one becomes fully conscious as that which is the object of intellectual regard. The intellect gives an outer revelation of matter ; intuition is the pulse of life as it throbs and in throbbing is felt ; and life is of the order of mind. Now it is the organism in action that is at the " intersection " of the two diverse orders of being. Here is the focus of solidarity. Here is the meeting ground of antitheses. Here memory of the one order glows to specific consciousness in choice ; here the automatism of the other order, itself the embodied product of memory, is guided to finer issues. Here the freedom of the one order overcomes the rigid determinism of the other. Here quality of the one order meets with quantity of the other. Here time (duration) of the one order comes into relation with space of the other. Here the flow of the one order is in vivid contrast with the stark immobility of the other. Here the dynamic impulse of the one order quickens the inertness of the other. Here process, change, progress—all that characterises life—is felt on the one hand, while on the other is seen in static immobility their negative antithesis. Here, in brief, memory of the one order is revealed as a kind of being that is, in all essential respects, the incommensurable opposite to matter of the other. Such is the outcome of hypostatising limiting concepts. May we not admit that this constructive hypothesis is much more picturesque and fascinating than ours?

Come now to some further application of the hypothesis. We must realise that memory gathers up and garners in its progress all records of its past activity. As memory it is the register which retains all memories " by the mere necessity of its own nature" (M.M. p. 92). But retention, though it may prolong a tendency, cannot initiate a change. Hence we must realise that it is mind, as vital impulse, that is the efficient cause of all organic process and of all behaviour. Mind is consciousness; but it takes, or may take, the form of individually conscious glow just when it is acting on, or into, or through, the organism which is the instrument it has progressively fashioned for its use. The connection of this conscious glow with the physiological processes in the brain is thus readily explicable. "Everything," as M. Bergson says, "seems to happen *as if* consciousness sprang from the brain" (C.E. p. 276, cf. M.M. p. 35). But everything does happen, he believes, because these physiological processes are the expression of the operation of the vital impulse which acts through the brain, and glows as it does so.

One is forced to have recourse to metaphor. Mind during its passage, as efficient in action, not only indwells, but envelops, surrounds, or overflows the organism after a fashion all its own—a fashion we cannot adequately describe since what happens is unique. And "the substance, or rather the content" of mind is memory. Herein all we have perceived, thought, willed, from the first awakening of our personal consciousness persists indefinitely. It is preserved even in its minutest details. Nothing is forgotten. But "the memories which are preserved in these obscure depths are for us in a state of invisible phantoms" (M.E. p. 94).

Furthermore, as Professor Wildon Carr says in his able advocacy of M. Bergson's doctrine, "We see in a living creature the preservation and activity of an illimitable past" (P.C. p. 178). Not only does this carry with it, albeit for the most part unconsciously, "personal memory-images which picture all past events with their outline, their colour, and their place in time, in the order of their occurrence" (p. 118), but "in the germ the past experience of the race is gathered up and exists" (p. 172). It is, however, in the vital impulse which acts through the germ that the garnered legacy of the past is preserved. For if it be impossible to suppose that, in our own lives, memory is carried along by us in our body, it is far more incredible that the memory manifested in organic evolution is preserved in the substance of protoplasm (p. 157).

On the hypothesis, then, that mind is a disparate order of being, M. Bergson reaches the conclusion that " all the facts and all the analogies are in favour of a theory which ... considers memory itself as absolutely independent of matter " (M.M. p. 232).

§ XXVIII. *Images at the Level of Pure Perception.*

A crucial question for any philosophy is : How shall we interpret the problem of cognition ? M. Bergson in large measure deals with it under his doctrine of images. He teaches that what he calls pure perception leads us into the very heart of the order of matter ; that recollection which is pure memory is at the very heart of the order of mind ; and that the cognitive relation is at the focus of solidarity in concrete perception where the two orders may be said to intersect.

In perception, as I have used the word, there is (*a*) something given in presentation (the sensory nucleus), together with (*b*) something else revived in re-presentation. This (*ab*) is what is minded under perception ; correlative to it is the process or act of perceiving. We cannot separate—we can only distinguish under analysis—the one from the other. In what we commonly speak of as the object of perception, the sensory nucleus (*a*) is interpreted as due to the stimulation of sensory receptors by some physical influence from the thing itself. But where the sensory nucleus, given in presentation, is not due to any stimulation from the thing itself, but involves, let us say, a receptor pattern due to its name, seen or heard, we commonly speak of having an image of the object of which the name is a sign. Of course, it is not only under the presentation of a name that images arise. If we use the word " pattern " in a sense that is not restricted to a *spatial* pattern but includes also *quality*-patterns—*e.g.* that of a chord, or that of chocolate—the percept implies nuclear stimulation of receptors on the plane of life ; the like pattern of an image does not imply actual stimulation then and there. It is centrally and not peripherally initiated. But, on the perceptual plane, it does imply (i) precedent stimulation of such a receptor-pattern, and (ii) some other pattern actually stimulated. For example the chocolate taste-image in the child is a revival due to sight-stimulation. To put the matter more technically ; an actual quality-pattern of taste, peripherally initiated, gives rise to an " engram " in the central nervous system, and the correlate of this engram and that which it involves is the percept. If a like engram be excited by an allied engram within the central nervous system its correlate is an image.

On this usage of the word an image is wholly re-presentative—a matter of revival. And, on the hypothesis above outlined, the image, as such, is not retained ; only the organic conditions involved in its coming into being are retained—subject of course to correlation. Such, in brief, is our hypothesis.

This meaning of the word "image" must be distinguished from that which M. Bergson bids us understand, at any rate at the outset of his discussion—and this is our present concern. In this usage of the word the material world around us is a world of images. And he tells us that any such image is more than what the idealist calls a *representation*, but less than what the realist calls a *thing* (M.M. p. vii.). It must be remembered that the word "representation" is here used as inclusive of what I have called presentation, and indeed, in the present context, is for the most part the objective presentation to sense. On this understanding it is M. Bergson's aim to show that matter is an aggregate of images. But we reach out to it through perception. As "a perception" (*i.e.* that which is perceived) an image is a veritable part of the thing itself; still, *qua* part, it is less than that which the realist calls the thing. But much of the thing itself may *be* without *being perceived* (p. 27). Hence the aggregate of images which is its "matter" is more than the actual representation with which the idealist deals.

M. Bergson, whose thesis is an interesting variant of phenomenalism, distinguishes between a "virtual" world of images—the world that *is*—from the actual images that are being perceived by some conscious being who is thereby raised to the status of a "privileged image"—one that is at the focus of intersection of matter and memory. His virtual images answer, I think, to the sensibilia of some authors, and to the "sensible qualities" of Mr. Stout. Might one say that the distinction is between images *in posse*, as perceptible, and images *in esse* as actually perceived by someone?

The material world, then, is a system of virtual images comprising far more than is given in actual perception. How then can we interpret the passage from the more to the less? Clearly the images existentially present in the world of matter are compelled to abandon something of themselves in order to become representations. And the distance between " presence " and " representation " seems just to measure the interval between matter and our conscious perception of matter (M.M. p. 27). None the less the image as perceived—the perception—is not other than an image existentially or virtually present as part of the material thing itself. It is only a selected part of the wider whole.

But how selected? One must consult *Matter and Memory* for the answer to this question. If I rightly follow the subtlety of M. Bergson's treatment one must combine a concept derived from the physical reflection which gives an optical image with that of the response of an organism in behaviour. There is some play on the word " reflection." A mirror suitably adjusted reflects an image back on to the source from which radiant influence comes. It gives back pretty much what it takes. But what it gives back is a selection from the total radiant effluence from the source. And only when suitably adjusted does it give *back* pretty much what it receives. Placed at other angles it does not give back but gives *away*. The stress, however, soon passes from the reflection of an optical image to the response of the organism in behaviour. Here is something quite in line with M. Bergson's reiterated emphasis on the supreme importance of action. When this comes well into view, we may say that the organism reacts to the image : one may say that this reaction is a reflection of movement received back on to the image from which the influence comes ; and one may say that through reflection there is selection of just that image which subserves behaviour. But the thing which both receives and reflects is itself an image. In so far, however, as it is a focus of intersection of mind and matter, it is a "privileged image." Such are we. There is not only "a perception"; there is also perceiving. In concrete perception there flow in memory-images of the order of mind. But to get at the matter-image, here under discussion, we must in theory abstract from this, though it is always there in concrete fact. We must take *pure* perception at its ideal limit.

Conceive an instantaneous snapshot of a momentary phase of such reflection and reaction as has been outlined. That gives pure perception in which the matter-image is isolated as such. "Perception in its pure state is thus in very truth a part of things" (p. 68). It is (1) a matter-image, (2) as selected through reflecting reaction, and (3) as a vision of matter which is both immediate and instantaneous. But *qua* vision of matter it is a representation. And a quasi-cognitive relation, emptied of all concrete cognition which implies memory, slips in. There is not only the pure perception as matter-image ; there is an isolated element in pure perce*iv*ing. There is an instantaneous factor in " the act constituting pure perception [which *must* here mean pure perceiving], whereby we place ourselves in the very heart of things " (p. 73).

I confess that I am " embrangled in difficulties," which, in part at least, centre round the application of the word " image " to that which is said to be constitutive of things as they verily are—even if it be what M. Bergson speaks of as " a concession to idealism." Fully admitting the charm of M. Bergson's brilliant treatment, admitting, too, that a familiar story can be told with seemingly unifying effect, in these unfamiliar terms, I think it questionable whether the concept of matter-images, as I have ventured to call them, tends to clarify the cardinal issue in the complex problem of cognition. In any case it seems to be a variant of phenomenalism.

§ XXIX. *Concrete Perception.*

Pure perception, considered in abstraction, is that factor in concrete perception which may be analytically distinguished from the memory-factor ; and the factors thus distinguished lead to the limiting concepts of disparate orders of being. As we have seen, the snapshot of pure perception affords a momentary vision of a veritable part of the material universe. Now a vision, even if it be immediate and instantaneous, may seem to imply a person for whom it is such a vision. And no doubt concrete perception does imply such a person. But personality involves memory in duration ; and this is just what we have thus far been bidden to exclude in distinguishing analysis. Hence pure perception, as such, is a wholly impersonal vision. None the less it is a perception that a consciousness would have if it were supposed to be ripe and full-grown, yet confined to the present, and absorbed, to the exclusion of all else, in the task of moulding itself upon the external object " (p. 24).

Empty this pure perception of its discrete snapshottiness as necessarily instantaneous, and it differs little from what I have spoken of as presentation to sense in that it affords the sensory nucleus of what we call a percept. But our presentation, no less than pure perception, is considered in abstraction from contributory re-presentative factors due to revival. Apart, then, from the interpretation I accept, let us now, in further reference to M. Bergson's thesis, restore to memory, hitherto banished " in theory," its rightful place in perception, no longer pure and immobile but living and concrete. For there is no pure perception in actual fact ; and there is no concrete perception which is strictly instantaneous. Memory in duration always co-operates, as a concurrent factor in a process which is continuous and, for M. Bergson, presupposes the fluent activity of *la durée*. If, then, we realise the duration of consciousness, we can readily understand that on the continuous string of memory there are threaded an uninterrupted series of instantaneous visions which, as snapshots, are a part of things rather than of ourselves (p. 69). Furthermore, the vision selected through action reflects in concrete fact the indetermination of the will—our free choice ; and this choice of reaction cannot be the work of chance. " Now a choice involves the anticipatory idea of several possible actions. Possibilities of action must, therefore, be marked out before the action itself. Visual perception is nothing else than this " (C.E. p. 102).

Incidentally one may note a seeming difficulty here. In pure perception the image is marked out and selected through action; and true action is genuinely new and unpredictable; but here we are told that possibilities of action are marked out *before* the action itself. That, however, need not give us pause. Just now, the chief point is that perception is no longer pure but rendered concrete by the influx of what memory has stored in duration. For choice is, we are told, likely to be inspired by past experience, and the concrete reaction does not take place without an appeal to the memories which analogous situations have left behind them. The indetermination of acts to be accomplished requires, therefore, if it is not to be confounded with pure caprice, " the preservation of the images perceived." " We assert then," says M. Bergson, " that if there be memory, that is, the survival of past images, these images must constantly mingle with our perception of the present, and may even take its place " (M.M. p. 70).

We have here what seems to be the most puzzling transformation scene in M. Bergson's treatment of perception; but I have some misgiving lest there be some link in the argument which I have unwittingly missed. In the foregoing section I sought to grapple with his doctrine of images in one sense of the word. How do we now stand? We have in some measure grasped that the world of material things is a system of images and that an image as purely perceived differs only from the rest of the world of images as the part differs from the whole. Thus far all goes passably well. But now we are told of the preservation of the images perceived, and are faced by the assertion that memory is the survival of past images. My armchair is an image in the world of material things; my perception (pure) is part of that very chair—just the part of the world that on some occasion interests me, and the part wherein, in action, I seat myself. Is it the image in this sense, or in either of these senses, that is preserved in memory? Such images are, we are told, veritable parts of matter. Can it be in this sense that there is in memory a survival of all the images that the instantaneous snapshots of pure perception have afforded in the course of my life? If memory be the survival of images and if memory be, as we are informed, " a power absolutely independent of matter "; then, one would suppose, the images preserved in memory must be irretrievably different from the matter-images of things or of pure perception. The two kinds are incommensurable. Why then call them by the same name?

In any case when the memory-image is introduced, as it must be in concrete perception, the impersonal vision is linked up with the personality which is a function of duration. It is no longer *a* vision, but *mine*. In other words the pure perception, " alloyed," as M. Bergson says, " with affection," becomes subjective in virtue of memory. For the subjectivity of our perception consists above all in the share taken by memory. "It is memory above all that lends to perception its subjective character" (p. 80). And if we turn from the pure perception as a partial image of matter, to the process of perceiving—as M. Bergson so often does without warning—then we shall realise that perceiving and remembering, though distinguishable under analysis, are nowise separable. As M. Bergson expresses it, they " interpenetrate " within the oneness of mind. "The two acts [note here *acts*], perception and recollection, always interpenetrate each other, are always exchanging something of their character, as by a process of endosmosis" (p. 72). Yes. As -*ing*-processes they are *in pari materia*. But can a pure perception, as a veritable part of things, interpenetrate with memory, which is veritably the flow of duration? And if " it is not only a difference of degree that separates perception from affection but a difference in kind " (p. 57), can we speak of " an alloy " of entities which are said to be different in kind? The expression " difference in kind," however, needs further elucidation. And it may be said that M. Bergson's " affection " (sometimes " sensation," sometimes " affective sensation ") is no less material than is his pure perception. It is *bodily* affection not mental. As he puts it: " We might say, metaphorically, that while perception measures the reflecting power of the body, affection measures its [note 'its'] power to absorb " (p. 57). None the less: " In this interiority of affective sensation consists its subjectivity " (p. 311).

§ XXX. *Memory Images and Recollection.*

It is memory that makes our consciousness what it is as personal and subjective. And if we could " eliminate all memory we should pass thereby from perception to matter, from the subject to the object " (p. 77). But surely only if we make play with the convenient ambiguity of the word " perception." For, as what is purely perceived, there is no need to pass from perception to matter, since it *is* matter ; and as perceiving it *is* duration and this cannot pass into matter. That would be to pass from fluent change to stagnant rest ; and these, for M. Bergson, are antithetical contradictories. He is, however, well satisfied with the outcome. " We leave," he says, " to matter those qualities which materialists and spiritualists alike strip from it : the latter that they may make of them representations of the spirit, the former that they may regard them only as the accidental garb of space " (p. 80).

I suggested above that the memory-image and the matter-image of pure perception are incommensurable. It is with the former that we are now chiefly concerned. But we have to distinguish two types of memories. The first may be called a condensation-image ; the second pure recollection. Let us now take the first. Pure perception is a matter-image, say my armchair. But this matter-image condenses on its surface just that which, as pertinent to action, can be drawn from the stores of memory in duration. And this condensation is a memory-image. Both what, as I should say, is presented in pure perception, and that which condenses thereon—which is, as I should say, represented—have a common function in subservience to action. Furthermore, as development proceeds the armchair as presentative nucleus may be replaced, let us say by its name, and, around *that*, memory-images may condense, and in condensation become materialised, or, as is commonly said, embodied. All imagination in one, and that a quite valid, sense, is embodiment ; that is where it differs from conception. " Literature," as Mr. Russell finely says, " embodies what is general in particular circumstances whose universal significance shines through their individual dress " (P.E. p. 74). So, too, in art. Mr. Luke Fildes embodied in his picture, " The Doctor," his conception of ministry, and much else. And my reader may have a memory-image of that picture condensed in revival through my words. This is what we may call " common form " in current discussion of such matters. There is nothing here that is peculiarly distinctive in M. Bergson's treatment save in so far as he links up all this with his philosophy in consummate artistry.

But whence come these condensed memory-images ? From pure recollection held in mind as duration. M. Bergson says that " memory is just the intersection of mind and matter " (p. xii). But elsewhere it appears that it is the memory-image that condenses at the point of intersection. Whence does it so condense ? From pure memory which is, as we are told again and again, not only at the intersection-focus. Now one might have expected that memory-images, so to speak crystallise out, on given nuclei, from solution in pure memory—from that " duration wherein our states melt into each other " (p. 243). But that is not so, as one gathers from many passages. They are already crystallised in duration. At any rate, they are very often spoken of as if they were pure and clear-cut memory-crystals. They seem to be already images, existent as such prior to condensation. " Memory chooses among recollections certain images rather than others " (p. 322). Here it is memory that chooses the memories (recollections) for condensation as memory-images at the focus of intersection. Elsewhere it is consciousness, in a more or less high state of " tension," that " goes to fetch pure recollections in pure memory in order to materialise them progressively by contact with the present perception " (p. 317). " Memory actualised in an image differs, then, profoundly from pure memory. The image is a present state, and its sole share in the past is the memory whence it arose " (p. 181). Might one not gather from this that merging interpenetration reaches, in pure memory, an ideal limit—that, in pure memory, there is pure solution and not pure crystals of recollection ? But turn to other passages. " True memory, co-extensive with consciousness, retains and ranges alongside each other all our states in the order in which they occur, leaving to each fact its place and consequently marking its date, truly moving in the past and not [like habit] in an ever renewed present " (p. 195). Surely, what Mr. Carr speaks of as " personal memory-images," which picture all past events in their outline, their colour, and their place in time, imply, in the language of metaphor, pure crystals and not pure merging solution. Can one say of merging solution that " all the events of our past lives are set out in their smallest details " (p. 218).

One would have thought that the use of the plural—(" recollections ")—would be inadmissible in reference to pure memory, if this be characterised through and through by interpenetration ; and that the antithesis would be between pure recollection—nowise cut up into distinguishable parts—and condensation images which are rendered discrete through their contact with matter under embodiment. And this may be at bottom M. Bergson's cardinal position. But, if so, many passages which imply retention of images, as such, must be read as not really meaning what they seem to say. For if " the memories which are preserved in these obscure depths, are for us in a state of invisible phantoms," it seems as if they were crystal phantoms rather than a phantom solution. And if they be genuinely interpenetrating, in pure solution, to speak of the retention of memory-images must be regarded as merely a concession to current modes of speech and in strictness, on M. Bergson's own principles, quite inaccurate.

Now, let us see how we stand. Either in merging solution, or as recollection-crystals—one *or* other—pure memory retains, in a past which is still existent, all that has happened to me and to my remotest ancestors. This, however, does not account for anything new ; since memory, though it can prolong a tendency, cannot initiate a change. It affords only that out of which something new can be fashioned. What, then, fashions? It is mind, which is also life, that fashions. And what "fetches" that which is so fashioned? It is life or mind that fetches. Here we have, in outline, the salient features of the whole comprehensive scheme. Mind as pure memory retains; mind (sometimes memory) fetches that which is so retained and moulds it to some matter-image; mind fashions into something genuinely new that which is so fetched and so moulded. On this hypothesis, one may admit, all the facts can be interpreted. It looks *as if* mind retains and fetches, and so moulds, as to give the emergently new. But what evidence is there that mind retains either in solution or as crystal-images—retains, too, in a past still existent in time (duration)—all that has happened to me and to my remotest ancestors? Can one find any reply save that it must be so if this hypothesis is to work? All that we—*nous autres*—ask is that a different hypothesis should be tried out on its merits. On that hypothesis there is no still-existent past which retains memory-images in such fashion as M. Bergson postulates.

There is, here, of course, no suggestion that, in what I may call departmental work, a specialist should be precluded from provisionally accepting for his specific purpose that "as if," which best subserves the end he has in view. In discussing *The Problem of Style*, Mr. Middleton Murry is fully justified in writing as if imagery were stored at call in the mind of the man of letters. Any other treatment in the field of literature would be intolerable. The specialist in psycho-therapy, too, is, as I think, quite free (under due safeguards), to deal with images *as if* they were retained in mind as such. But when either one or the other says that what he postulates for departmental purposes must be accepted as the settled verdict of philosophy, he takes up a wholly different position. Now M. Bergson writes, not as a departmentalist but as a philosopher, and as such he would, I take it, wish to be judged.

One must remember, however, that, on his own principles, M. Bergson, has the very difficult task of expressing in logically discrete terms the fluency of alogical process in merging duration. What was said above on " crystal recollections " is, it may be urged, wholly beside the mark. For, of course, " all the *events* of our past lives " as " *set out* in their smallest *details*," cannot be said of merging solution or duration. But how else can one express the inexpressible ? What M. Bergson is doing his best, with the only tools at his command, to help us to *feel* through intuition in synthesis is that mergency which can only be very inadequately *described* in the chopped-up terms of the abstract and analytic speech which the intellect has devised for practical purposes, and in such wise as to turn our regard away from the fluency of fact as it really is within the order of duration. This opens up a problem, the consideration of which must be reserved for its place in the second course of lectures. We may there find that mergent interpenetration is true in respect of mind*ing* which is thus and nowise else " enjoyed," as we say, or, as M. Bergson says, " known " ; but that what is mind*ed* is partial and discrete, since that is the nature of the non-mental which we acknowledge, and on which the minded is initially moulded. For us then discrete parts and " chopped-upness " is not a falsification by the intellect, either in common-sense treatment or in logic, but just as much rooted in the nature of things as mergency is rooted in the nature of enjoyment.

Reverting now to the vexed question of the storage of memories, may I here parenthetically comment on the futility of adducing as evidence of this or that interpretation of retention and revival a statement of the facts which have, in some way, to be interpreted ? It is sometimes said that if only one were less culpably ignorant of psycho-analytic revelations, one's views of the whole matter would be profoundly modified. But, quite obviously, *all* the facts, so long as they be facts, must be taken into consideration and given their full weight. Of course, they are part of the evidence—but evidence of what ? Of this or that constructive hypothesis ? Not so. Of this or that array of facts for the interpretation of which some such hypothesis must be suggested. No doubt, the easiest course is to suggest that nothing is forgotten ; that everything is retained. Then the question is : How does " memory " fetch just that which will subserve some present purpose ? How does it select from the full store of " memories " those which have some utility or value for the conduct of life ? That it does so select is part of the hypothesis. Given, then, a store of all racial and individual memory-images in the mind which has made and uses the body of any organism—oak-tree or man—and given the capacity of selecting therefrom that which is at any moment *ad rem*—the hypothesis is bound to work. In that sense it is a supposal that fits the facts. And this may be—pragmatists assure us that it is—the only criterion of the truth of the supposal. But there are other supposals which claim to fit the facts. How, then, is one to decide which is true? The question may be unanswerable. But this, I think, one may say: that the supposal for any given thinker must fit not only the facts but the philosophic creed. Even here the trouble is that the " facts " are almost inevitably conceptualised in the reflected light of the creed. So at bottom the alternative seems to be this creed or that. Hence each of us must say all that he can in favour of the creed which he has been led to accept.

In conclusion, let me try to put the views that may be held with regard to the status of images, in a rather different way.

First, with regard to my own position—as part of my philosophic creed. Images are re-presentative. They are objectively minded. As such they only exist as complementary to a process of minding. Of minding, I shall assume, the only unimpeachable evidence that we have is the felt enjoyment thereof. Memory-images are, therefore, only in being when they are actually minded (remembered) by someone minding (remembering). Now when this or that is presented to sense there is advenient influence from some acknowledged physical thing, to which, as its effluent source, the presentation is referred. But when this or that is re-presented, in the absence of presentation of the thing, there is then no such advenient influence. It is a revival from within the organism. It may, however, be projiciently referred to its specific place, and projectively referred to a time, within the revived situation as a whole ; and under reflective contemplation it, and its situation, may be referred to a spatio-temporal frame or scheme. The gist of the contention is : Nothing is objectively minded under imagery in the absence of an actual and current process of minding ; the image, therefore, that is not minded *does not exist*. Hence, there is no storage of memory-images that are not being remembered.

Secondly, M. Bergson's contention is, or from many passages seems to be, that memories are so stored. In any case, that seems to be a view that is widely accepted by believers in the " new psychology," but in their case, I think, rather as a policy than as a creed.

Thirdly, it may be contended that, in accordance with one form of new-realism, we must acknowledge with Mr. Alexander, the continued non-mental existence of images in a past that has not ceased to *be*, though it has, of course, ceased to *be present*. The mind, it is said, is " compresent " with these images just as it is " compresent " with things that are now existent. All that it has to do is to apprehend them in suitable fashion.

Furthermore, it may be contended, in accordance with the modern doctrine of relativity, that all talk of time as if there were " a time " for unambiguous reference, is hopelessly out of date—a relic of " classical " treatment. We should speak now of " local times " (cf. Russell, A.M. p. 128). There is thus no reason why an image should not act causally (under " mnemic causation," cf. § XLVII.), out of what old-fashioned folk are pleased to call the past. I find some difficulty in applying this modern concept to the very definite memory-image of a pond into which I fell some sixty-three years ago—one that generally comes at the bidding of the scent of violets with which the old garden in Hornsey was then redolent. But as will be seen later on, my interpretation of " local times " under projective appearance is such as to lead me to regard as invalid the relativist argument and the hypothesis of mnemic causation.

What bearing, if any, has any hypothesis of the status of images on the dependence of all things—images included—on God? I have little to say; and that little scarcely more than a repetition of what has already been said.

If images be survivals, or revivals, of that which has been in some way given in prior experience, they must be considered *sub specie temporis*. But if God subsist *sub specie aeternitatis*—if here the universal present tense be alone applicable—can we properly speak in this connection, of the origin of images under past conditions, or of their value for the guidance of future action? At the level of reflective thought in us, a plan of action precedes execution in action. Cognitive regard of the intellectual order, and volition, as in modern phrase conative, are implied. Does any such implication hold in what we may anthropomorphically speak of as the eternal wisdom of God? Spinoza thought not, and therefore denied that in Him there is intellect or volition. To many good people this seems to be outrageous, and to savour of what they may deem the disguised atheism of Spinoza. But before they pronounce a damnatory verdict they should carefully weigh all that may be said for the defence. No one who is a defendant in this cause is likely to deny that intellect and volition are manifestations or expressions dependent on God, or that *their instances* exist in time, *i.e.* that they imply temporal terms in the relations of before and after. The question at issue is whether (as *we* may put it), under the doctrine of ultimate dependence on God, the plan of emergent evolution preceded the progressive advance of events, admittedly incomplete and developing within a space-time frame of ideal construction but referable to our world. Difficult as may be the concept embalmed in the phrase *sub specie aeternitatis*, there should surely be nothing to offend the most delicate susceptibilities in contending that the question whether the plan precedes the execution has really no *locus standi*. If, by the word " eternal " we mean timeless, for God the plan and execution just *is* one and indivisible.

LECTURE VII. TOWARDS REALITY

XXXI. From "as if" to "is." XXXII. A Mark of Reality. XXXIII. Qualities and Properties. XXXIV. Intrinsic and Extrinsic Reality. XXXV. Levels of Reality.

§ XXXI. *From "as if" to "is."*

ACCORDING to Professor Dewey (H.T. ch. vi.), the first step towards overcoming a difficulty is to locate it—to put one's mental finger on the exact spot at which it arises. Then there may come, if one is rightwise constituted by nature and under nurture, a suggestion of a way out of the difficulty. This, however, may need further development in view of the problem as a whole. Often it is found to be of little use, and not worth following up. It has then to be abandoned as one of the "strangled ideas with which the path of human thought is strewn." But suppose that it passes this preliminary examination, the suggestion must then be put to the test in every way that can be devised. Its consequences must be followed up in practical affairs or in prolonged research. If it stand the test, or tests, it may be accepted, at least provisionally, as the solution of the problem in which the difficulty arises. The located difficulty asks a definite question; the accepted suggestion, duly tried out, affords a probable answer.

Now the suggestion generally starts business as a more or less plausible assumption. When it comes, supposing that it does come; when under further elaboration, it passes the preliminary examination for candidature; one's attitude is: It looks *as if* this may be the means of overcoming the difficulty. And should it win through the more rigorous tests to which it must then be subjected, the final attitude of more or less confident acceptance is: I believe that this *is* the solution of the problem, or the probable answer to the definite question.

The wise man is very cautious in passing from " as if " to " is." Furthermore, he learns to distinguish, under Sir J. J. Thomson's guidance, between the acceptance of " is " as a policy, and its acceptance as a creed. Accepting as a policy means regarding the tested " as if " as a sufficient basis—the best for the immediate purpose in hand—for continued enquiry and research, reserving full freedom to accept some other basis which may hereafter be suggested if it afford a better policy for the prosecution of further research. Accepting as a creed, in the naturalistic sense, is more difficult to characterise. But if, in terms of emergent evolution, the aim of a constructive philosophy be to trace the inter-relations of all events, psychical as well as physical, under one comprehensive scheme, the outcome of that endeavour may perhaps be regarded as a creed. Even so it differs from a policy chiefly in the nature of its acknowledgments. Should this provisional distinction be valid, then, as was urged at the close of the foregoing chapter, it may be legitimate to accept as a policy in some specific branch of departmental enquiry that which need not be accepted—may perhaps be rejected—as part of a more comprehensive philosophical creed.

To apply this distinction ; no one is likely to question the common-sense policy of regarding the external world—represented for the nonce as the rainbow R.W.—as existent with its very own proper form, orderly colour-scheme and appealing beauty, quite independently of someone's experience thereof, for which *rw* may here stand.

Fig.3.

This is, as some say, fully endorsed by that experience ; it carries the pragmatic sanction of working remarkably well. What more can be required ? Nothing more perhaps on this plane of enquiry. It is part of common-sense policy. But one may still ask : How far should it be accepted as part of a philosophical creed ? I take it the position, on this wider and deeper plane, is this. When a person, as enminded body or embodied mind (I accept Mr. Alexander's distinction between "person" and "subject" (S.T.D. I. p. 103)) is, under suitable conditions, compresent with RW, there occurs in him *rw*, and all that this involves. The located difficulty is to account for the passage, in some manner, from one to the other. Now for suggestions of ways out of the difficulty. There may be either (1) transference of the characters of RW to the person compresent with it. The suggestion here is that RW just has all those characters the receipt of which, under apprehension, gives *rw*. Or there may be (2) projicient reference (cf. § viii.) of the characters of *rw* to the acknowledged thing out there. On this suggestion, it is the acknowledged thing that is in receipt of the characters that *rw* gives it. Both these suggestions are based on the acknowledgment of a physical thing existent in its own right. But this may not be acknowledged, save as a convenient policy for purposes of physical science. It may be said : No doubt it looks *as if* there were such a physical thing ; and no doubt you are justified in accepting it in your departmental enquiries and research. But, from the point of view of a critical philosophy, does not your so-called acknowledgment illustrate the too ready and facile passage from " as if " to " is " ? Thus arises another suggestion (3) of a way out of the difficulty. May not RW be just an objective construct ? May it not be fundamentally a differentiation of our experience of phenomena or appearances ? May not this be all that we are justified in accepting as a philosophical creed ?

These several suggestions, and perhaps some variants thereof—*e.g.* under (3)—must be submitted to such tests as are available and applicable. But it is not here a question of which of them works best as a common-sense policy, save in so far as the first may seem to be the simplest ; for all may work equally well. And common-sense should be reminded that in complex matters the simplest interpretation is often too naïve to be accepted forthwith as the most probable. The question for us, at any rate, is not : Which works most easily in the departmental affairs of daily life ? but Which should be accepted as part of our evolutionary creed ?

§ XXXII. *A Mark of Reality.*

As part of that creed I acknowledge the physical thing—*i.e.* an orderly cluster of physical events the foundational existence of which is quite independent of any construction on my part or that of other persons. On the basis of this credal hypothesis one has to ask whether what we commonly call the properties of an object belong only and wholly to the acknowledged thing. And one suggestion (that which I shall accept) is that some of them demand for their very existence the relatedness of that thing to such persons as we are. The grounds on which this suggestion is accepted will be given in due course.

If this hypothesis with regard to some of them (clearly not all of them on this basis) should be tenable in the light of our evolutionary creed, does this imply any diminution of their reality ? I take it that this question cannot be answered unless we can come to some agreement as to what we mean by reality. An agreement to which all philosophers will subscribe ? Probably not ; one may perhaps say, certainly not. That would be too much to hope for. What then ? An agreement among evolutionists of our peculiar brand ? I hope something more than this, if less than that. One may not be able to define reality; but one ought to be able to indicate some character the presence of which may serve as a mark of reality, not only for us, but for sundry others whose views, save in this, are not accordant with ours.

From what was said in the third lecture it may be gathered that, on the interpretation I seek to develop, *relatedness* is an essential feature of reality. Comprehensively it is that which obtains throughout what I have called the pyramid of emergent evolution and is characterised by such coherence and consistency as is found therein.

Part of my contention was that, within any field of relatedness, the *terms* (in my restricted sense of the word) are homogeneous with their relation; but that the same *entity* may stand in many relations and may function as just so many different terms in different and co-existent fields of relatedness. This does not mean that an entity is other than a system of terms in intrinsic relations, for herein lies a mark of its reality. It means rather that we are to take this for granted so that we may analytically distinguish some special part that it plays in some wider field of relatedness.

Among such fields is that which we may call a purely logical field—one which is objective to reflective thought and which is predominantly a matter of ideal construction. And it is, I take it, in such a field that coherence and consistency so obtain as to give to that field of relatedness a claim to reality. So long as such a field subsists in accordance with the strict laws of logical construction it affords an instance of possible reality. But the entities which function as logical terms therein, subject to the nature of the logical field, may function also as terms in many other relations in the actual reality of the existing world with which we are acquainted on the basis of observation. And whereas what we may speak of as logical reality is (in a sense which will, I trust, not be misunderstood) independent of the facts of the actual world, what we may speak of as pyramidal reality is not only dependent on this relatedness but involves also other kinds of relatedness therein. Hence pyramidal interpretation—that of emergent evolution—is, figuratively speaking, under double constraint ; (i) that imposed by the constitutive structure of nature, and (ii) that imposed by the regulative structure of a logical field as such.

There is one more point on which very briefly to comment, so as to clear the ground before we pass on. I spoke of such coherence and consistency as is found within the pyramid of emergent evolution. But it is sometimes urged, or so it seems, that the emphasis on what we are to call real should be on incoherence and inconsistency. The real world, it is said, is an aggregate of pluralistic factors, which in detail are loose-ended, raggedly frayed out, untidy, and hopelessly incalculable. We may not like it, since it is the antithesis of the logically ideal ; but whether we like it or not, that is what it really is. If we be sufficiently toughminded we accept it without whining.

One cannot parenthetically discuss so large a question. There is, however, surely no call to ignore such loose-endedness as we find. In the evolution of organisms there have been many and varied lines of advance ; some of them have made good, and still make good, as viable lines ; a far greater number have not made good. Biological history shows very many loose ends in this sense, racial and individual ; and psychological history, could it be written, would show perhaps a far greater number of loose ends in this sense. Furthermore, what *can* be written is bound to show much untidiness due to lack of knowledge adequate to the task of unravelling so terribly complex a web of events. All this must be reckoned with in any discussion of reality. But the deeper question is whether we can find any loose end of which it can confidently be asserted : Neither intrinsic events nor extrinsic events suffice to account for this instance of untidiness. The world is ragged, it may be said, because it eludes all the kinds of natural relatedness, on which you rely in your naturalistic interpretation. You will, if you be honest, have to confess that raggedness, loose-endedness, untidiness, wholly escape the mesh of your net of natural causation.

If, by stress on untidiness, a protest be entered against prematurely forcing a tidy scheme on a set of facts which do not admit of *that* scheme's tidy neatness—well and good. This is a wise reminder of the imperfect nature of our generalisations (which must express what is *salient*), in view of the extraordinary complexity of the factual texture as we rise to higher pyramidal levels in emergent evolution. But if it mean that " in reality " there is no consistent and coherent scheme for naturalistic interpretation—that, I should urge, is an assumption which is tantamount to a fatal bar to progress in scientific interpretation. At all events emergent evolution proceeds on the hypothesis—to be tried out on its merits—that there is a natural, coherent, and consistent plan of relatedness to which its interpretation has reference ; and that belief in any fundamental untidiness (if this mean absence of causal order), should have no place in a philosophical creed of any constructive worth.

Hence emphasis on orderly relatedness as a feature of reality worthy of such emphasis forms a plank in the platform of emergent evolution. But I expressed a hope that some such view of reality might be more widely, though not universally, accepted. The philosophical doctrine of neo-idealists is in many respects quite divergent from our interpretation. Is it so in this respect ? Of neo-idealism Mr. Wildon Carr says that, from its philosophical standpoint, " reality in its fundamental and universal meaning is mind or spirit. Mind, in this universal meaning, is not an abstract thing opposed to nature, or an entity with its place among other entities in space and in time, it is concrete experience in which subject-object, mind-nature, spirit-matter, exist in an opposition which is also a necessary relation. Apart from their relation the opposites are meaningless abstractions... Experience is analysable but cannot be dissociated into constituent elements " (P.A.S. 1921-2, p. 124). Here it is urged, in effect, (1) that all experience is subject to relatedness, and (2) that all relatedness is experiential. Those who are not neo-idealists may accept (1) and reject (2). But that, important as it may be, is not just now the point. The point is that relatedness, as I call it, is, in the neo-idealist doctrine, an essential feature of reality.

Common to neo-idealism and to new realism (at any rate in one of its forms) is the acceptance of phenomena or appearances, within experience, as themselves real, and indeed, for such new realism, as the only reality with which science is concerned. They can thus combine forces against those who acknowledge physical events as existent independently of experience. Thus Mr. Wildon Carr, on the one part, says that " to constitute a common object it is not necessary to place the existence of that object outside experience and independent of it ; all that is necessary is that one individual should be able to refer to an object in his experience which corresponds point to point with the object in another individual's experience." And Mr. Percy Nunn, on the other part, says that " physical objects are but syntheses of, or constructs from, sense-data." New realists (of his persuasion), he tells us, " have taught explicitly that the varying appearances of the ' same thing ' to different observers are not diverse mental reactions to an identical material cause, but are correlated sense-data, or ' events ' belonging to a single historical series " (P.A.S. 1921-2, pp. 125-128).

I may be concerned to advocate an evolutionary interpretation of the facts different from that which the phenomenalist accepts. But such divergence of view is not *ad rem* just now. The point rather is that the kind of co-relation on which new realists of the phenomenalist school so often, and rightly, insist, falls under the rubric of relatedness. Their position is not quite that of H. Poincaré who acknowledged " real objects which nature will hide for ever from our eyes." But they would, I think, endorse his stress on relatedness. " The true relations," he says, " between these real objects are the only reality we can attain, and the sole condition is that the same relations shall exist between these objects as between the images we are forced to put in their place " (S.H. p. 161).

It seems, then, that we shall not be ploughing a lonely furrow in proceeding on the basis that relatedness, fundamentally orderly, is a cardinal feature of reality.

§ XXXIII. *Qualities and Properties.*

Of emergent evolution, in so far as it claims to be a philosophical system, idealists say that, instead of explaining (as any self-respecting philosophy should explain) the world in terms of mind, it vainly endeavours to interpret mind as itself the outcome of an evolutionary process.

Can we find here any common basis of agreement? I take it that both parties do agree that *our knowledge* of the world depends on experiential relatedness. Where, then, is the locus of disagreement? The idealist says that the existence of the world, as a going concern, depends on experiential relatedness. The evolutionist says that experiential relatedness involves the existence of the world in which, very late in the course of events, it has appeared. The one says that the world itself depends on knowledge ;

the other says that knowledge involves the prior existence of a world to be known. The one says: Apart from knowledge (in some sense) the world would be non-existent (cf. Lord Haldane, R.R. p. 30). The other says: Apart from a world independently existent (in some sense) there could be no knowledge thereof. We are in presence of alternative " as ifs." Each hypothesis has to be tested and tried out on its merits, so far as the nature of the problem permits. It is of little avail for the supporters of this one or of that to be petulantly impatient of the alternative hypothesis, as is too often the case in both camps.

The evolutionary view, with which as advocate I am concerned, demands, I think, the more patience on the part of those whose considered and impartial verdict is sought. For they are asked not to rest content with accepting experiential relatedness as *the* one concrete fact on which to build, but to hear what may be said in favour of the claim that there were prior kinds of relatedness which afford the foundations of this building. I must therefore crave patience. I beg leave to consider certain foundational distinctions which, as I think, are common to all kinds of that relatedness which is, for us, a mark of reality. We shall then be in a position to apply the conclusions we reach to the specific problem of experiential relatedness.

Revert, then, to the distinction, already adverted to (§ IV.), between intrinsic and extrinsic relatedness. As organisms we are (under acknowledgment) things in extrinsic relatedness to other things with which we cannot become directly acquainted save through some extrinsic physical influence from them. This means that our intrinsic goingness is in some way modified in the manner of its going by such physical influence as is advenient. So, too, the intrinsic goingness of any one of them may be modified by the extrinsic influence of others. Now the intrinsic relatedness of inner events which is the very own nature of any given thing is its intrinsic reality. This may never be *separable* from the modifications it undergoes under extrinsic influence. None the less it may be *distinguished*—just as we distinguish a body's own motion in translation from acceleration due to extrinsic influence. One may often be able to distinguish, say, ninety per cent. of the given goingness of a physical system, during some short span, as intrinsic and grounded in its own pre-existent go, from ten per cent. due to modification of this under extrinsic conditions.

Let us connect this with another distinction which I propose to draw. We commonly speak of the characters, properties, and qualities of things; and these words are often used interchangeably. In the light of what has been said above I shall, for the purpose in hand, earmark the word " qualities " for characters that are grounded in what I have called intrinsic relatedness, and reserve the word " properties " for those which get their distinctive status from extrinsic relatedness. That leaves the word " characters " for the class which includes both qualities and properties as sub-classes.

Now we will assume that a thing affords evidence of " possessing " some qualities. This may here be taken to mean that what we comprehensively call the thing is (*a*) the sum of its qualities, and (*b*) their intrinsic relatedness. The Schoolmen spoke of the qualities as attributes, and of their intrinsic relatedness—their going-together within the thing—as the substance. But for them substance was also an efficient cause. Hence they regarded substance as that which holds the attributes together, *i.e.* the relating Activity to which their intrinsic relatedness is due. In some measure we carry on their tradition by saying that the thing " possesses " its qualities.

We have, then, to deal with its qualities. As such they are its very own ; as such they have status independently of any extrinsic relatedness. What qualities, then, may we attribute to things with acknowledgment of rightful possession. They will include certain characters of purely spatio-temporal order within the confines of the thing under consideration—namely the proper figure, size, and motion of parts, which Galileo called *primi e reali accidenti*, and which are generally known, through Boyle and Locke, as " primary qualities." In dealing with them we do not need to consider relation to any contextual environment. But, if we accept emergent evolution, much more than this will be included under the qualities of a thing ; there will be included also all characters expressive of the physico-chemical, physiological, and (imputed) psychical relatedness, *qua* intrinsic,—all those characters which give to a thing, an organism, or a person, its status in the evolutionary hierarchy. To the primary qualities must be added those that may be called " constitutive qualities." These, too, belong of very own right to the thing, or the person, under contemplation. Hence I have followed Mr. Alexander in speaking of life and consciousness as qualities.

But some of the characters that we habitually attribute to a thing imply effective relatedness to some other thing or things (or at least to an environing context) by which it is in some way influenced. Can one, for example, attribute weight to a thing apart from the earth with which it is in gravitative relation? Can one attribute to it resilience save under impact? If one speaks of the hardness of a mineral, is not relation to something other than itself implied—to one's thumb-nail or one's knife? More technically, perhaps, one means that it will scratch a mineral below it on the Mohs or other " scale of hardness," and be scratched by one above it. Can one speak of the refractive index of a crystal irrespective of the transmission of light? And so on. Extrinsic relatedness of the effective order is, in all such cases, presupposed—not in place of but as well as intrinsic relatedness. I here speak of such characters as properties, and that without denying that they are closely co-related with intrinsic qualities. Nor need the extrinsic relatedness be effective. When we pass on to experiential relatedness, I shall urge that all perspective appearances as such, and all secondary characters, are properties. The real shape of a penny (under acknowledgment) is one of its qualities. Its perspective appearance, whether as round or elliptical, is (I shall contend) one of its properties. The mark of a property, in the sense I intend, is that it cannot either be, or be considered, apart from some mode of extrinsic relatedness. But it is none the less real. However distinguishable, under analysis, qualities and properties may be, the former have no greater and no less claim than the latter to reality in relatedness.

§ XXXIV. *Intrinsic and Extrinsic Reality.*

It will not, I trust, be supposed that I dream of suggesting that qualities and properties lead a charmed life each independent of the other. That is very far from my meaning. Mainly restricting myself, here and now, to levels of relatedness below that of consciousness itself, and tacitly taking for granted such cognitive relatedness as may obtain, what I do mean may be expressed as follows. Let us analytically distinguish (i) the own intrinsic goingness of a system or thing from (ii) some modification of that goingness through extrinsic influence. Let us consider the own goingness in some given brief span of time quite irrespectively of the past history of its origin—which is another story. Then and there it is just a matter of intrinsic relatedness, or current changes of such relatedness within the system. One need not go outside the system to get at its character as a quality. What one has to do is to install oneself inside it—to live (so to speak) in close and intimate touch with all the intrinsic changes that are in progress, and to deal reflectively with them. M. Bergson has rightly insisted on the importance of some such procedure. Here I follow him whole-heartedly. Assume, then, that one can do this with some measure of success, so as to get at the existing go of the system as it is, in and for itself—through empathy if you like. What one must speedily realise is this : that one cannot interpret all the changes in current goingness on a wholly intrinsic basis. As interpreter one is forced to say (putting it picturesquely) : It looks as if there were some extrinsic influence which is a causal condition of some of these changes in current goingness, since I cannot account for these changes as grounded in intrinsic relatedness only. I have done my best to interpret what happens on the supposal that the relatedness, $T_R T^1$ is wholly of origin from within the system. I find it won't work. There are facts for which that hypothesis does not adequately account. They present a serious difficulty. My suggestion of the way out of it is that I must also consider extrinsic relations to something outside the system. That means that, in applying the formula $T_R T^1$, I must regard the T as attaching to the system, and the T^1 as attaching to something outside it. This must be so if the relatedness be extrinsic as defined. But the system then assumes a new status in virtue of its function as T. As term it now earmarks the system in extrinsic relation to some other system, or systems, or some context, outside it. The system becomes, so to speak, a debtor through its indebtedness to some other system for some of its characters. One wants a comprehensive name by which to designate that which the system gains in becoming a term in extrinsic relatedness. Under suitable definition the word " property " serves, as I think, this purpose. I therefore speak of properties of a thing, and urge that as such they are existent only in virtue of extrinsic relatedness.

Such is the position as I see it. Now dive inside again. Ignore all that is happening outside which you may infer to be the extrinsic cause of certain changes in goingness. Just take the intrinsic changes of relatedness in the system within which you install yourself at their face-value, so as to be in close touch with the current go which is their intrinsic reality. What will this reality include? It will include space-time-event relatedness as primary quality; it may include physico-chemical relatedness so far as intrinsic only; it may also include life; it may include the quality of consciousness. How much it will include in any given case will turn on the level at which one places the given system in the scale of emergent evolution—that going system in the heart of which one installs oneself. But whatever we so regard as intrinsic to that system will belong to it of its very own right. That is its mark as quality.

But when we dive inside—installing ourselves as best we may in the system under consideration—we must do so, not only as a means to realising what is going on, partaking, so to speak, of its process as though we were immersed in it, but we must do so as interpreters also. We must strive to get both current touch with it and a more detached intellectual view of it. And we have seen that, *as interpreters*, we should soon be led to infer that an extrinsic origin of some of the changes in the current passage of existing goingness is demanded in order to account for all the facts. The further question then arises : Is something also demanded in order to account for the existing goingness independently of such modification by extrinsic influence ? And if so what ? The answer is that what is demanded is *au fond* retention of the goingness of a moment ago, and other preceding moments. This opens up the " other story " to which allusion was made near the beginning of this section. Retention is intrinsic ; but the change of go that is retained is often of extrinsic origin. Hence the importance of an adequate interpretation of retention. This has already been attempted in the fifth lecture (cf. §§ xxiii.-xxv.).

Regarding the matter, then, from the point of view from which goingness is in focus, may one say that any extrinsic modification of the existing go of a system is, in a comprehensive sense, an " acquired character " thereof ? This may be retained in some primary, secondary, tertiary, or lower inorganic fashion. In so far as thus retained it will henceforth form part of the intrinsic go of the system so long as retention holds. Thus there is provision for the evolutionary and historical development of qualities in existing systems at different emergent levels. But any such quality, in so far as it needs no extrinsic renewal, persists *within the system*, and is part and parcel of its intrinsic reality. Space-time-event relatedness, as part of intrinsic reality, is always within any given system under consideration; sundry chemical transactions are within a more highly evolved system ; that kind of relatedness which the quality of life expresses is no less within the organism ; emergent mind is within the personal system, and nowhere else. The given system is the home of all the intrinsic reality which is its very own—belongs to it "absolutely," since it is no merely external view thereof (cf. Bergson, I.M. p. 2).

I ventured incidentally to suggest in the foregoing section that in any given integral system the specific gotogetherness may be regarded as the substance of that system in its entirety. In this naturalistic sense it may be said to be the principle of unity ; but, if so, it must be distinguished from such a Principle of Unity as plays the part of an integrating Activity—*e.g.* in T. H. Green's philosophy. With any such Agency naturalism, with which alone I am at present dealing, has no concern.

Provisionally grant, then, that the gotogetherness in a manner distinctive of the emergent level of relatedness in this or that integral system, may be spoken of as substantial. We then ask : What is it that thus goes together ? I should reply : It is the stuff of the system that thus goes together. In one sense of the formula H_2O, the stuff of the molecule is indicated—*i.e.* the atoms of hydrogen and oxygen; but in a richer sense more than the stuff is implied —namely, as I put it, the substantial gotogetherness of the stuff in a quite specific way so as to constitute the molecule. Even so, as molecular stuff, the atoms are no longer what they were in prior independence. This holds throughout all the ascending levels in the pyramid. That which becomes the stuff at a higher level of emergence is never quite what it was at the lower level from which it was derived—otherwise one would have resultants only and not emergence. Under emergent evolution there is progressive development of stuff which becomes new stuff in virtue of the higher status to which it has been raised under some supervenient kind of substantial gotogetherness.

I think I am here expressing in my own way what Mr. Alexander has expressed, perhaps better, in his. It is not easy to express—though I believe it to be common form in much current thought—partly because one cannot have substance without its appropriate stuff; and partly because the stuff is what it is—let me say as emergent stuff—in dependence on its appropriate substance. There is, too, progressive advance from some stuff which we take to be ultimate at the base of the pyramid to the emergent stuff at this or that level in the hierarchy. Furthermore, while the stuff is regarded distributively and peripherally, the substantial gotogetherness, in this or that specific way in accordance with evolutionary status, must be regarded as centrally integrative. Thus, it is that, naturalistically, the stuff goes together in a collective entirety. This precludes the view that the emergent stuff can adequately be dealt with in distribution *only*—that is, apart from central integration or substantial gotogetherness.

We may now pass to correlation that we may ask in due course what is the stuff and what the substance of a psychical system. It will be well, so far as is possible, to restrict our view here and now to those instances at the level of mind wherein there is, as we think, some positive, though necessarily rather indirect, evidence that such correlation obtains.

L.M.E.

Even so it must be remembered that our full acknowledgment is that of unrestricted correlation at all levels of emergence.

What, then, do I mean by correlation thus restricted for present purposes to man and some of the higher animals? I mean that the whole physical system from bottom to top is also from top to bottom a psychical system. Of this total psychical system in its entirety the emergent quality of mind is high-level only; but all lower levels are psychically, as well as physically, involved. Consider, then, this psychical system with emphasis on the supervenient stage of evolution when the status of mind is attained What does this mind comprise?

My reply to this question must be different from that of Mr. Alexander; for, as will be remembered (§ VI.), I include " in mind " that which is there " by way of idea," as well as that which is there " by way of attribute." I include in mind all that is objectively minded as well as processes of minding, Mr. Alexander includes only the latter. For me, therefore, the emergent stuff of the mind is afforded by the distributive and peripheral items as minded; the substance of the mind is the psychical gotogetherness of all such peripheral *-eds* as are on the *tapis*. For him these peripheral *-eds* are non-mental —the *-ing* alone is mental. That this central and substantial *-ing*-relatedness is of supreme importance I do not deny. Nay, rather it will have been seen that it is the substantial factor in relatedness that makes *any* integral system, physically or psychically regarded, what it is in its entirety—for what it thus is depends on substantial gotogetherness. This must

TOWARDS REALITY

suffice to show on what general basis of interpretation I am led to include all that is minded as constituting the emergent stuff of mind, subject always to its substantial gotogetherness in the psychical system as an integral whole.

Revert now to what was said a little way back. I said (p. 191), that space-time-event relatedness, as part of intrinsic reality, is always within the given system under consideration; sundry chemical transactions are within a more highly evolved system; that kind of relatedness which the quality of life expresses is no less within the organism; emergent mind is within the personal system and nowhere else. I wish this to be taken quite literally as inclusive alike of stuff and substance. Not only is all minding but all that is minded intrinsic to the psychical system. Stuff and substance of it— -*eds* no less than -*ing*—belong to a personal biography (as some put it) yours, or mine, or another's.

Now if we take up this position and feel constrained or content to abide therein, there seems to be no escape from solipsism. But under our primary acknowledgment of a physical world, there is provision for advenience of physical influence. This again I take quite literally. There is extrinsic relatedness of the person, *qua* physical system, to things, as likewise physical systems, in the acknowledged world of physical events. But what reaches the former from the latter is advenient influence only—*e.g.* that which is the external stimulus to which some receptor-pattern is due—this and nothing more. This, however, affords no provision for the *objective* world in which we live—a world richly dight in colour, and scent, and sound—what we may call a rainbow world of perceptual experience and not only a physical source of electro-magnetic and other advenient pulses. How comes there to be such a rainbow world, rich with the reality of extrinsic relatedness to us? Through projicient reference. That which is perceptually minded—inevitably intrinsic to the psychical system that one is—affording the distributive stuff of the mind—is also a set of signs, including Berkeley's language of vision, which, primarily, for purposes of behaviour, are referred to centres of physical effluence thereby signified. The centre from which advenient influence comes on the plane of matter is the centre to which there is projicient reference on the plane of mind.

I know full well that new realists, and not they only, will summarily reject this concept of projicient reference, and will say that direct apprehension offers a far simpler interpretation of the facts. But perchance the problem is too complex to admit of so simple a solution. The crucial question, I think, is: What is advenient? In the light of a critical philosophy that takes evolution seriously the reply to which I am led is: Sundry kinds of physical influence only. If this be so, some such concept as that of projicience demands careful consideration.

For those who accept it, there is a double escape from solipsism; (1) through the concept of advenience, if a physical world be acknowledged; (2) through the concept of projicient reference of that which psychical signs signify, to those centres from which advenient influence comes. Thus for us the colour-sign *red*, part of the psychical stuff of the mind, correlated with a specific chemical process in the organism, has projicient reference to occurrences (thereby signified) in the physical centre from which electro-magnetic influence is advenient.

Enough now, for the present at least, with regard to projicient reference. What does it come to? All substantial minding, all emergent stuff as minded, is within the personal system. Only through reference does that which is so minded attach, as a sign, to occurrences thus signified in some system extrinsic to the personal system; but under acknowledgment of a physical world, there is adequate provision for such attachment in the genesis, through behaviour, of that which we speak of as perception.

We need, however, yet another avenue of escape from the solipsistic position. Here is a psychical system—yours or mine—within which all minding and all that is objectively minded, is intrinsic. But if you and I are to escape from psychical solipsism, I must somehow get at your psychical system and you must somehow get at mine. I suppose few are likely to deny that one does " impute " (to use Mr. Alexander's word) to one's neighbour a psychical system of like nature to that with which one has immediate or, as some say, intuitive acquaintance, as intrinsically one's own. And I suppose there is little doubt that, as the outcome of a very elaborate process, of the reflective order, in large measure inferential, one does eventually (1) frame an objective construct of oneself which more or less tallies with that self which one can only enjoy directly in immediate acquaintance; and that one does (2) refer some such construct to one's neighbour who is thus regarded as a person, no less than one is oneself. Such an elaborate construct of the psychical order, a very late outcome of reflective thought, W. K. Clifford called an " eject."

Such an eject, as an imputed self of ideal construction, comprises, I should urge, both the stuff and the substance of the mind under contemplation —comprises not only minding " by way of attribute," but also that which is at some given time objectively minded " by way of idea." A gifted historian said in my hearing that he only began to be in touch with some given period of our history when he could jostle the folk in Fleet Street, chat with the country gentleman over his wine, talk with the waggoner in the wayside inn, and share the modes of thinking and the current enthusiasms of the day. Did he not here include as " in mind " not only substance (modes of thinking) but such of the peripheral stuff as he considered *ad rem* ?

But is there not a far earlier and much more primitive stage of some such reference on the perceptual plane of mind ? Does not the infant and the animal seem somehow to get—M. Bergson would say through instinctive sympathy—some dim inkling of mind (say in the mother) other than its own ; and this at a time long precedent to that at which any reflective constructs are framed ? I think I am at one with Mr. Alexander in believing that there is some such primitive process, though we may interpret its outcome with a difference. I venture to name it *ejicient reference*—craving pardon for doing so. If such a process of ejicience—whether we call it by this name or another—be entertained, then we may say of ejicience, as Sir Charles Sherrington says of projicience, that it initially occurs, "without elaboration by any reasoned process." This is no doubt implied in M. Bergson's "instinctive sympathy." But "sympathy" needs careful definition; and nowadays the word "instinctive" has half a dozen quite different connotations.

If, then, the inelegant word "ejicience" be provisionally allowed to pass—of course under protest—at what level is ejicient reference emergent? Only, as I think, at the level of mind. Ejicience no less than projicience is a differentiated kind of reference; and I have urged that reference proper only begins when the level of mind is reached. There is neither projicient nor ejicient reference at any lower level, even granting that there are psychical systems at such lower levels.

But when the level of mind *is* reached, this ejicience, or something of the sort—founded, as I think, on an observable differentiation of behaviour towards enminded systems on the one hand and mindless systems on the other hand—affords a perceptual avenue of approach, under genetic treatment, towards (1) such correlation of the physical and the psychical as some comparative psychologists accept as a provisional working hypothesis or a policy; and (2), through this, to the acknowledgment of unrestricted correlation as part of a constructive creed. This further step, be it noted, admittedly goes beyond the positive evidence. Such is the nature of a creed. Such I hold to be the characteristic feature of what I call acknowledgment subject always to the proviso that it embodies nothing contradictory to such positive evidence as can be adduced.

Taking, then, correlation as a policy of interpretation accepted by many comparative psychologists who have no use for a so-called philosophic creed, let us ask : On what observable difference of behaviour does it look *as if* projicience is supplemented by ejicience ? The trouble is that as a policy of interpretation it is based on a number of observations on the part of those who have been in close touch with many and varied nuances of behaviour. Recital therefore of this or that instance is not likely to produce the effect that many instances produce on the observer himself. And here only one can be cited. A and B are two chicks and x a worm. As the outcome of prior behaviour the sight of x evokes a taste-revival in A and B respectively (cf. Fig. 2, p. 134). This taste-sign is projicient on to the centre of physical effluence. So far there is projicience common to A and to B ; and it seems to those who are not behaviourists only as if the way in which each acts is in some measure dependent thereon.

But carefully observe the further course of behaviour, a little later in life, of the two chicks in presence of a worm. It looks as if each seems to realise, however dimly and vaguely, that the other wants that worm. I transcribe from my notes. " B [seven days old] and another in corner of pen. Dropped small worm near them. B drove other off ; then ate worm." Here it looks as if B's act was in part determined, as the result of what we call prior experience, by the behaviour of others in presence of a worm. But no doubt the observation *can* be interpreted in behaviouristic terms, *i.e.* irrespective of any psychical correlation.

If, however, such correlation be accepted as a policy of interpretation, then how does ejicience come into the picture? In what respect does it differ from projicience only? In brief: Projicient reference runs from A or B to x; ejicient reference runs from " A with projicient x " to " B with projicient x." Here I must leave the matter *sub judice*, merely adding that such a psychical factor (if it be granted) is ejicient *into* B; nowise as such advenient *from* B. Physical influence only is advenient from B.

If correlation be admitted at all we need some genetic interpretation of the transition from " I want x " to " you want x." Something of the sort, however crudely the exigences of language force us to express it, lies at the critical turning-point from merely individual behaviour to that which is incipiently social. Reduced to its simplest terms for evolutionary interpretation it looks as if the transition is interpretable on the hypothesis of what I call ejicience.

Let us now ask one more question of rather different import—one which naturally arises if we may still regard relatedness as a mark of reality. Is correlation itself a kind of relatedness? I think Mr. Alexander would say: No, it is fundamentally identity. None the less it is identity expressed in very diverse attributes and given through quite different modes of acquaintance. Grant that we may still—fundamental identity notwithstanding—regard correlation as a kind of relatedness. We must then ask : Of what nature is its connection with other kinds ? Is there spatial relatedness, so that we may say that the physical system is here and the psychical system there ? Is there temporal relatedness, so that we may say that the physical event either precedes or succeeds its correlate ? Is there physical relatedness if the one be of the physical and the other of the psychical order ? Or is there psychical relatedness of terms that are heterogeneous in attribute ? In each case the answer, for us, must be in the negative. What one means by this is that there is no spatial distance nor temporal interval between the physical event and its correlate. In these respects there is fundamental identity. Nor is the one either the cause or the effect of the other ; as Spinoza long ago urged. If the one event be fundamentally identical with the other, can one well speak of causal relation between them ? What then is there ? Can one say more than that there is just correlation of this attribute with that. If it be a kind of relatedness, it is *sui generis*, and stands alone of its kind. Within *each* attribute there is a hierarchical order of involution and dependence ; but as between attributes there is just that one kind of relatedness, at each given level, which I seek to distinguish by the specialised use of the word " correlation." That is why in Fig. 1 (p. 11) correlation is represented by the horizontal dotted line (cf. § v.).

§ XXXV. *Levels of Reality.*

It is clear that, on the constructive philosophy of emergent evolution which I seek to develop, there are levels or orders of reality in respect both of intrinsic and of extrinsic relatedness. This does not, of course, imply a scale of more or less reality, as such, for relatedness as a mark of reality obtains at all levels. It does, however, imply (1) that there is increasing complexity in integral systems as new kinds of relatedness are successively supervenient ; (2) that reality is, in this sense, in process of development ; (3) that there is an ascending scale of what we may speak of as richness in reality ; and (4) that the richest reality that we know lies at the apex of the pyramid of emergent evolution up to date.

From what was said in the foregoing section, it will be understood that what I mean by richness characterises both stuff and substance as we ascend through the hierarchy of levels. It is no disparagement of the achievements of modern physical science to say that the stuff and substance with which it deals are, in the sense intended, less rich than the stuff and substance with which the biologist has to deal. It is no disparagement of the achievements in biology to say that the stuff and substance with which it deals are far less rich than that with which the student of human affairs has to deal. And if Mr. Alexander be right in contending that the quality of deity is only attained within some human persons —which does not preclude preeminence in one along this central line of nisus—then here we have the very richest product of emergent evolution.

Now one of the cardinal implications of emergent treatment is that the richer cannot adequately be interpreted in terms of the poorer; that life cannot be interpreted in terms of physico-chemical relatedness only; that human affairs, which depend on the quality of mind, require something more than biological interpretation; and that conduct when deity is emergent depends for its guidance, in the naturalistic sense, on that which is expressed by this richest of qualities.

I know full well that there are many who cannot allow to the quality of deity, in Mr. Alexander's hierarchical scheme, a place in naturalistic treatment. To accept this with natural piety means, they say, a surrender to nature of all those values whose Source is nowise discoverable in nature. A resolute stand, they think, must be made somewhere; it may be, with Descartes, at the level of reflective consciousness when the Rational Soul took command over precedent automatism; it may be at the lower level when Mind was first introduced; it may be at the level of Life with its *Elan* or Urge. At one or more of these levels there is an inflow into nature of that which belongs of right to a disparate order of being. Such explanatory views do not lack able advocacy. All that we—*nous autres*—have a right to ask is that a hearing—patient and so far as possible unprejudiced—should be given to our version of the world-story we all seek to read aright.

What just now I am anxious to emphasise is that on our view, be it right or wrong, when we reach the quality of deity we attain to the level of natural reality which is the fullest and richest of all that we know. It comprises more than there is at any other level; the more is emergent and not only resultant; it involves the less of all other levels; on the less the more is built; by the more the less, right-down to the least, is transformed. All this we accept on the basis of what we deem to be a purely naturalistic interpretation.

Here we may stop. Here naturalism with its attendant agnosticism is bound to stop; for the attitude of natural piety is frankly that of agnosticism expressed in more homely and less repellent phrase. We reach a naturalistic level at which the enrichment is due, let us say, to the presence of ideals of value on which the shaping of conduct depends. They are emergent; and they are to be accepted for all they are worth, nowise slighted or slurred over to the impoverishment of the person who is "qualitied" by them, whose status in the hierarchy is, in and through them, just what it is. It is the business of naturalistic ethics to render an account of their natural genesis. Are they real under the rubric of relatedness? Assuredly they are real in the fullest naturalistic sense. They are the emergent stuff of which the natural gotogetherness at the level of deity is the substance.

What more need one ask for? Is not such a scheme of interpretation complete?

Let us enquire of the critics of naturalism in what respect they regard it as incomplete. They say that it is incomplete since it not only ignores but disallows the concept of *Activity*. Now I am one of those who hold that, for purposes of naturalistic interpretation, this concept is quite useless, and that all the facts—those of life and mind included—can be adequately described without invoking Activity of any sort from start to finish. None the less from the point of view of a constructive philosophy, I, for one, am unable to see how one is to explain all that goes on from start to finish without it. At every upward stage of emergent evolution there is increasing richness in stuff and in substance. With the advent of each new kind of relatedness. the observed manner of go in events is different. In a naturalistic sense each level transcends that which lies below it. Thus we reach the level of deity which in its richness transcends all others. From bottom to top, then, there is continuous redirection of the course of events. The more loyally we accept a naturalistic interpretation, say, of an emergently new (anabolic) rise of the evolutionary curve on the advent of life with consequent provision for new modes of the storage of physical energy, or " the apparent paradox that ethical nature, while born of cosmic nature, is necessarily at enmity with its parent " (H.E. IX. p. viii.) ; the more clearly we realise that Huxley's agnostic position in regard to *Evolution and Ethics* was fundamentally consistent with his earlier teaching *On the Physical Basis of Life* (I. p. 130) (notwithstanding much mistaken talk about " recantation ") ; the more steadily we remember " that evolution is not an explanation of the cosmic [or the ethical] process but merely a generalised statement of the method and results of that process " (IX. p. 6) ;—in brief, the more adequately we grasp the naturalistic and agnostic position, the more urgent is the call for some further

VISION AND CONTACT

This receptor-event is to be regarded, on the plane of matter, as physico-chemical. As such, on this plane, it is closely analogous to that which occurs in a photographic record. It is emergently at a higher level than that of the electro-magnetic influence which evokes it ; and, as record, it affords the first step upwards towards vision in the person. *In the person* the receptor-event happens, and beyond the confines of the person it has no being. Since it is that which is involved in sensation it is that which the biologist must regard as the " sense-datum " or " sensum," if he should elect to retain the use of this ambiguous word. Hence, the difference between Mr. Russell's statement and mine.

Thus far I tell in brief a purely physical story of the events involved in vision. This first chapter of a very complex bit of evolutionary history brings us up to a very highly specialised kind of receptors to which Sir Charles Sherrington has given the name " distance-receptors." The name implies that, under physical interpretation, there is a space-interval between the place of the effluent event and the place of the receptor-event to which influence is transmitted with the velocity of light, and since this velocity is finite, there is also a time-interval between effluent departure and influent arrival. If we call the centre from which the effluent event proceeds, the source of influence, the points for emphasis are these :

    (i) What the distance-receptors are immediately up against is the influence that arrives ;

(ii) They are only mediately in relation to the effluent source from which such influence has departed some time ago, however brief,

but

(iii) That to which the behaviour of the person is directed is the source from which the influence comes ; and

(iv) If conscious reference is to have any value for such behaviour it must be directed to that source.

Under (iii) we pass to the biological chapter in the story of events. One can only indicate here its salient motif. It seems pretty well established that the physiological outcome of the stimulation of any group of distance-receptors (which will include those for radiant influence, for sound, and for odorous particles—each after its kind) may become linked with any adaptive response which has value for behaviour towards the effluent source. Such neuronic linkage has been provided in the course of long ages of evolution. In vertebrates it has reached its highest level in the central nervous system and finds expression in the integrative action of the brain. " *The brain*," says Sir Charles Sherrington with the emphasis of italics, " *is always the part of the nervous system which is constructed and evolved upon the distance-receptor organs* " (I.N.S. p. 325). So far the interpretation may be frankly behaviouristic, for, biologically, the brain is *par excellence* the organ of the guidance of behaviour.

But, according to emergent evolution, vision,

VISION AND CONTACT

of objects ; there are all the varied contributions, under revival, in terms of other experience than that which is visual, *e.g.* those which are derivative from manipulation through touch, perhaps contributions re-presentative of smelling, tasting and so forth. All these are intervenient *in the organism*, and through this intervenience involved on the plane of life, make projicient reference, under correlation, what it is on the perceptual plane of mind. It is in virtue of all this that Sir Charles Sherrington speaks of the brain as " evolved upon the distance-receptors." To ignore all this would betray sheer ignorance of the topic one pretends to deal with. Is it not set forth in the text-books (cf. Stout, M. Bk. III. Pt. ii. ch. 4) ? In any case so much of all this as is pertinent must be taken as implied when I speak of projicience.

Projicient reference, on the plane of mind, thus affords the subject-matter of the third chapter of the complex story I briefly summarise. How comes it that it works so wonderfully well as a guide to behaviour ? To this question evolutionists seek to give an answer based on prolonged research. The net result seems to be : Because it has been endorsed by the survival of those organisms in which so serviceable a process obtained.

It follows that there is : (i) the assigned place of effluent events ; there is (ii) the assigned place of receptor-events under influence ; and there is (iii) the located place of projicient reference which may, and often does, approximately coincide with the assigned place of effluent events, but need not do so, and frequently does not (cf. § VIII.).

Let it then be understood that vision is always an affair of distance-receptors and that everything we see is subject to projicient reference. I shall urge that *visible* shape or size does not afford the best avenue of approach towards the acknowledgment of the intrinsic reality of this or that shape or size.

One need not repeat in detail the oft-told story of the coin with manifold variations of apparent figure and bulk from different points of view and at different distances. Each such appearance, without exception, is a matter of projicient reference, subject to the conditions of extrinsic relatedness which then and there obtain. They are properties of the coin which no doubt may be clues to the intrinsic qualities which we acknowledge as its own (cf. § xxxiii.).

Now it would conduce not a little to the analytic interpretation of the facts if we could (at any rate initially and provisionally) wipe mind and its projicient reference off the slate. Let us try to do this, and to deal only with what occurs in the recipient organism—Mr. Whitehead's "percipient event" (C.N. p. 152). We grant to the thing, under acknowledgment, its own intrinsic shape. There are two systems in extrinsic relation, (i) the said thing with its proper figure, and (ii) some other thing in which a record is produced through influent events, effluent from (i) as their source. In the organism such a record is a pattern (the so-called "image") on the retina ; and the pattern thus recorded is itself a figure correspondent to that of which it is a record. But the recording system need not be the retina of a person ; it may be some other recipient such as a sensitised photographic plate, which gives what I shall call an optical record. In this case the terms in extrinsic relation—figure of thing and recorded figure—are both frankly spatial systems with comparable relations of the spatial order. Given then, on a film, successive snapshots of a coin rotating on a selected axis, and one has an optical record giving figures closely comparable to the " images " on the retina at similar intervals.

Reintroduce now the conscious percipience which we have banished for awhile. What happens? Under projicience the proper figure of the retinal " image " or of the record in the film, is referred to the coin as a direct or indirect object of vision. *Qua object* it extrinsically acquires the perspective property of the shape projicient from the record. But of the intrinsic figure of the coin (let us say) vision as such can give no assurance—only a clue to be elsewise followed up. Not along the lines of projicience (the *only* lines open to vision) can intrinsic reality be reached. The world of vision is always a world of appearance—objectively real in extrinsic relatedness, but affording no voucher for intrinsic reality, though it may give a clue thereto.

We have, then, as distinguishable (*a*) projicient or apparent shape subject always to " point of view," and (*b*) intrinsically real figure, under acknowledgment. And the projicient shape may differ from, or in some cases it may accord with or correspond to, the intrinsic figure proper to the coin. The correspondence, if it obtain, is that between figure of coin and figure in record (retinal or optical), both circular, but always differing in size owing to the part which is played by the lens.

§ XXXVII. *Contact*.

The argument thus far is that projicient vision affords a valuable clue to the intrinsic spatial relatedness which obtains within the thing that I see out there ; but that it is incapable, as such, of affording more than a clue to the determination of what the spatial relatedness is in and for itself. What, then, does afford, under acknowledgment, something more than a clue ? I think that the old answer is still that which can establish the best claim to acceptance. It comes in effect to this. We must build on a basis of contact-receptors which is the primary basis of measurement.

Let it be admitted that the spatial characters of some given system other than myself—say that of the room in which I sit, or that of the cube on my desk—is for our reflective knowledge a construct to which suitable data are contributory. I urge that the suitable data are *derivative from contact*. I say " contact " because I wish here to abstract from *manipulative* touch which implies much intervenient process.

Consider the glass cube. Any two minute areas of its surface which I choose to mark with ink-spots afford spatial terms, in the spatial relation of distance within the confines of the cube. As a relation this distance is indivisible ; but it may be co-related with a measured stretch or length on some conventional scale (cf. § xii.). Hence one may substitute for any indivisible distance-relation its co-related scale-length. There are an indefinite number of such instances of spatial relatedness within the cube. We deal with them methodically in the light of what we have learnt through manipulation under the guidance of reflective thought. Only then have we the analytic data on which to frame a synthetic construct. One may assume that we have long ago done something of this sort in such manner as to understand what is meant by saying that we are dealing with that which we agree to call a cube.

Now primarily and fundamentally all direct measurement of the kind we are considering is based on superposition under contact. By means of suitable instruments—calipers, rods and the like—two terms in one system are, within narrow limits, at the same assigned places as two terms in the other system, and their distance-relation is, under acknowledgment, the selfsame distance. What seems to be essential is that, under such terminal contact, the analytic data obtained by measurements of the recording system and of the system recorded are one and the same. This is never so where the distance-receptors of vision, on the hither side of the lens, play their normal part as record. Under contact each of two systems may be regarded as reciprocally functioning as record to the other. In vision there is no such contact.

Let me put the matter thus. I superpose a suitable surface of my body on a suitable surface of not-me in contact therewith. I consider the end-points in contact. I regard these end-points, in me and in it, as substantially coincident—*i.e.* as lying within a small area ; and I regard the spatial distance " between them," *i.e.* their spatial relation, as substantially the same under acknowledgment. I then superpose the second " length or stretch," derivative from spatial relatedness intrinsic to me, on some third surface, say the wall of my room. And I accept the supposal, which seems to have pragmatic sanction as a basis of measurement, that the length *a-b* intrinsic to me, the length *a'-b'* intrinsic to the " foot-rule," and the length α-β intrinsic to the wall to which I apply this foot-rule, are, *qua* length, what we may call one and the same, or, if it be preferred, equivalent. Thus I can " install," as I put it, a little bit of my intrinsic spatial relatedness in the little bit of intrinsic relatedness which belongs of right to the wall of my room. It is a piecemeal business. That's where the construct comes in.

One must not minimise in all this the guiding value of projicient reference under vision. That would be to ignore, not only patent facts, but the pragmatic " end " which distance-receptors subserve in evolution. I sit in my room and scan the ceiling, floor, and four-square walls, as seen in perspective. It may be that here and now I employ no contact-treatment. I do not, through manipulation, actually bring some selected bit of my intrinsic relatedness, through the intervention of a foot-rule, into touch with any selected bit of its intrinsic relatedness. But I can do so on occasion. And I can, here and now, do so imaginatively. That is where the projicient experience of vision comes so helpfully to my aid. I can, so to speak, throw a little bit of my physical self, or my foot-rule, on to this, that or the other selected instance of intrinsic relatedness within the room. With the aid of the clues afforded by vision I can bring it imaginatively within the field of contact. But can one not do more than this? Can one not, by a further and more resolute effort, install oneself in the total spatial relatedness intrinsic to that which one reflectively contemplates? Can one not imaginatively expand or contract oneself and fit oneself as record, to the thing, room, cube, or what not—so as to *be*, *pro hoc*, one with its total system of intrinsic spatial relatedness? I have been told by an architect (when he grasped my uncouth phraseology) that this is just what those in his profession who are worth their salt do as a matter of course. "One must somehow," he said, " get at the building as it is, and not merely as it will look from this or that point of view— important as that of course is." I believe that it is by imaginative processes of this sort, that the worthy man of science, dealing with his special province, succeeds in interpretation where the hodmen of his trade fail. I well remember how, years ago, a physicist of note, from whom I sought help in certain questions of double refraction, said : "You will never get the matter quite clear till you can sit inside a crystal so as to feel the course of the rays of light as they pass through you."

The upshot, then, comes to this. Our knowledge of the shapes and sizes of external things is no less a constructive product than our knowledge of such properties as colour or scent which we attribute to such things. But on the basis of contact-treatment we seem justified in believing, or as I say acknowledging, as part of our evolutionary creed, that, so far as spatial relatedness is concerned, what a thing is known as *under contact* that it veritably is. The figure and bulk of a given quartz-crystal is, I believe, intrinsic to that thing and is nowise dependent on its extrinsic relatedness to some percipient person.

I am doubtful, however, whether, even through the avenue of approach afforded by contact-data, the intrinsic spatial relatedness within the crystal is susceptible of irrefragable proof. After all, it may be said, you are dealing with " appearances " to the sense of touch ; you have insisted with frequent reiteration, that all such appearances, as minded, are within the mind—no doubt, as you put it, objectively ; a tango-receptor-pattern on contact, no less than a distance-receptor-pattern in vision, is something that has place in the organism and not beyond its confines ; and yet you speak of a belief in the intrinsic nature of that which confessedly lies beyond those confines ; you may have narrowed the gap but you still have the " fatal leap " from what you call person to thing. Furthermore, you admit that the real shape of a thing as we come to know it, is a construct ; you speak of imaginatively " installing " yourself (*i.e.* the intrinsic order of spatial relatedness involved in your own bodily structure) in the cube or the room ; and so forth. Here you emphasise the necessity of taking your fatal leap.

It is just because I grant all this—nay, more, because I urge its validity—that I must still speak of acknowledgment. So I put the position, which I am concerned to put as clearly as I can, in summary fashion thus : (1) It looks very much *as if* this line of approach leads me towards intrinsic reality in things external to me ; (2) I shall take the risk of acknowledging this to be a feature of the physical world as it veritably *is*.

§ XXXVIII. *The Property of Beauty.*

In the foregoing section there is at least an approximation to a frankly realistic view of spatial relatedness as specifically intrinsic to this or that thing in an external world. It is no doubt true that, under the conditions of projicient vision, many things thus appear to which the application of direct contact-measurement is impossible. Take, for example, the rainbow which in § XXXI. stood for our world. We cannot apply calipers or foot-rule to measure its breadth. None the less we may acknowledge that it has its own real or intrinsic breadth, *i.e.* the distance between some rain-drop, rays from which stimulate the cones on the upper edge of the retinal pattern, and some other rain-drop, rays from which stimulate the nether edge of that pattern. By indirect means this distance can be measured or co-related with a measured length ; and on the basis of data derived from contact-treatment one may infer spatial relations which are not directly susceptible of contact-measurement by superposition.

Now we distinguished not only the form, but the colour, and the beauty of our rainbow. Can the beauty and the colour be interpreted realistically on lines similar to those of our interpretation of form or shape? Are the beauty and the colour intrinsic qualities of the bow, or are they properties acquired through extrinsic relatedness to some person? Divergent answers are given to the question thus differently expressed. Let us lead up to colour through beauty considered only in the light of this question.

That which has beauty thereby possesses value for aesthetic treatment. Professor John Laird, as representing a philosophy of realism, contends that this beauty is valuable in itself whether any personal mind appreciate it or not. Let us, then, take it as our chosen example of value. Mr. Laird says: "A romantic revival may be needed to reveal the stateliness of Gothic cathedrals or the serene grandeur of Alpine summits, but this beauty and the worth of it belonged to the Alps and the sanctuaries all the time" (S.R. p. 126). Delight, no doubt, enters into the recognition of all beauty; and things may certainly be beautiful when they bring this delight. But " the beauty (and therefore the value) of these delightful things is a predicate of them just as certainly as their lustre is a predicate of my lady's diamonds" (p. 135).

On this distinctively realist view beauty is intrinsic to that which is said to possess it. As a *quality* it must be claimed for the thing in its own right. The alternative view is that beauty, and every kind of value, demands for its existence (real existence but in a non-realist sense) extrinsic relatedness to some person in whom reflective consciousness is emergent and is therefore in our sense a property. No doubt, under realist interpretation the beauty is, in some sense, referred to the thing (Alps, or rainbow, or diamond), for " the primary function of consciousness is to refer beyond itself " (p. 154). But this has little in common with projicient reference. Nay, rather it emphasises the difference between projicient reference and direct apprehension. For under projicient reference a property is bestowed on the thing which thus acquires a new character. But under direct apprehension the quality of beauty is nowise bestowed on, or acquired by, the thing. It is " revealed " or " disclosed " to the mind which is aware of it and grasps it in a manner all its own. Hence we find that the realist doctrine of beauty implies a doctrine of mind wholly different from ours.

Not all realists, however, acknowledge beauty as a quality intrinsic to the thing that is said to possess it. According to Professor Alexander, though colour *is* such an intrinsic quality, in my sense of these words, beauty is not. " In our ordinary experience of colour," he says (S.T.D. II. p. 244), " the colour is separate from the mind and completely independent of it. In our experience of the colour's beauty there is indissoluble union with the mind." The contention, I think, comes to this. Colour resides in the thing seen, with which an organism having the quality of consciousness may or may not be compresent. Whether it be so compresent or not makes no difference to the non-mental existence of colour as such, because that colour is intrinsic to the thing as its own emergent quality. On the other hand, beauty resides, not in the thing only in its intrinsic independence, but in the " whole situation." This we may bracket thus (coloured thing *in extrinsic relation to* compresent person with quality of aesthetic consciousness). In that relation " the object has a character which it would not have except for that relation " (p. 240). The doctrine of internal relations (cf. § XIII.) is, it seems, accepted where beauty is concerned, and rejected in respect of colour. Beauty and colour are not alike in kind and demand different kinds of treatment. In other words : If the beautiful object be one term and the person the other term, the former gets an acquired character or property (*qua* beautiful but not *qua* coloured), in and through its extrinsic relation to the latter.

Thus the beauty of an object is interpreted as, " a character superadded to it from its relation to the mind in virtue of which it satisfies or pleases after a certain fashion, or aesthetically " (p. 245). And, within the relational situation, " the beauty is attributed to the object " (p. 246). Mr. Alexander says that " it is the paradox of beauty that its expressiveness belongs to the beautiful thing itself and yet would not be there except for the mind " (p. 292). But is not this just the paradox of all acquired characters as properties that have being through extrinsic relatedness ? Quite irrespective of beauty, or other value, the coin which hangs from my watch-chain has weight which belongs to it as expressive of its gravitational relatedness to the earth ; it has, for my projicient vision here and now, the property of elliptical shape as expressive of its extrinsic relatedness to a pattern of stimulation in my retina ; it has, too, as I believe, the *property* of colour distinctive of a late eighteenth century guinea-piece.

§ XXXIX. *The Property of Colour.*

In regarding colour as a property of the guinea-piece bestowed thereon under projicient reference, and not one of its intrinsic qualities revealed or disclosed to the mind's native power of apprehension, I must to my regret part company, not only from Mr. Laird, but from Mr. Alexander, and from many others with whom I would fain travel in quest of reality. But I cannot go with them ; and I must give reasons for treading an older path which they have left.

Let me first clear the ground a little. Beyond question we *act* " as if " colour belongs to this thing or that of its very own right. To act otherwise would generally result in hopeless confusion. The " as if " works admirably. It has pragmatic sanction to the full. This, I think, no one seriously denies. But I, for one, cannot pass from " as if in the thing " to " is in the thing in its own right " with an easy conscience.

There is a pretty long chain of events between what actually goes on in the acknowledged thing out there, and what actually goes on in a fairly definite area of the occipital cortex. Somewhere, either in the whole chain, or in one or more than one of its links, correlated colour-vision, in its aspect of minding and of that which is minded, emerges. And within the chain certain intervenient physical and physiological changes are involved. Now I urge, to begin with, that no matter where its physical basis " really is "—in "the whole situation," or in any specific part of it, at one end, or the other, or somewhere between them—colour *must*, for practical purposes of behaviour, be referred to the thing and located therein, if it be endorsed by the pragmatic sanction of working so well in its guidance of behaviour. Refer it anywhere else and action inevitably goes astray. I conclude, therefore, that this pragmatic sanction does not take us one step towards a confident assertion that the colour is intrinsic to the thing itself.

Taking " location " of colour in the thing and nowhere else for granted as matter of common agreement, the question is whether, on other and more cogent grounds, we should " assign " (cf. § VIII.) colour, as such, to an intrinsic place in the thing as one of its own qualities. Let us revert to my lady's diamonds with their lustre and their brilliantly changing play of refraction-colour. She and others delight in their beauty which in part involves these kaleidoscopic colour-changes as the gems are moved under suitable illumination. But for adequate interpretation we must trace the stages or levels of involution from top to bottom. At top is my lady's appreciation of an object of beauty, involving her perception of the colour-changes which are characters attributed to that object. Colour-perception involves certain physiological changes in the brain at the level of life; this again involves (if any reliance can be placed in the outcome of research in the field of colour-vision) certain specialised physico-chemical changes in the retina, or the choroid, or (more comprehensively) in the retino-cerebral system; and this under acknowledgment is due to transmission of electro-magnetic influence from the diamond. Thus at top we fringe off into correlated consciousness, aesthetically "qualitied," and at bottom we fringe off into physics. There is an enchained set of events, subject to emergence, from bottom to top. Strike out *any* of the relevant events, at bottom or at top, and the beauty of colour is struck out; strike out any of the relevant events between electro-magnetic influence and the events with which percipient consciousness is correlated and colour, as such, vanishes and surceases.

If the idealist assert that colour lives only at top, in the mind, irrespective of physical correlates in the organism; or if the realist assert that it lives only at bottom, in the thing, irrespective of psychical correlates in the organism; I respectfully submit that each goes beyond the evidence. According to the evidence (if I do not misread it) colour lives *in the whole situation*; in other words, it has being in virtue of the extrinsic relatedness of person (body-mind) and thing; but that which has being in virtue of extrinsic relatedness I call a property, not a quality intrinsic to the thing. And if either person or thing, which thus function as extrinsic terms, be absent there is no colour (as Mr. Alexander admits there is no beauty) in being.

Such in brief is my main thesis. Turn aside from it for a moment. In scientific research on the salient features of colour-vision it is justifiable policy to deal with those links of the chain which are chiefly *ad rem* for the purposes of such research. The departmental question is thus narrowed down to this : What are the specific physico-chemical processes that are involved ? Colour as experienced is here taken only as an indication of the presence of these processes under advenient electro-magnetic influence. Just where they occur is a question that arises in the course of that research. But no physiologist or bio-chemist would seek for them outside the organism. If, however, these highly-specialised processes be in the organism, and if colour as experienced be an indication of their presence, it seems to follow that, for emergent evolution, the person (body and mind) is an essential factor in colour-vision. Rub the person off the slate and the physico-chemical processes are not in being, and the colour-experience that indicates their presence under correlation cannot exist.

This little digression serves, I think, to lead to a conclusion in support of my main thesis. What may be said in support of the antithesis ?

First it may be asserted that it is not electro-magnetic influence, as such, but colour as such— *i.e.* an emergent quality of that influence—that determines the physico-chemical events. If so we must ask for the grounds of this assertion. Is it the expression of a fact which must be accepted with natural piety ? I think not. I believe that I am wholeheartedly with Mr. Alexander in this matter of natural piety. At any rate we both agree that whenever and wherever emergence occurs it is to be accepted in " the reverent temper which is the mood of natural piety." In this mood we both accept colour as an emergent quality. But then, unfortunately, we part company. He says that it is an emergent quality intrinsic to the ruby *qua* radiant thing ; I urge that, like beauty, it emerges within the bracketed relatedness of ruby and person, and is a property referred to the ruby as objectively minded under projicience. Now this I urge is not a matter for acceptance, one way or the other, under natural piety. It is a matter of interpretation of the facts that are common to both views. One such fact is this—that in order to see the ruby as coloured there must be an eye wherewith to see it. But Mr. Alexander says that the eye is the instrument for apprehending the colour which nowise depends on such instrumentality. "When a physical body is such that the light which it sends out to our eyes has a determinate wave-length, that body is red" (*Hibbert Journal*, XX. p. 614). It is that body in itself that has the quality of redness. It is colour, as such—an emergent quality of the ruby as a physical thing—that determines the physico-chemical events. Here again I ask : What are the grounds of this assertion ? And then, so far as I can ascertain, it is said that our experience of this colour is a matter of direct visual *apprehension*. What it is as experienced, that it is in itself. Since we assuredly apprehend it as there, there it must be ; and if there, it will exercise influence, after its kind, on the eye evolved for its reception. Colour intrinsic to a thing is directly apprehended by a mind, should that mind be compresent with it. If no mind be compresent, it is not apprehended ; but it is none the less *there*. And if we ask for further information with regard to this apprehension we are told, in effect, it is that through which the realistic world as it is in itself is revealed or disclosed.

We thus open up a further question which, crucial as it is, cannot here be discussed. One can only indicate its import. For Mr. Alexander mind is mind*ing*. All that is mind*ed*—at any rate under perception—is non-mental. " Compresence " obtains between a person so minding and that which is, *qua* minded, non-mental. The crucial question (to be reserved for future consideration) is this : Is there differentiation in such minding—say, in perceiving red, or green, or violet, so as to keep within the field of vision ? Mr. Alexander says (he will perhaps correct me if I misapprehend his teaching) : There is no differentiation in such minding. All the differentiation is in the non-mental colours as minded. The mind just apprehends for 'tis its nature to do so. All I can here say is that I wholeheartedly disagree. I shall hereafter contend that there is just as much differentiation in the minding as substance of the mind as there is in that which is (in my sense) objectively minded as stuff of the mind. Differentiation in the *-ed* and the *-ing* is strictly complementary. If there be so much in the one attribute there is that much (no less and no more) in the other attribute. To regard percipient mind as blankly apprehending is—to paraphrase Mr. Alexander's saying with regard to time—

not to take seriously the evolution of mind as substance. It robs mental evolution, on the plane of perception, of its distinguishing features. Under a doctrine of direct apprehension the mind is regarded as an interested spectator in the evolution of our richly-coloured world. Under projicient reference mind, even at the perceptual level, is a participator in that evolution. Nay more; it is, in a sense, creator of our objective world with its colour, its aroma, its music, and its beauty. A skeleton world of physical events there is—independent of us under acknowledgment. From its purely physical events there is advenient influence. But it is through projicient reference that it becomes for us a rainbow world, with the scent of the shower that has passed by, or the patter of retreating raindrops. Such is the corollary from the conclusion that secondary characters are properties extrinsically real in relation to our persons—not our minds only but also our bodily organisation, as recipient of advenient influence and as the seat of intervenient processes and thus contributory to projicient reference.

§ XL. "*The Bifurcation of Nature.*"

What has been said above will no doubt be regarded as open to Professor Whitehead's criticism of such views, namely that they imply what he speaks of as a " bifurcation of nature," and introduce the notion of " psychic additions."

Mr. Whitehead is concerned to keep nature, as he defines it, wholly uncontaminated by mind.

Nature is the intricate and orderly game that is played by non-mental events ; mind is an interested spectator, recorder, and interpreter. Clearly the " nature " thus characterised does not include mind. It is that from which a mind receives information, primarily through sense-awareness visual and other. When, therefore, we are thinking " homogeneously " about nature we are not dealing with the relation of nature to thought ; and " this means that nature can be thought of as a closed system whose mutual relations do not require the expression of the fact that they are thought about " (C.N. p. 3). " The understanding which is sought by science is an understanding of relations within nature not of the relation of nature to mind " (pp. 41-47). Clearly on this view mind is no part of " nature " as defined.

Well and good. Here is the mind that, somehow, has awareness of nature and seeks to interpret it ; and there is the nature of which the mind is, in some way, aware, and which is to be interpreted. That seems all right so far if the definitions expressed or implied be accepted. But the trouble Mr. Whitehead finds is that what he calls " the modern account of nature " " is not, as it should be, merely an account of what the mind knows of nature ; but it is also confused with an account of what nature does to the mind " (p. 27). Now what nature does to the mind it is supposed, he says, to do through causal influence ; this is supposed to entail mental appearance, say colour ; and then this appearance is thrust upon nature through " effluence." Such an effluent character thrown by the mind on to nature is thus a " psychic addition." Under this bifurcation of nature an attempt is made to exhibit apparent nature as an effluent of the mind when it is influenced by causal nature. It is thus supposed that " no coherent account can be given of nature as it is disclosed to us in sense-awareness without dragging in its relations to mind " (p. 27).

Now Mr. Whitehead says that " the philosophy of the sciences—conceived as one subject—is the endeavour to exhibit all sciences as one science " (p. 2). " We leave," he says, " to metaphysics the synthesis of the knower and the known " (p. 28). But he uses again and again such an expression as " disclosed to sense-awareness " ; and this, since it expresses, however naïvely, the relation of known to knower, is clearly, on his own showing, a bit of metaphysics in his sense of the word. Subject to correction, I take Mr. Whitehead's position to be this : In so far as there is direct apprehension of " nature " there is, when it occurs, this relation of " nature " to mind. But being so apprehended makes no difference to " nature " which is (as defined) just what it is and as it is whether it be so apprehended or not. Hence we are justified in restricting attention to that, and that only, which is, or may be, apprehended. Now colour is something that is, or may be, so apprehended ; colour therefore is part of " nature." To say that it is not so, is to say that colour is a psychic addition, effluent into " nature " from mind—or, in other words, to accept the vicious notion of a " bifurcation of nature."

What " modern account of nature " Mr. Whitehead has specially in view I cannot tell. What he says calls up reminiscences of the long-ago days of my youth. Then people did talk of what nature does to the mind, and did speak as if there were some sort of flowing forth of colour from the mind into nature. In what exact sense they used such expressions I need not stay to consider. My concern is with the bearing of Mr. Whitehead's criticism on the interpretation I seek here to render clear.

Much, of course, turns on our widely divergent views with regard to the status of mind. For Mr. Whitehead, as I gather, mind is an order of being wholly disparate from "nature," and affords the subject matter of metaphysics as distinguished from the physics of "nature." For me, in the good company of Spinoza and his followers, mind is within one of the two "attributes" of nature. It is the natural correlate of certain physical events which belong to the other attribute. There is, for us, no effluence from either attribute to the other; nor is there any causal influence of the one on the other. There can, therefore, be for us no psychic additions to physical nature. What there are, if I may so put it, are psychical signs attaching to certain physical events—the sign in one attribute, the physical events in the other. Colour is such a psychical sign in the correlated attribute which accompanies certain processes in the physical attribute when both attributes reach a late stage of evolutionary development.

Where, then, are the physical events with which colour-signs are correlated? I am content to reply that they are the correlates of a chain of organic events extending from the retinal receptor-pattern to the "visual centre" of the occipital cortex. As I read the evidence (of course it may be otherwise read), when the central factors in such and such a chain of physical events are in being—no matter how they are physically called into being—such and such colour-signs, correlated therewith, are also in being.

But of what is such colour the psychical sign? We must here distinguish that of which it may be the sign for the interpreter from that of which it is the sign for the conscious percipient. From the point of view of the interpreter it may be the sign (*a*) of the physiological events in the visual centre with which it is correlated ; or (*b*) of other events within the organism that are involved—*e.g.* the chemical changes in the retina or the choroid. But from the point of view of the conscious percipient it is, as a matter of primary genesis and to the end of behaviour, a sign of the presence of some *thing* in the external world which has become an *object* of vision. The sign is within the person and is correlated with very complex and highly differentiated chemical processes within the organism. But what is signified for the percipient is not within the person; nor is it within the organism. What is projiciently signified is a source of advenient physical influence.

Now the value of a sign is that it shall have reference to something signified. But surely this does not imply, or even suggest, that the sign is in any valid sense effluent on to that which is thereby signified. The red which is the psychical sign of certain physical events in the ruby is no more effluent to the ruby than is the word "red" or the name "ruby" effluent thereto. Herein lies the point of much that Berkeley said concerning visual language. It is a sign *of* something quite different from that which, as sign, it *is*. Hence it can be a psychical sign of physical events. This we express by saying that the sign has reference to that which is signified. And the good of such reference is that the sign shall serve as a guide to behaviour towards the thing that is signified. Hence the evolutionary stress on behaviour, on the plane of life—genetically purely "behaviouristic"—as the natural precursor of reference on the plane of mind. I speak of the sign as "projicient" to emphasise (1) its correlation with that which occurs within the person, and (2) its reference to something signified at a distance from that person.

In its primary genesis, then, this projicient reference is to a source of advenient physical influence. But when the visual centre of the occipital cortex is secondarily excited along some neurone-route from other parts of the brain, there is the psychic sign in the absence of the external source of effluence normally signined. None the less there is projicient reference of the sign to some located position in the external world and there is a visual image. Its location is probably due to the substantial similarity of the complex set of intervenient events concerned in such location—*e.g.* focussing of the eyes, but also much else.

Let us descend to a little detail. On waking this morning my eyes fell on the window through which streamed brilliant sunshine. I closed them swiftly.

After a brief interval there appeared at the same distance a full rich violet-purple after-effect, window shaped, round-headed, and crossed by a dark horizontal band, nearly neutral grey with a soupçon of green, answering to the lower frame above the open part of the window. It moved, jerkily, with the movements of my closed eyes, but preserved the same apparent distance under location. After another brief interval it became (still at the same distance and of the same shape) a fainter rather dirty green or greenish yellow ; and so on. I speak of these colour-effects as projicient, just as all visual images, as such, are projicient.

It may now be comprehensible why I should not speak of the colours which appear in the positive or negative after-sensations, as psychical *additions to physical nature*. None the less they may be spoken of as psychical correlates, of something that does occur in nature (as defined by Mr. Whitehead), *i.e.* of something going on somewhere. Then where ? In my retino-cerebral system. And how evoked ? Primarily, by electro-magnetic influence from some effluent source. Also, as physico-chemical changes consequent thereon, *i.e.* as after-effects not due to further influence from without. Secondarily by revival of neural process in the visual centre. There *may* also in this case be renewal of chemical processes in the retina or choroid through an outstroke from the brain ; but whether this is so, or not, it is difficult to determine. In any case the colour is referred to something, however intangible, outside us. I speak of this colour as projicient, but if I speak of it as *effluent into physical nature*, I speak inadvisably, even if (as I suspect) I am not talking nonsense from the standpoint of my own interpretation. I am well aware that there are other interpretations—that, for example, according to which all images are not only objective but also non-mental; but I am here concerned to make mine as clear as I can.

Now, suppose, instead of after-effects, or of images, one considers the red of the ruby, or the hues of the rainbow, or the colours of thin mineral slices under a polarising microscope—it matters not which—colour-signs are, in each case, the psychical correlates of the cortical occurrence and all that this involves in certain highly specialised physico-chemical events *within me*. If there be no such events, there are no such correlates. But these correlates are also the psychic signs attaching to electro-magnetic events in things outside me which are thereby signified. It is for the physicist to determine the exact nature of these events. *They* may continue indefinitely whether they be perceived or not; but only in certain organisms do they evoke those specialised physical and physiological events which have, as psychical correlates, modes of colour-experience.

On the above showing I regard it as equally inadmissible to say that colour, as such, is effluent *from* " nature," or that it is effluent *into* " nature," as defined by Mr. Whitehead. It is a projicient sign begotten of the psychical correlates of processes that occur in the organism.

VISION AND CONTACT

NOTE.

Lest it be said that I shirk details as to the kind of chemical process that is inferentially involved in colour-vision, I may add that my own provisional interpretation (stated with the utmost brevity) is something like this:

(1) The specific event is a "reversible" chemical process, or the net result of two such processes, say $\alpha+$, $\alpha-$, and $\beta+$, $\beta-$.

(2) These processes are due to light-waves (electro-magnetic pulses) ranging, say from d to j; where d may be something like 400 billion vibrations *per sec.* and j. something approaching 800 billion *per sec.*

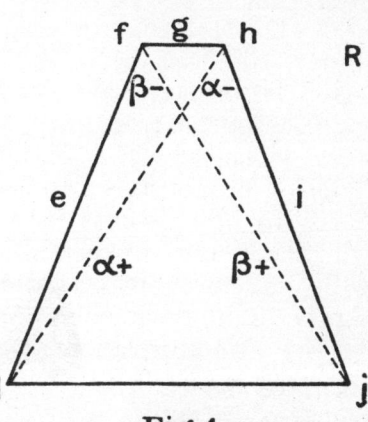

Fig. 4.

(3) Express the suggested relation of light influence to chemical changes in the diagrammatic form of a truncated pyramid (Fig. 4).

(4) Now tabulate these results and introduce the correlated psychic colour-signs.

Light Influences.	Chemical Process.	Psychic Colour-sign.
d	$\alpha+$	Red.
e	$\alpha+\beta-$	Orange-yellow.
f	$\beta-$	Yellow-green.
g	$\alpha-\beta-$	Green.
h	$\alpha-$	Blue-green.
i	$\alpha-\beta+$	Blue.
j	$\beta+$	Violet.

This gives the range of the colours of the spectrum.

L.M.E.

(5) Any combination of wave-lengths (say f and h) which gives $a-\beta-$ (in due proportion) gives also its correlated colour-sign (say green).

(6) Now the table given above leaves out of account purple, which does not occur in the spectrum. But it also leaves out of account the combination $a+\beta+$.

(7) We must, therefore, add to our table one more item, thus:

d and j $\qquad a+\beta+ \qquad$ Purple.

(8) If we have, say, 75% $a+$ with 25% $\beta+$ we get a reddish purple; or say, 25% $a+$ with 75% $\beta+$ we have violet-purple. Similarly with, say, $a+\beta-$ in differing proportions; and so on.

(9) In other words, and more generally, any colour will shade into its neighbouring colour in accordance with the proportional amount of a-process and of β-process in their positive and negative phases.

(10) The correlation of $a-$ with blue-green, and of $\beta-$ with yellow-green may not be accepted. And the truncated pyramid of my diagram may be rejected. It serves (as I think) to afford an avenue towards the reconciliation of the so-called " four-colour " and " three-colour " theories, and will presumably find acceptance with neither party to a long controversy.

But the cardinal questions are these: Are chemical processes involved in colour-vision? If so, can the psychical colour-signs correlated therewith properly be described as effluent either *from* or *into* nature under Mr. Whitehead's definition of nature?

LECTURE IX. RELATIVITY

XLI. Spatial Frames.   XLII. A Space-time Frame.
XLIII. Classical Treatment.   XLIV. Special and
General Relativity.   XLV. Relativity subject to
Projicience.

§ XLI. *Spatial Frames.*

The burden of my contention in the foregoing lecture may be expressed under two clauses:

(1) That contact-treatment affords an avenue leading to acknowledgment of such intrinsic qualities as are exemplified by the proper figure and the size of a thing, *i.e.* the spatial relatedness within it ; and

(2) That projicient reference under vision, founded on Sir Charles Sherrington's treatment of distance-receptors, is a better policy for the interpretation of apparent shape, and of colour, than is direct apprehension under the alternative doctrine of vision.

In approaching the difficult topic of this lecture we have first to distinguish in some way relativity from relatedness. The concepts are not coterminous. Relatedness embraces more than the relativity we have now to consider. May one say:

(*a*) That relativity characterises a feature of *extrinsic* relatedness;
(*b*) That it deals with the relation of some *record* to events which are thereby recorded; and
(*c*) That what is chiefly on the *tapis* of recent discussion is some *visual* record; or some *optical* record which gives, so to speak, vision at second hand?

Thus Professor Einstein predicts what will be given in the optical record of certain events which will occur during a solar eclipse.

One must try to lead up through instances of what Mr. Einstein calls the " principle of relativity " to the special and the general " theory of relativity." Let us revert, then, to the glass cube in our room which has already been used for purposes of illustration. Positions, as terms in intrinsic spatial relatedness, were then tacitly, and should now be explicitly, regarded as *occupied*—let us say by events. The cube is not only an orderly set of purely geometric relations of purely spatial terms; it is an orderly cluster of events which go together within the boundaries of this figure.

It is unnecessary to enter more than a reminder here that, in dealing with the figure of a cube or other contemplated thing, a special construct has classical sanction. A frame of three planes perpendicular to each other is erected within the spatial system under consideration. These three planes of events within the system are selected, under device of method, as a frame of reference for other events therein. The assigned place of any event will be given by the lengths of three Cartesian co-ordinates (x, y, z), dropped from that place on to the three selected planes. This scheme and its Euclidean implications will be familiar to all who are likely to read these pages.

Thus a 3-dimensional frame may be constructed within the cube as an aid to the determination of its own proper figure and the assigned positions of events within it. But the cube is also in extrinsic relatedness to other acknowledged things beyond its confines. And when we go outside the cube and install ourselves in the larger system in which it is set—and this is what we do in reflective thought— we need something more than the cube's own frame. Suppose, for example, we see it turned about, or set a-spinning. We then perhaps say that it rotates " in space." What from the common-sense standpoint do we mean by this? We mean, I suppose, primarily, that it rotates in the room. So we think of the room, which, as we say, contains the cube (and much else, *including ourselves*) and construct it on *its* 3-dimensional frame. The interpretation of the observed facts may then run thus: The cube with its frame (which after all is only a selected part of its intrinsic structure) rotates relatively to the room with its bigger frame. The fact that it is bigger does not much matter. The more important point is that the room with its frame is taken by common-sense as fixed in orientation, so that we speak of the rotation of the cube as relative to the unchanging frame of the room.

But is this more than a prejudice due to our naturally taking our own " point of view " as we sit pretty securely attached to the floor of the room ? What about that of the cube ? Imaginatively I install myself within it. *Pro hac vice* I am it. There occurs some strange convulsion of nature. Looking out through my glass walls I exclaim : How that room is whirling round ! Projicient vision will objectively locate the spinning motion in that which I see from a point of view extrinsic to it. If I identify myself with the frame of the room (which I commonly do since I am sitting in it) I am recording the spin of the glass cube. But if I identify myself with the cube (and imaginatively sit in it) I record a spinning of the room. In each case I can do no otherwise. It is the evolutionary nature of projicience in its primitive and unreflective form to refer *from* the record, which we *are* actually or imaginatively, to that which gives the record.

Which then is right—projicient reference from the room as record ; or projicient reference from the cube as record ? The essential and indubitable fact is just relative spin. That is given in each record. Can we so long as we just keep to this fact then and there immediately in evidence—without straying into extraneous considerations regarding other natural facts—can we get beyond and behind *this* basal fact of relativity ? We can never, I think, do so through the avenue of vision only.

Note here in passing that we can in a measure wipe conscious vision, as *directly* concerned, off the slate. Let the cube and the room be fitted with suitable sensitised plates in suitable photographic cameras, so as to record what takes place during, let us say, one-tenth of a second. Each will record, so to speak, a streak of relative movement of some point in the other more or less in focus. Neither can afford evidence of aught but relative motion.

On this understanding, then, let us frankly accept the relativity which is inalienable from vision and from optical records. And let us revert to the question : Which " really " spins, cube or room ? Common-sense, still clinging to an interpretation based on classical treatment (the foundations of which are not only visual), may regard as the saner view that the room records an acknowledged spinning of the cube, rather than that the cube records a " real " spinning of the room. If adequately instructed the " plain man " may pertinently ask whether, in the person installed, another kind of record—that of receptors in the " semi-circular canals "—might not forthwith decide the question. That person who had such a receptor-record would be the one who was " really " in motion. That person who had no such receptor-record would be really at rest, so far as rotation is in question.

It is worth noting, again in passing :
- (1) That the data afforded by such a receptor-record are naturally and naïvely referred to the rotation of oneself as the person who has them, and
- (2) That a curious and interesting touch of relativity comes in here.

Seated in a closed cupboard (so as to exclude all view of surroundings) on a turn-table running quite smoothly on ball-bearings, one is rotated, let us say clockwise. One feels the turn quite distinctly. But so long as rotation continues at that rate one is quite insensible to its continuance. It feels as if one were at rest. Quicken speed. One feels an added turn clockwise; but is again insensible to continued rotation at that speed. But now let the speed be slackened by an operator in control. What one feels is an anti-clockwise turn. So long as that diminished speed is maintained one is not sensible of any rotary movement. But slacken speed again. One feels a further anti-clockwise turn. And so on. What one feels, then, on the data afforded by the receptor-record in the semi-circular canals, is *relative* change of rotary motion. And though the movement in rotation is felt as one's own it is, in us at least, subject to projicient meaning. If one assume the most unreflective attitude possible to a being so reflective as to participate in such enquiries, still one cannot (or I cannot) get rid of and annul all reference to a context of a surrounding world in extrinsic relation to which I am turned this way or that. Projicience, on our interpretation, is always the outcome of individual experience in a world which is for us predominantly objective through vision. And it is relative to that world that the modes of experience I have briefly described take definite form.

But this kind of thing may perhaps be regarded by the physicist as mere psychological whimsy, and *nihil ad rem*. Let us then return to our main theme.

There the point is that, if we rely on visual or on optical data only, then, in taking the room as stable, and the cube as spinning, we yield to natural prejudice or we accept an " as if " based on other considerations than those which are strictly in evidence.

Even so, is this good enough? Common-sense, still under the sway of classical treatment, quite realises that the room is part of the earth-system which is in rotation and revolves in its orbit. It is quite prepared to admit that we require for adequate interpretation a greater natural system (though its size does not much matter) and a frame of things more stable in orientation (the more essential feature). On astronomical grounds it is commonly assumed that within this more stable frame, the lesser system of the room with its frame spins, just as does the cube within the room. The pole-star (nearly) marks the direction which determines the setting of the frame with reference to which events in our solar system run their course. What we speak of as " in space " is comprehensively within this " larger room." But if we mean by " space " a specific mode of relatedness named " spatial," it is clear that no system, small or great, is strictly " in space " ; nay rather " space " (*i.e.* spatial relatedness) is *in the system.* Space as a limitless receptacle or container has, I take it, been relegated to the limbo of discarded notions.

Now, if we could only be sure that the pole-star is an ultimate fixture, we could construct an absolute frame of spatial relatedness with known orientation—that to which all subordinate positions are referable.

But we cannot; for we are assured that the pole-star is not fixed " in space." What then are we to do? We want to get a 3-dimensional frame in which the three selected planes are absolutely and ultimately determinate with immutable axes. And that, it seems, is just what (even on the basis of an *a*-device) we cannot get. There is no use in whining about it; and it is scarcely worth while to boast of our incompetence. We must be content to accept the position.

§ XLII. *A Space-time Frame.*

Thus far we have taken " time " more or less for granted. We must do so no longer. We have in some way to link up spatial and temporal relatedness within one constructive scheme.

Consider how far it may be said that, from the evolutionary point of view, it is with the advent of distance receptors, at a fairly high level of development, that the chief data are afforded from which are derived the twin concepts of *objective* space and time. Picture a lowly organism—amoeba or the like—moving sluggishly over the surface with which it is in contact. There are touch-data here and there on the surface of the organism. In this respect neither passage of events from a distance nor location of events at a distance comes within its ken. In this respect, for its almost inconceivably primitive mind (if such it may be called), there would be no " space " beyond the surface of actual contact common to it and that over which it moves. Space as objective and beyond the range of contact would be unknown. If we grant a kind of memory there would be duration within it—what M. Bergson would call " lived time." There would be little or no " projection " of time into an external world beyond its surface ; and such is the time we have now to consider.

This is not the occasion to elaborate the thesis thus adumbrated, or to qualify a statement admittedly crude. Nor is it necessary. It suffices to emphasise the view that what one may speak of as external time—M. Bergson would say spatialised time as distinguished from duration—is in large measure projective. I use the word " projection " in this temporal sense, as distinguished from " projicience " in its spatial reference, where such a distinction may serve to make my meaning clearer. The point of emphasis, in our present context, is that, in visual events, both temporal projection and spatial projicience demand careful consideration.

Let us here pause to note that, since the velocity of light is finite, the starting-time of the effluent event is never simultaneous with the arrival-time at which the influence reaches the distance-receptors. Mr. Russell says (cf. p. 210) that two places are associated with every " sense-datum " ; that at which it is, and that from which it is perceived. Similarly two times have to be considered in respect of every optical event ; that at which effluence starts and that at which influence is received. There are two occurrences in temporal relatedness—say one in *Nova Persei* and the other in someone's retina on our earth. Which occurrence, then, is to be called the " sense-datum " ? Mr. Russell may say : That in Nova; the biologist may say: That in the distance-receptors. In any case no visual "sense-datum" in the one sense is ever simultaneous with that in the other sense.

To proceed. The classical doctrine, with which we are at present concerned, presupposes the uniform flow of external time (at any rate Newton did so) under the passage of which things either persist without sensible alteration or undergo change in some respect. The kind of change of predominant classical interest is motion. Uniform flow of time, it was assumed, has continued and will continue always and everywhere, *i.e.* in all that happens within some absolute space-frame. Mr. Alexander bases his world-interpretation on the hypothesis that time is fluent.

Another line of interpretation, still following classical tradition, but with a difference, might be roughly but inaccurately expressed by saying that it may be a better policy to regard events as flowing through time than to regard time itself as fluent. This, however, lends colour to the notion that time is a special sort of container of events which are thus said to be "in time" as well as "in space," the other sort of container. That is unsatisfactory; for temporal no less than spatial relatedness is *in events*. Both sorts of container must be relegated to the limbo of discarded notions.

Some method of treatment must therefore be devised which shall afford a yet better policy. We must bear in mind:

(1) That just as positions (places contracted almost to vanishing-point) are terms in

RELATIVITY

spatial " here-there " relatedness, so too are instants (durations likewise contracted) terms in temporal " now-then " relatedness ; and

(2) That although temporal relatedness (for which the word " time " is shorthand) is, for classical treatment, *utterly different from* spatial relatedness (for which the word " space " is shorthand), yet both kinds of relatedness inseparably co-exist in all events and in every event.

Hence the aim of fruitful method should be to treat these two co-existent and co-related kinds of relatedness on quite similar lines and within one comprehensive construct of conceptual thought. Such a construct is the 4-dimensional continuum, with x, y, z, t, as co-ordinates. To whom the first suggestion of such a world-scheme, in which there is provision for indicating the time at which any given event occurs and the place which it then occupies, I do not know. But a personal reminiscence may here be of interest.

Some half-century ago, in the early 'seventies, W. K. Clifford, with what seemed to a young student extraordinary brilliance and clarity, was discussing 4-dimensional space. He paused ; and said with emphasis : " Mind you ; I'm talking of a purely imaginary *space* of four dimensions. Our actual world may well be regarded as 4-dimensional, with time as the fourth dimension "—or words to that effect. I was puzzled, and afterwards asked Frederick Guthrie (who was present when Clifford spoke, and under whom I was then working) what it meant. " Well," he said, " something like this. Just as in the conventional space-time diagram one so arranges matters as to take the space-factor in one dimension, and plots in time in the second dimension on the plane of one's paper, so can a man like Clifford conceive, though even he cannot picture or make a model of, a sort of mental scheme, in which all three spatial dimensions, and a fourth time-dimension, are so combined as to enable him to deal mathematically with the space-and-time course of anything in motion."

A point for special notice is that one can neither picture nor make a model of a 4-dimensional continuum—for all picturing and modelling are 3-dimensional. If, however, one is dealing with two spatial dimensions only, *i.e.* with events on one spatial plane, and introduce time as a third dimension, one can picture, or make a model of, *that* mental scheme. One just spatialises time as replacing one of the three spatial dimensions of our ordinary world. Suppose, for example, a mouse pursues a sinuous path as a flatlander, along the floor of my room. Of course as a 3-dimensional thing the mouse is not " really " a flatlander ; but one may legitimately discount this. Then one gets rid of all *vertical* here-there relatedness " in space," and one can substitute the now-then relatedness " in time." In our model of the space-time frame of what happens, the mouse will be at different levels from its spatial floor at successive instants. My room thus becomes a space-time model of the mouse's line of advance " in space and time." If he be so far above the spatial floor that will mean so much time-interval from his start. The scales of space and time will need conventional adjustment. A purely natural scale has been suggested and may be worked out ; but, like the vertical and horizontal scales on a map, some conventional adjustment is in most cases more profitable.

Now if snapshot records be made from the four corners of the spatial floor of our model all will be different. Each record gives appearances from selected " points of view " and some of them will be foreshortened in perspective. This foreshortening will be projiciently referred to the mouse's sinuous course.

Furthermore, since the velocity of light is finite, there are differences between times projective from the record—the times of appearance—and the " real " time of the events recorded. Moreover, the projective times—so-called " local times "—are not the same from different recording standpoints. Time-intervals are subject to projective foreshortening. Two pulses of *influence* on the record are " now " and " then " with a time-interval irrespective of the distance of their effluent sources. But if the " now " and " then " be projectively referred to effluent events, m and n, *at different distances*, the time-interval between departure of effluence from m and from n is not the same as that between the arrival of influence from them on the record. Events are warped for visual appearances—spatially under projicience, temporally under projection. Even the space-time frame itself, constructed four-square, or Euclidian, to fit the " real facts " for classical treatment, may seem to require some non-Euclidian distortion, and some borrowing, so to speak, from " space " or from " time," to fit the no less real facts for visual appearance *viewed through the record*.

In ordinary events projective time-distortion is negligible. Still there is always some difference; and in events of more than ordinary velocity it ceases to be negligible.

§ XLIII. *Classical Treatment*.

Let us now introduce time-relatedness into our picture in what is perhaps a simpler and more elementary way. Let us take two systems or bodies in relative motion as the one moving and the other (relatively, of course) at rest. Each has its 3-dimensional space-frame which is in relative motion as a whole. It travels with its system or body. We are to observe one system from the other. Under device of method one may so arrange matters that the direction of motion to be dealt with is in one dimension only, say x. This means that a measured length along y or z, as observed from the other system, is not affected by the relative motion of either system. And we will assume, under classical tradition, that the time-relatedness of events is uniform and common to both systems. In the two systems, then, y of the one and y^1 of the other, z and z^1 remain constant for the observer. That leaves us to deal only with x and x^1.

What we want to get at is this: How can an observer on one of the two systems so bring the length x^1 into relation to x that he can pass from

RELATIVITY

one to the other with assurance. Those who have solved this little problem show that (to allow for relative motion), we must here take into consideration velocity v (say in feet per second) during so many seconds as a value of t. In other words, one has to use a "classical" (Newtonian or Galilean) transformation thus expressed $x^1 = x - vt$. This is discussed and justified in the classical text-books. It works well in all cases of moderate velocity, up to, and a good way beyond, that of the earth in its orbital sweep.

On this elementary plane of more or less familiar experience, a long-ago recognised form of relativity comes in where there is cross-reference to different records as registered in different frames. Take the illustration with which Professor Einstein and others have made us at home. A stone is dropped from the window of a train in motion. It participates in the onward movement of the carriage, and there is no relative motion as between stone and train in that direction. The relative motion is entirely downwards with increasing velocity as the stone falls. And this will be recorded, visually or optically, in the train.

But let there be also an optical record secured by someone on the platform which the train passes. Relatively to *its* frame, the "stone-motion-record" is quite different—namely a parabolic curve on a suitable plate on the platform. Its parabolic form betokens acceleration in fall. Similarly the fall of a stone on the platform is relatively to its frame wholly downwards, as records will there show. But the record thereof on a suitable photographic plate attached to the train will be a parabolic curve. The stress, therefore, is on different frames of reference. May one, then, say :

> (1) That optical and visual records will, under suitable precautions, give correspondent results *within any given frame*, whether relatively at rest or in motion ;
>
> (2) That records *in one frame of what occurs in another frame*, give results different from those obtained under (1) when the two frames are in relative motion ;
>
> (3) That this relative motion—*e.g.* of " train " and " earth-rail-platform " will be inferable from optical records of what is seen or, as Mr. Einstein so often says, " judged " to occur, in the one from the standpoint of the other ; and
>
> (4) That *which* " really " moves—train-system or earth-system—cannot be determined if visual or optical observations be restricted to just these two systems in relative motion. In all this " classical treatment " suffices.

If, therefore, one who is still under the sway of classical tradition be asked : which, then, is really in motion ? How will he reply ? He might, I take it, say : You know the order of nature which men of science have worked out, not wholly without success ; our earth rotating on its axis and revolving in its orbit round the sun ; trains running over its surface ; stones falling towards its centre, and the rest. Does not this—stated perhaps with added refinement—give a sufficient answer to your question? Or do you want more? Do you seek to know what, on our view, is the absolute frame of reference, how it is oriented, and what is the motion, say of the stone in reference to it? I do not know what may be the orientation of an absolute frame of reference, and I frankly say so. But if you will kindly supply me with sundry data—such as compass-direction, latitude, time of year and a few more—I can give you a closely approximate answer in reference to a provisional pole-star frame, subject to the universal uniformity of time-relations which we accept as a policy, or (if you will) as part of our classical creed.

§ XLIV. *Special and General Relativity.*

a. Special Theory.

In the special theory of relativity there is much that need not concern us, notwithstanding its great value and its splendid achievements. One must try to get at the gist of a difficult matter, bristling with technicalities, only so far as it affects our evolutionary interpretation.

The chief point for emphasis is that, when the physicist has to deal, under vision or in optical records (and he can deal no otherwise), with uniform velocities of translation approaching that of light (some 300,000 kilometres per second *in vacuo*) classical treatment *does not work*. His task, therefore, is to find a transformation formula that does work.

The position, I take it, is something like this. Given uniform translation at velocities from say 3 to 30 (or even 300) kilometres per second, the Newtonian, or classical, transformation gives, by calculation, results which accord with observation. But given velocities from, say, 300,000 down to 30,000 kilometres per second, that transformation formula does not give results which are accordant with observation. The problem, therefore, is to find a formula that does give accordant results.

Now the steps by which the call for a new formula was rendered imperative and the way in which it was suggested as the outcome of electro-magnetic research form a most interesting chapter in the recent history of physical science. But its recital does not fall within my province. Is it not told in many books and papers by those who have the requisite knowledge—and, unfortunately, by some who have not? For us here the essential point is that, under certain special circumstances, the classical transformation *does not work*. For records dealing with uniform velocities approaching more or less closely to that of light, (c) a more complex transformation (Lorentzian) is required. In place of the $x-vt$ of the classical equation one must write

$$\frac{x-vt}{\sqrt{1-\frac{v^2}{c^2}}}.$$

Then all goes well under the restricted or special theory of relativity—*i.e.* that which quite legitimately disregards, or abstracts from, fields of acceleration.

Does this mean that at some critical velocity there is a jump from the classical to the Lorentzian equation? Surely not. Under this special mode of treatment, dealing, say, with optical records, the Lorentzian formula admits no exceptions. But for moderate velocities the $\sqrt{1 - \frac{v^2}{c^2}}$ may for all practical purposes be expunged. Since its value then very closely approximates to 1, it makes no appreciable difference in the result—say one part in 200,000,000 even in the case in which the earth's orbital velocity of some 30 kilometres per second comes into the reckoning. Is it surprising that the old classical folk were unaware of its existence? Should one say in strictness or in fairness that Galileo or Newton have now been proved to be wrong?

Whatever, then, may be its calculable value, great or small, negligible or not, the Lorentzian factor is *there* in the visual or the optical record, *and is thence, on our view, projicient as an acquired property of that which makes the record.* Revert to the illustration of the train and the platform. It follows from Lorentzian treatment that the length of a metre-rod, as measured in the train, is judged through the record on the platform to be less than a metre, but, for the trains of our daily and current experience, less by a very minute and quite negligible amount. Conceive, however, an ideal train travelling at 100,000 kilometres per second. Then apply, if you have this moderate amount of training, the Lorentzian transformation to the length of a metre in *that* train as judged from the platform; or the length of a metre on the platform as judged from a record in that train; and make a note of how much shorter it is judged to be. Work out just a few examples. Then you will appreciate Mr. Einstein's statement that, under such judgment, " the rigid rod is shorter when in motion than when at rest, and the more quickly it is moving, the shorter is the rod " (T.R. p. 35).

But, in accordance with Lorentzian treatment, not only is an x-transformation required; a t-transformation is also required. This follows quite prettily. But here it must suffice to say that just as spatial distance is judged to be diminished, so is time-interval judged to be greater. A time-interval of 5 minutes *in* the train is judged *from* the platform to be more than 5 minutes; and so much more in accordance with the speed of the ideal train. It follows that, subject to judgment from the record, " as a consequence of its motion the clock goes more slowly than when at rest " (p. 37).

β. *General Theory.*

In the special or restricted theory of relativity uniform motion in translation, as given in optical records registered within a different frame, is the subject-matter of discussion. Acceleration is left out of account, under abstraction quite legitimate. In the general theory of relativity acceleration, so conspicuous a feature in nature, is deliberately brought into the picture, and matters already complex enough are rendered very much more complex. I can only give a bare indication, simplified by the omission of some important details, of the kind of change which comes over the physical scene requiring for its treatment new modes of mathematical device.

If one conceive around a magnet a field of influence (*i.e.* something physically describable) varying in density or intensity with the distance from the magnet, the observed motion of certain entities in that field can be interpreted, in terms of that generalised " description " which science now employs. Similarly, if one conceive around the earth a gravitative field (likewise describable) anything, no matter what its so-called material substance—anything that has mass or inertia (which must here be identified, cf. Einstein, T.R. ch. xix.) exhibits accelerated motion, within that field, in accordance with the varying density of some given small area through which it moves. A *de facto* field of acceleration thus replaces a " force " supposed to be in some sense active. But many physicists have for fifty years and more dropped overboard any such notion of " force " as active or operative.

As we have seen, the recorded behaviour of " clocks and measuring rods," as judged from the frame of reference of the optical recipient, is such that the time-intervals in the swiftly-moving system appear to be lengthened, and the space-intervals appear to be shortened, in accordance with the Lorentzian formula. But in any field of acceleration, matters are much more complicated.

In illustration, Mr. Einstein (ch. xxxiii.) takes the field of acceleration in a rotating disc. The " density " of the field in this case is *nil* at the centre and increases with the distance therefrom as we proceed outwards. How about " clocks and measuring rods" at various positions on the disc as judged from a non-rotating reference-frame outside it? Clearly, a clock near the periphery of the disc will be judged to go slower than one near the centre—all others at intervening positions will be judged to go at different rates, each according to its station. Clearly, too, measuring rods, placed tangentially to concentric circles, will be judged to be shortened by an amount accordant with their several speeds in conformity to their distances from the centre; but those placed radially will appear unaffected. Hence, the classical π of Euclidian geometry can have no status *in respect to these judgments*, and must, so far as they are concerned, go by the board.

Well, then (asks the somewhat bewildered " plain man "), what is to be done? Tell us, I beseech you, the gist of it. I think the gist of it is that just as classical treatment does not suffice where uniform velocities approaching that of light are in the record, but must be replaced by Lorentzian transformation; so here, where acceleration is in the picture, this transformation is no longer good enough, and must be supplemented by new methods of treatment based on " Gaussian co-ordinates " or on " tensor transformation " which, perhaps, a few score of mathematicians can securely wield.

§ XLV. *Relativity Subject to Projicience.*

That the modern doctrine of relativity should unreservedly be accepted as a policy no one is likely to deny. Splendid results stand to its credit in this respect. But whether it should be accepted as a philosophical creed is another matter. And this, I contend, turns on the acceptance of visual apprehension on the one hand, or of projicience and projection on the other hand.

One must realise to how large an extent, not only the special and the general theory of relativity, but the relativist position at large, in its modern development, depends on vision, and involves optical records. Two intertwined issues should be distinguished. Let me put the matter thus. First strike out from Mr. Einstein's masterly exposition (in T.R.) all that implies some optical analogue of the distance-receptors, as a recording instrument, and consider how much, or how little, remains. Secondly, mark all such expressions as " judged from this or that frame of reference " and weigh carefully their exact import. Thirdly, ask whether in those more direct statements where " judged from " is not explicitly inserted, some such concept is not implicitly inferable, though unexpressed. Thus when we read " the rigid rod is shorter when in motion than at rest," or, " as a consequence of its motion the clock goes more slowly " (pp. 35, 37), may we, or may we not, preface each statement with " as judged from another frame of reference," and still preserve the spirit of such statements ? Fourthly, if the question just asked be answered in the negative, consider on what grounds the jump from " is judged to go more slowly " to " goes more slowly " is justified.

What, then, are the intertwined issues ?

 (1) That of recipient record in relation to some occurrence at a distance therefrom ;

(2) That of "judgment" (to adopt Mr. Einstein's expression) having reference (in some sense) to the occurrence at a distance.

With regard to (1), the primary difficulty is that the only means of getting at what the occurrence at a distance intrinsically *is*, apart from the record, is through this record or other such records. To this I shall revert. With regard to (2) we must clear the ground a little. May we take the word "judged" as equivalent to "perceived," in the sense that what is so judged would be perceived had we organs of suitable refinement? That, I think, is partly what is meant, in perhaps rather a metaphorical sense. But only in part. For, I take it, the aim of the physicist is to abstract from percipience as a mental event—in other words, to deal with the whole matter irrespectively of the so-called relativity of knowledge—quite a different story. Unfortunately, some writers introduce the words "objective" and "subjective" to trouble not a little the waters of exposition. Now, all that is in any way perceived is objective, at any rate as I have used this word; but my contention is that not all that is objective, in that sense, belongs of right to the thing which is said to be perceived. As to "subjective," unless the word be defined in some such way as Mr. Russell suggests (A.M. pp. 130-295), (which empties it of much of its usual connotation) it is better to eschew it altogether. In fact, both words—objective and subjective—should be reserved for use, under careful definition, in con-

If for "has" we substitute "appears to have under optical or visual treatment," all will agree. On these terms passing events in the Minkowski-Einstein world-frame are "warped" or non-Euclidian from the point of view of visual appearances or phenomena. Hence, the exact determination of this warping is of prime scientific importance. *This* warp may well be a property of a gravitative field ; *that* warp a property of an electro-magnetic field as judged from records of events therein.

Since then the whole problem turns on what appears from the record's perspective, the validity of relativist policy for strictly scientific interpretation is unimpeachable. At the present juncture no other policy is admissible.

But if the relativist claim, at the bar of philosophy, not only that there are as many apparent lengths and times as there are frames of reference in relative motion ; not only that scientific policy in this domain of research demands a universe of warped events ; but that he thus takes us one step nearer to an interpretation of *intrinsic* reality in the world as it is *apart from perspectives*, the grounds of his doctrine of direct apprehension, or revelation through vision, must be firmly established before any such conclusion can be accepted—I repeat at the bar of philosophy. According to those who accept some such alternative doctrine as that of projicience these grounds are open to criticism.

One must again urge that, so far from being a primitive mode of acquaintance with the world, vision is one of the least primitive modes of approach. Evolved as a premonitory guide to coming, through behaviour, into direct contact with things; acquiring, step by step, the pragmatic endorsement of working so well; affording to the full the extrinsic reality of appearances; supported in this by the verdict of relativity; it is, from first to last, subject always to that projicience which is, on the one hand, the secret of its success, and, on the other hand, the condition of its failure to get into touch with intrinsic reality. Such is our evolutionary view—to be subjected, of course, to counter-criticism.

On its success as a guide to behaviour in a world which is, for us, so largely one of ever-changing perspectives, it is needless to enlarge. But on its failure, as such, to give aught but appearance as a clue to that intrinsic reality which it is, of itself, incapable of reaching, the evolutionist is bound to insist. As I look up from my desk in the corner of my room there is scarcely a thing whose apparent shape even approximately accords with the acknowledged configuration of that thing in its intrinsic spatial relatedness. In all, save some specially selected instances of accord, where what we may speak of as the plane of the retina is parallel with the plane of events recorded, vision so distorts the thing it renders objective, that it is unsafe to rely on judgment based only on optical records, for knowledge of the intrinsic course of events in that system, having visual depth, which lies at a distance. The new relativity does but point the moral of this old tale.

May I now, at the risk of some repetition, be allowed to emphasise the contention that we must be careful to distinguish between a scientific policy and a philosophic creed? As a policy physical relativity is to be accepted at the present juncture with the most cordial sympathy. It has shed brilliant light on the interpretation of phenomena as revealed in optical records. It entails non-Euclidian reconstruction of the spatial frames in terms of which such phenomena must be interpreted if the policy of physical science is to be carried on to further stages of advance. It entails, too, a revised treatment of objective time as incorporated in 4-dimensional frames. There is assuredly nothing here to which the philosopher of any school, if he have some tincture of wisdom, should take exception.

But if it be said that this warping of the universal frame as revealed in optical records reveals also the intrinsic space and time plan of the universe; if it be said that temporal relatedness in events can no longer be distinguished in the nature of its being from spatial relatedness; if it be said that since thus are things given in the record, thus also must they be given apart from the record; if, in brief, it be claimed that a successful policy must be the one true basis of an acceptable creed; then the whole position is different.

Those whose researches have lain in other departmental fields of science may ask whether the physicist has weighed with due care the biological and psychological evidence in matters of vision, and of optical records as necessarily interpreted through vision; whether, in view of the results obtained within this field of scientific enquiry, new realists are quite sure that, on the evolutionary evidence, the policy of accepting direct apprehension at its face-value is the only policy, and therefore the unambiguous platform of a creed; whether, on broader lines, they are fully satisfied that their epistemological foundations are secure.

It is, I know, the fashion among some new realists to relegate epistemology—the basal problem of knowledge—to a quite subordinate position. Mr. Whitehead, I think, would say that it is one for " metaphysics " and not for science to discuss. None the less, a rather naïve solution of the problem is too often accepted without any serious discussion of its merits. If it be a problem for " metaphysics " let it be metaphysically discussed, and let full references be given to such discussion so that it may be quite clear what reasons are assigned why this metaphysical solution, and not another, is to form the basis of scientific procedure. For us, however, the problem is not " metaphysical " in the sense intended. For us any definition of nature according to which mind and knowledge are other than natural is out of court. And, if this be so, the epistemological problem falls within, and nowise outside, the purview of scientific enquiry.

If it be said : Science has no concern whatever with what you are pleased to call a philosophic creed ; then I must ask : If reference *from* the record casting a more or less warped shadow on to that which is thus recorded be *a policy* alternative to that of direct apprehension *by* the record of that which is intrinsic to physical nature ; should not an interpretation based on the former policy receive serious consideration whether it be accepted or not ?

But one of the claims of relativists is that the modern doctrine entails a thorough revision of our concept of the intrinsic structure of the physical universe. And this is hard to distinguish from what I have spoken of as a philosophic creed in respect thereof. Is it as a policy *only* that we are bidden to regard the inevitable warping of visual and optical constructs as revealing the actual course of events in nature itself? May we still subscribe to the essential tenets of the Newtonian creed? Many physicists will reply that we may no longer do so. We have to reckon with a new scientific creed.

In attempting to discuss—I hope without grave errors of presentation—a cardinal issue that is raised by modern physicists, I have taken relativity on its own terms as concerned only with what new realists speak of as the non-mental. I have therefore said nothing on the further issue which idealists regard as foundational—the so-called relativity of knowledge. They urge that any sundering of the apprehended from apprehending is false and meaningless. Wedded in synthesis, no analytic decree of divorce can separate them. Each is what it is in relation to the other. I regard this, however, as a matter that falls under relatedness rather than relativity. Furthermore, so far as I can judge from much that has been written of late, this further problem cannot profitably be discussed on the same platform as that on which the advocates of physical relativity take their stand.

LECTURE X. CAUSATION AND CAUSALITY

XLVI. A "Common-sense" View and that of "Exact Science." XLVII. Cause as precedent to Effect. XLVIII. Ground and Conditions of Change. XLIX. Causality distinguished from Causation. L. The Position reviewed.

§ XLVI. *A "common-sense" view and that of "exact science."*

I SEEK in this lecture to distinguish between causation and Causality; to indicate on what grounds I regard such a distinction of service in the discussion of causal problems; to show that the concepts to be distinguished under these names belong to different universes of discourse; to urge that they are nowise contradictory; and to state some conclusions which seem to me to follow from my whole method of treatment.

To this end it will be convenient to start with some general statement, such as this: Given a thing or a system of things which is, in some relative sense, either (*a*) at rest, or (*b*) changing; then if that which is at rest begins to change, or that which is changing does so more, or less, or in some different way, this change in the one case or altered change in the other may be regarded as an effect recorded in the thing or system. The problem is to ascertain what is, in some sense, the cause of this effect. Here we come into touch with what has been said with regard to effective relatedness.

There is, I suppose, little or nothing in the foregoing statement (apart from crabbed wording) to which the so-called " plain man " would raise very serious objection from what he regards as the common-sense standpoint. He might perhaps say that it does not sufficiently emphasise the feature of uniformity (where it obtains), and that it fails, in so abstract a form, to distinguish different kinds of cause, e.g. Force in the physical world, Life as a cause of the changes which occur in organisms, and, above all, Mind as causally operative in human affairs. In all cases, he might add, to *be* a cause it must *do* something. Unless it does something there will be no effect. Nothing will happen.

There is little doubt that most people thus regard the cause as operative or active in bringing about the change as effect. They hold that the effect produced is proportional to the given activity of the cause, which may, however, have in reserve power to produce other and greater changes. Under what they take to be the teaching of science, they accept, in physical matters, strict uniformity of connection between the cause, as then and there operative, and the observable change which results from its operation. They look upon changes wrought by the will of man as due to a cause which is in a high degree and very characteristically active, but which is, owing to our freedom, in a less degree, or at any rate not so characteristically, uniform. Hence it is taken for granted as scarcely open to question by practical folk, that mind is pre-eminently a cause of certain noteworthy changes in the face of nature, and is in a very special sense active—so much so that the activity we feel, when through exercise of the will we are ourselves causes, best illustrates what is meant by causal activity. Carry this a stage further, lifting it to a higher plane of thought, and we have the widely accepted belief that ultimately all observable change is due to some form of Spiritual Activity.

Turn now from such an opinion as this to the view that is advocated by some exponents of exact science. By them we are told that the concept of activity, if not that of cause itself, is to be cast aside. Half a century ago W. K. Clifford spoke of " such an interdependence of the facts of the universe as forbids us to speak of one fact or set of facts as the cause of another fact or set of facts." And again : " The facts of one time are not the cause of the facts of another, but the facts of all time are included in one statement and rigorously bound up together " (L.E. Vol. I. pp. 111, 123). Ernst Mach says : " I hope that the science of the future will discard the idea of cause and effect, as being formally obscure " ; and he adds : " In my feeling that these ideas contain a strong tincture of fetishism I am certainly not alone " (P.S.L. p. 254). More recently Mr. Bertrand Russell has urged that the word " cause " is so inextricably bound up with misleading associations as to make its extrusion from the philosophical vocabulary desirable (M.L. p. 180).

This as it stands may seem an extreme view. But in what sense extreme? Extreme only as expressing a method of interpretation in exact science within the carefully restricted universe of physical discourse. One is dealing with the changes which are observable at the basal level of emergent evolution and with kinds of relatedness that obtain therein; one fixes attention on a relatively isolated situation in which all disturbing conditions coming from beyond it are excluded or, if this be impossible, allowed for; one conceives this whole state of matters as affording a field of relatedness; the more one knows about this field the more confidently can one say that what happens is an invariable expression of the nature of the field and the nature of that which lies therein, and the more adequately can one summarise the net result of many observations in a law, or express it in suitable equations. All reference to force as an agency through the operation of which the changes occur is barred because it is quite valueless for purposes of exact science. The word "force" may still be used, but not with this meaning. In one such usage it expresses the measure or degree of some observable change in some specific field of relatedness.

There is another reason why the word "cause" is so sparingly used in physics, if it be used at all. Part of the commonly accepted connotation of the word, as it occurs in what may be called the historical sciences, is that the cause, or some part of it under analysis, precedes the effect. But such historical treatment is not the primary aim in physics. The aim is rather so to reduce the time-interval to a minimum as to say, " X now causes Y now." If this be so, the use of the word " causation," which commonly implies antecedent cause and subsequent effect, may not be desirable save under some suitable re-definition.

Now, if we may say that an essential feature of causation may be thus expressed : Given a field of effective relatedness that which observably happens under the existent go of events is an expression of the nature of the field and the nature of this or that which lies within it ; then it is clear that the higher we ascend in the evolutionary scale the more complex are the concrete problems of causation. We have a progressive superposition of level on level. Higher kinds of relatedness—chemical, vital and conscious—are each in turn supervenient on those that stand lower in the scale ; but they do not supersede them in the sense that, when some higher kind of relatedness comes, the lower kinds go. It is just because they do *not* go—because the lower still remain, in such measure as to afford foundations for the emergent superstructure, that all higher level treatment of causation becomes increasingly complex. And if the manner in which lower level events run their course *depends on* the higher kind of relatedness co-existent at the supervenient level, this does but emphasise the effectiveness of the relations which obtain at that higher level.

§ XLVII. *Cause as Precedent to Effect.*

Whatever may be said for or against the retention of the concept of causation in the more exact branches of science, it is in matters of common experience, dealing with the net result of concurrent events at many, or perhaps at all, levels, that the words " cause " and " effect " are chiefly of service. Nor, sanctioned as they are by long usage, are they likely to be discarded. We are interested in the sequence of events ; and it is, in daily life, mainly this interest that decides what event, or component in a system of events, we select as that which is to be regarded as " the cause " of some other event. We must satisfy ourselves that it is relevant ; and the discarding of irrelevant events (such as spilling the salt at breakfast) is a first step towards realising that there is some kind of connection, other than temporal sequence, between cause and effect. Relying on a somewhat vague and general, but gradually strengthening, notion of uniformity in natural routine, we search for the cause of something that happens in order that we may promote or prevent its recurrence ; or, if the cause lie beyond our control, that we may place ourselves or our belongings out of reach of the effect. The wider our practical experience, and the fuller our knowledge of routine, the more complex does the concept of cause become. Not one condition only, but quite a number of conspiring and concurrent conditions have to be taken into consideration. Still we may, as a matter of emphasis, lay stress on one as *the* cause—meaning that of chief interest. Sometimes we may discuss which of two conspiring conditions is in this sense *the* cause. We may, for example, ask whether the outburst of vegetation in the Spring is due to increasing warmth or to longer and stronger light-illumination. The man of science may say "both," and may seek to assign a value to each. The student in any scientific laboratory has, moreover, to learn that the more obvious and salient facts are not the only conditions to success in his experiments. He thus gradually grasps what Mill meant when he said that, "the cause is the sum total of the conditions positive and negative taken together—the whole of the contingencies of every description which being realised, the consequent invariably follows" (S.L. Bk. III. ch. v. § III.). And with this in view, part of his aim, under analysis, will be to distinguish the contributory from the counteracting conditions when both are in evidence. Where the contributory or positive conditions would, as he judges, be effective if certain counteracting or negative conditions were absent, he may speak of a "tendency" in the cause to give rise to an effect which, as a matter of fact, does not follow. Thus the earth has a tendency to pursue a course tangential to its orbit.

One need only notice in passing what Hume spoke of as "Rules by which to judge of causes and effects" (agreement, difference, concomitant variations, residues, and so forth). They were developed by Mill, and used to be fully discussed in text-books of logic. Such rules are of value as a means to discovering the chief factors in the causation of some given event. On these terms our knowledge of causation may be discussed under probability. Hence Professor Broad has suggested some such statement as this: "To every true proposition that asserts the happening of an event at a time there is a set of relevant true propositions such that, relative to the whole of them, the probability of the event happening is 1 " (P.P.R. p. 154).

Without attempting to follow up this matter in its more recent developments, it suffices here to say that if, under analysis we may regard as a near approximation to 1 the probability of the proposition : *When* and *where* the total relatedness under consideration obtains is irrelevant ; then it follows that the prediction of future events may be trustworthy even if these events be new to human experience—as was exemplified in the discovery of Neptune. But must we not add as a proviso that the characters we deal with are *resultant* ? If they comprise also evolutionary emergents in some measure, in that measure they are unpredictable. In the total set of relevant propositions which are referable to the cause, there are certain propositions which are, from the nature of the case, not yet known. Hence the basis on which the probability of the effect is logically founded, is *de facto* an incomplete basis.

The question for us then arises : May we bring emergence itself under the rubric of causation ? The reply turns on our answer to a further question : Is emergent evolution itself the expression of an orderly and progressive development ? If so (and such is my contention), then emergence itself takes rank, as Mill and Lewes also contended, among the " laws of nature." We may be unable to predict the probable nature of a character that is emergently new. We could not have foretold on the basis of physico-chemical events *only* what the nature of life would be. But that is due to our ignorance before the event of the law of its emergence. May we, then, say :

> (1) That where resultants, and resultants only, are concerned, the probability of the uniform continuance of the routine of the past approximates to 1, and thus would enable an adequately instructed Laplace to predict with assurance and success ;
> (2) That such approximation to 1 is taken to *be* 1 under acknowledgment ;
> (3) That genuine novelty under emergence precludes, in the measure of its presence, such confident prediction ; but
> (4) That, if there be a natural plan of emergence, then every effect is strictly determinate in accordance with the nature of that plan ;
> (5) That novelty itself is thus caught up in the web of causal nexus under suitable acknowledgment ; but
> (6) That such novelty is for us unpredictable owing to our partial knowledge of the plan of emergence up to date, and our necessary ignorance of what the further development of that plan will be ?

Important as this question is for us, it may be regarded as parenthetic. To revert, then, to more detailed discussion, we have seen that for historical treatment some part of the cause as the sum total of the conditions, is precedent to the effect. But we have also seen that, in the more exact science of physics, the time-interval between cause and effect is reduced to a minimum. They are in touch at some " now " in the current situation.

In historical treatment, wherever there is transmission, we refer the cause to some effluent event which precedes the arrival of the influent event; under scientific analysis we focus attention on what happens at the moment of arrival of this influence. Only where there is transmission does the effluent event precede the arrival of influence. This may not be so in a gravitative field which has therefore to be treated under the concept of varying " density" in that field. Here causation in the historical sense is out of place and the word " causation " is seldom used (cf. Russell, M.L. p. 180).

Where transmission obtains, then, as in the case of all optical records, the effluent event *always* precedes the influent event, and there is time-interval between the one and the other, with passage of events in transmission. It is, however, a corollary from relativist theory that classical and old-fashioned notions of temporal sequence must be discarded. One may no longer speak of time but of " local times." Hence one is hopelessly out of date if one says that the past is non-existent now (cf. Whitehead, P.A.S. 1921-2, p. 132). For the past may, and still does, exist in some other local time than that of the record.

Out of this, in part at least, arises Mr. Russell's hypothesis of " mnemic causation." He urges that the traditional antithesis of mind and matter as diverse in the nature of its ultimate stuff cannot be accepted. " The dualism," he says, " is not primarily as to the stuff of the world " (for him sensations) " but as to causal laws." " The causal laws of psychology are *prima facie* very different from those of physics" (A.M. pp. 137, 172, cf. p. 121). In what then does this difference lie? Mr. Russell replies that the difference lies in this ; that in mnemic causation, as distinguished from physical causation, the proximate cause consists not only of a present event, but of this together with a past event (p. 85). In more formal terms instead of asserting : " X now causes Y now " we should say : " A, B, C, . . . in the past, together with X now, causes Y now " (p. 87). The emphasis is on causal events *in the past* : and this is to be taken literally. " I do not mean merely," he says, " what would always be the case—that past occurrences are part of a *chain* of causes leading to the present event. I mean that, in attempting to state the *proximate* cause of the present event, some past event or events must be included, unless we take refuge in hypothetical modifications of brain structure " (p. 78).

The alternative view is that the past has ceased to exist, though its enchained effects persist, unless we take refuge in the relativist hypothesis of " local times," (p. 128) under conditions, it would seem, which render the Lorentzian factor negligible. For us such local times are matters of projective appearance. As at present advised I must therefore reject mnemic causation. But I may close on a note of possible agreement. When Mr. Russell says that "the state of the body and brain is proved to be necessary but not sufficient" (p. 91), he gives expression to that which is fully accordant with the contention of emergent evolution. That contention is that there is more at the conscious level, in spatial projicience and temporal projection, than there is in the set of events at the level of life, or *a fortiori* that of physical matter. I too should agree, then, that what is involved is necessary but not sufficient.

§ XLVIII. *Ground and Conditions of Change.*

We have seen that, according to Mill, the cause is the sum total of the conditions, positive and negative, taken together; and that according to Mr. Broad, our knowledge of the cause is a set of propositions, expressing the conditions, which is implied by the proposition which expresses the effect. But we have still to consider in what sense the word "conditions" is to be understood.

In several passages Mill distinguished between events and states. Discussing, for example, the case of a man who eats from a dish of contaminated food and dies in consequence, he says: "The various conditions, except the single one of eating the food, were not events but states possessing more or less permanency; and might therefore have preceded the effect by an indefinite length of duration, for want of the event which was requisite to complete the required concurrence of conditions." So, too, "when sulphur, charcoal, and nitre, are put together in certain proportions and in a certain manner the effect is, not an explosion, but that the mixture acquires a property by which, in given circumstances, it will explode" (S.L. Bk. III. ch. v. §§ 3, 5). Now, although Mill regards the more or less abiding state, or the constitution, as part of the sum total of conditions, he does here draw an important distinction. It will be helpful to emphasise this distinction by naming the "state" of the system the intrinsic *ground* of the change which occurs within it when certain extrinsic *conditions* are also present. In popular speech the cause is commonly identified with some salient feature in the set of conditions. Thus warmth during incubation is regarded as the cause of the hatching of a chick ; the ground of development—the intrinsic constitution of the egg—is taken for granted. On the other hand the embryologist may take the external conditions of incubation for granted, and direct his attention to the constitution of the fertilised ovum as the ground of that which specifically happens.

That factor in the changes within any given system which has its ground in the constitutional nature of that system is sometimes spoken of as attributable to *immanent* causation ; while that which is due to conditions extrinsic to the system is attributed to *transeunt* causation. When gunpowder explodes, a spark may be the condition of the disruptive change under transeunt causation. But if it be asked how it is that under such conditions gunpowder explodes though charcoal does not, the reply is : Because such is the constitution of gunpowder. The two kinds of causation, methodologically distinguished, are here co-factors. When an organism behaves in such and such a manner a describable pattern of extrinsic influence may afford the transeunt conditions. But if it be asked : How comes it that under substantially the same external influence *this* organism behaves thus and *that* organism quite otherwise ? The reply is : Because the immanent ground is different in this organism and that. Even what we call the same organism may respond differently to like stimulation on some subsequent occasion. This is because the ground of behaviour, *i.e.* the constitution of the organism, is no longer the same. In human life the distinction is familiar under the headings of character and circumstances.

If there be any talk of " proportionality " of cause and effect it is essential to comprise under the cause intrinsic ground no less than extrinsic conditions. We need not discuss in what sense such talk is wise when we are dealing with events— *e.g.* emotional events—which are not in strictness *measurable* ; or any events of which some *estimation* of their intensity is all that we have to go upon. Assume for the nonce that there may be some sort of proportionality in some liberal sense of the word. Then, even so, if we restrict the word " cause " to extrinsic conditions only—sometimes spoken of as the releasing cause (cf. Bergson, C.E. p. 77)—then there is no proportionality. An explosion of gunpowder is not proportional to the spark that ignited it. In such a physico-chemical matter one must consider the intrinsic ground of what happens, *i.e.* the constitution of the gunpowder ; one must consider, too, the change of so-called potential to kinetic energy in the mass of powder throughout which the disruptive change spreads ; and so on. At a much higher level, as Sir Robert Ball used to say in his popular lectures with a piquant touch of Irish intonation : " If a boy in the audience runs a pin into his neighbour's thigh the consequent commotion is nowise proportional to *the size of the orifice.*" When we pass to the reflective level of human consciousness quite astonishing conclusions, animistic or other, have been drawn from the fairly obvious fact that a very slight difference in advenient influence (*i.e.* in extrinsic conditions of vision or hearing) may make a profound difference in consequent conduct. Of course they often do so ; in accordance with the intrinsic ground which includes (under correlation) the character—the total mental constitution as an integral whole—of the person who is the recipient. Or given the same person : a slight difference in what falls on the retina may induce a marked difference in that person's mental attitude. If owing to mishap a letter drops out ; and if instead of the text, " We shall all be changed," one reads " We shall all be hanged " ; the outcome, whatever it may be, and however it is interpreted, cannot, with any sense of propriety, be said to be proportional to the elided letter *c*. The essential point is that (if there be proportion) intrinsic ground has in all such cases far more weight than extrinsic conditions.

The distinction, then, between ground and conditions must be borne in mind. And if we introduce some notion of proportion we must include under cause the immanent as well as the transeunt factor in causation. But we have also to remember that the distinction is methodological in its application ; methodological because it depends on what natural system we so isolate under attention as to regard the changes therein as intrinsic thereto. If, to take but one example, we regard the nervous system of an animal as such a system (and the biologist often does so) then other occurrences in the body have transeunt influence on that system. On these terms, when science has given the fullest possible account of the constitution of any given system as immanent ground, and of all the transeunt conditions of some given change therein, its task (up to date) is accomplished.

Now we may regard the total goingness of any given system as its activity—in the sense of " something doing " as contrasted with " nothing going on." Or we may, and commonly do, apply the word " activity " to intrinsic go—that part of a system's own doing which is not merely impressed on it from without—the active go of an aeroplane or a thoughtful man compared with the passive go of a drifting balloon or of a man at the mercy of every wind of doctrine. It is not activity in either of these purely naturalistic senses that is barred in science. It is not of such activity that Mr. Broad says that " (1) it is perfectly useless to science, and (2) no kind of observation of external things or their changes could prove it " (P.P.R. p. 80). In what sense, then, *is* it barred ? In the sense of Activity as that which makes events go as they do go. It is this Activity that is quite useless in science and is nowise susceptible of scientific proof. The causation with which I have been dealing has nothing whatever to do with it.

But philosophy, throughout the ages, has had very much to do with it. For those who acknowledge God the concept is essential. Much that has been written on causality implies it at every turn. Well then, since we have two differing concepts, and two different words, it seems not unreasonable to suggest that causation should be reserved for the one and Causality applied to the other. I differentiate partly by using a capital letter. This usage, though perhaps inelegant, is convenient where we have no different words while the underlying concepts are quite different—*e.g.* in determination under causation and Determination through Causality; or, as above, the activity which characterises a going system and the Activity on which the passage of all events in the universe, manifested in diverse ways, is ultimately dependent.

§ XLIX. *Causality distinguished from causation.*

I believe that the " capital " distinction I thus draw on methodological grounds is traceable throughout modern philosophy and has its roots in precedent systems of thought. A brief impressionistic sketch may serve to show what I mean.

Descartes interpreted under causation all physical events and included under his doctrine of automatism, such processes as perception, imagination, and memory in animals—included also, even in man, all that could be regarded as independent of

Guidance by the Rational Soul. Defining "substance" as that which has being in such manner as to require no other being in order so to subsist, he urged that this can be imputed only to God. There are indeed (1) corporeal substance (*res extensa*), and (2) mental or thinking substance (*res cogitans*) ; but they need for their being the concurrence of God ; "*Dei concursu egent ad existendum.*" Apart from this common Dependence on God neither is dependent on the other ; for if it were so, neither would be substance under the definition. Furthermore, this common Dependence on God excludes both, in strictness, from the status of substance. Still, in virtue of the Rational Soul, Causality is attributable to man. It remained for Descartes' disciples, Malebranche and others, to attribute Causality to God alone. All merely "occasional" causation is subject to His Determination.

Spinoza—in so far as he dealt with "modes," *i.e.* concrete things or events—taught that each is determined from without (*per aliud*) under transeunt causation. But any given system of events, though it is thus partially, and *qua* mode, determined by extrinsic conditions, is also determinate from within, *i.e.* in virtue of its intrinsic ground or "essence" (immanent causation). Now the totality of all such events is nature. Taken as a whole it cannot be determined from without, for there is nothing external to it. It must, therefore, be determinate wholly from within, that is, in virtue of its constitution or essence. Thus we get *natura naturata*. But is not this, too, Determined? If so by what? By *Natura naturans* under Causality. Here God is not only the one Substance in that He exists by the sole necessity of His nature ; He is the one Free Cause in that He acts by the sole necessity of His nature (*Eth.*, Part I. Prop. 17, Corr. 2).

According to Spinoza what transeuntly determines this or that several event, or mode, as it *is*, must be sought in other external and relevant events which it is *not*. This renders them finite. But nature comprises *all* finite events; hence in its essence it is not thus finite. The constitution of nature in its essence (and of any given system in essence) is infinite. But since modes, as finite, are determined *ab extra*, they are constrained. Now the antithesis of such constraint is freedom. Nature, therefore, as totality of events, is free, since there is nothing to constrain it from without. And any given system is in essence free in so far as what happens therein is the outcome of its own intrinsic constitution. Its freedom, however, is that of a determinate system and differs from the Freedom of God under Causality. The former, Spinoza calls freedom after its kind ; the latter absolute Freedom. Constraint is *ab extra* and is determinant of modes ; freedom is *ab intra* and is determinate in essence ; but Freedom is *Ab Intra* and characterises God as *Natura naturans*—characterises man, too, in so far as he expresses *sub specie aeternitatis* the Immanent Activity which is Divine Causality at its ultimate Source.

For Berkeley causation is swallowed up in Causality. The so-called " causes " in any empirical discussion of " causation " are falsely so called. Any supposed connection between " cause and effect" is no more than the observed conjunction between the sign and that which is signified, Dependent on the arbitrary, but nowise capricious, Causality of God, who has chosen this means of admonishing us with regard to what we may expect. But we too, as Spirits created by God, are endowed with our measure of Causality. And if he be asked what assurance we have of Activity, Berkeley replies : Look within ; we most assuredly know that we are Agents, and on this knowledge is based all our notions of efficiency and relation. We have only to raise these notions to their absolute limit and God stands revealed. Such in brief is Berkeley's argument.

But here David Hume intervenes and roundly asserts that, on looking within, he finds nothing on which such notions can be based. He finds primary " impressions " and secondary " ideas " derivative therefrom, often very complexly ordered in ways we must accept as we find them. These in their given clustering constitute us. And we are all that there is in Hume's radical phenomenalism. " We never really advance a step beyond ourselves, nor can conceive any kind of existence but those perceptions which have appeared in that narrow compass." And here conjunction under the empirical sway of custom is all that can be found. The uniform rules of conjunction are what we deal with under causation which suffices for all interpretation of matters of fact. Other matters are intellectual constructs with laws of our imposing. For Hume, Causality is barred save in so far as it may be accepted on non-rational grounds. " Our most holy religion is founded on faith and not on reason." That was his form of acknowledgment—genuine, as I think, but in need of more systematic development.

In so brief an outline sketch I have passed over Hobbes, and also Locke in whose often-revised discussion of Power the emphasis falls on Causality. Leibniz could hardly be summarised without entering in some detail into his elaborate scheme ; but an adequate disentangling of the warp of causation and the woof of Causality would, I think, serve to throw light on his system of philosophy, and on his exact meaning when he said that " in the phenomena of nature everything happens mechanically, and at the same time metaphysically." The word " mechanically " must here be read subject to his denial of all transeunt causation ; " metaphysically " subject to his doctrine of pre-established harmony. He might have been content to substitute for divinely imposed harmony a " natural plan " of accord in the whole system of monads which constitute a natural hierarchy wherein one is supremely domiant. But was he ? It is matter of controvesy.

Let us realise to how large an extent Leibniz, in his hierarchy of monads, anticipated the ascending order of levels which is a cardinal feature in emergent interpretation. In man at his highest and best there is the quality of deity. Hence through his relation to God he becomes a supreme monad. But as a member of the progressive hierarchy he is still only *primus inter pares*. He still remains in some measure weighted with matter which sets limits to the Activity expressed through him. God alone is free from all such limitation—as *Actus purus*. And so, after the manner of his time, Leibniz strives to give proof of the God he acknowledges as the ultimate fount of Causality. Even if perchance we agree with Mr. Bertrand Russell (P.L. ch. xv.), that the proof lacks cogency, we may still acknowledge that which lies beyond logical proof or logical disproof. On this understanding we may see what Leibniz meant when, in addition to saying that everything in nature happens both mechanically and metaphysically, he declares that " the source of the mechanical is in the metaphysical " (Letter to Remond, Edn. Erdmann, III. 607).

Little can here be said with regard to Kant. For him the distinction is rendered explicit as that between " natural " and " free " causality. His upward path lay through emphasis on " synthesis " in that human experience from which he sets forth in his quest for truth. Such experience is both objective and subjective in synthetic relatedness. Independently of us the objective world cannot be as it is for us; independently of a world rendered objective for us we should not be what we are. Kant's detailed treatment of causation is purely empirical, and justifies his claim that " truth is to be found only in experience." It justifies, too, his stress on the synthetic or ampliative nature of all propositions in which discoverable connections are predicated, even in mathematics. It might seem, then, that for Kant Causality is out of court. But in the " thesis " of the third antinomy he says : " Causality in conformity with the laws of nature is not the only causality from which all the phenomena of the world can be derived. To explain those phenomena it is necessary that there is also a free causality." In the " antithesis " this Freedom is denied. By Freedom is meant the power of bringing something into existence spontaneously. It implies the capacity of making an absolute beginning ; of doing one as easily as the other of two opposite things. It belongs to that which he calls the " intelligible " realm of noumena as contrasted with the empirical world of phenomena. In the one we have Causality ; in the other causation. I substitute these words in the following passage from the solution of the third antinomy. " May it not be that, while every phenomenal effect must be connected with its cause in accordance with empirical causation, this empirical causation, without the least rupture of its connection with natural causes, is itself an effect of a Causality which is not empirical but intelligible " ? The trouble is that " between the sensible realm of nature and the supersensible realm of freedom a gulf is fixed which is as impassable by theoretical reason as if they formed two separate worlds." Hence it is in the practical reason, and in the domain of ethics, that we must seek those principles through which the two realms may in some measure be united. How far Kant succeeds in establishing a valid union, and in what manner he attempts to do so, need not here be discussed. After all, this meagre sketch is only intended to illustrate how a methodological distinction, in more competent hands, might be applied.

§ L. *The Position reviewed.*

In such more competent hands I must leave the solution of the third antinomy which may be suggested on the lines of Hegelian dialectic. I suppose it may be said that contradiction begotten of difference disappears in the reconciliation of a higher synthesis (cf. Caird, C.P.K. II. p. 63). I should urge, however: (1) That it is only *apparent* contradiction that is susceptible of reconciliation, and (2) That causation and Causality are *not* contradictory in any strict sense.

They do not belong to two realms or to different orders of being; nor is there any gulf. There is one realm within which both are always present. And this, I think, though I speak with diffidence, accords with the spirit of Hegelian treatment.

If this be so there is no reason why both may not be accepted, each in its appropriate universe of discourse. Let me now review the position:

Emergent evolution works upwards from matter, through life, to consciousness which attains in man its highest reflective or supra-reflective level. It accepts the " more " at each ascending stage as that which is given, and accepts it to the full. The most subtle appreciation of the artist or the poet, the highest aspiration of the saint, are no less accepted than the blossom of the water-lily, the crystalline fabric of a snow-flake, or the minute structure of the atom.

Emergent evolution urges that the " more " of any given stage, even the highest, involves the " less " of the stages which were precedent to it and continue to coexist with it. It does *not* interpret the higher in terms of the lower only ; for that would imply denial of the emergence of those new modes of natural relatedness which characterise the higher and make it what it is. Nor does it interpret the lower in terms of the higher. If it be said that I have myself urged that how things go depends on the level of relatedness at which events run their course, this means the full recognition of the kind of effective relatedness which obtains at the level in question. It does *not* mean, for naturalistic treatment, dependence on kinds of relatedness *not yet emergent*. If physical changes be explained in terms of life ; or physiological changes in terms of unreflective consciousness ; or this in terms of guidance by reflective consciousness ; when there is no sufficient evidence that these respectively higher kinds of relatedness have yet emerged ; *then* the interpretation is not consistent with the tenets of emergent evolution ; it is not in accordance with generalised description under causation.

But if we may acknowledge on the one hand a physical world underlying the phenomenal appearances with which we are acquainted by sense, and, on the other hand, an immaterial Source of all changes therein ; if, in other words, we may acknowledge physical events as ultimately *involved*, and God on whom all evolutionary process ultimately *depends* ; then we may, with Kant, but on different grounds, accept both causation and Causality without shadow of contradiction. I claim that such procedure is legitimate in philosophy, and that it furnishes a consistent scheme. I have confessed my doubt whether either acknowledgment is susceptible of strictly logical proof. But in neither is there, so far as I can see, aught discrepant with the evidence. In regard to both one can only ask : Does the postulate so work that I am prepared to adopt it, and to run the risk of being mistaken in doing so ? In my belief in God, on Whom all things depend, I am certainly not alone. I would fain not stand alone in combining with this belief, and all that it entails, that full and frank acceptance of the naturalistic interpretation of the world which is offered by emergent evolution.

Emphasis on relatedness still seems to be essential ; and this is implied in both involution and dependence. Of God in isolation from the world—of God apart from what Mr. Alexander calls the emergent quality of deity supervenient near the summit of the evolutionary pyramid—I can form no adequate conception.

An adaptation of the use of a current philosophical expression of old standing may serve to bring out more clearly a salient feature of the position. Suppose we are dealing with some lowly plant as a natural system that has reached the level of life with its keynote of vital integration. There are physico-chemical events, and there is emergent vital relatedness. If then we deal with its materiality in abstraction from the supervenient life—or with its life apart from a physical basis—in either case we are concerned not with the concrete whole in accordance with its level of emergence, but with a *res incompleta*. The *res completa* is the living organism, nothing less but nothing more. Similarly, man, the highest natural system that we know, is a *res incompleta*, if considered in abstraction from those emergent qualities which give him, in alliance with all that is involved, his status as *res completa* ; and of these the highest is what Mr. Alexander calls the emergent quality of deity.

So far we have an interpretation in accordance with emergent evolution. Introduce now acknowledgment of Dependence. If this be accepted, then we may urge that apart from God—some Hegelians may prefer to substitute Reason, or Thought, or Knowledge—what I spoke of, at the outset, as the pyramid of emergent evolution is still a *res incompleta*. A constructive philosophy demands the *Res Completa* which is Reality.

But if we acknowledge God we nowise *supersede* interpretation under emergent evolution ; we *supplement* it by accepting something more in a richer attitude of piety. We supplement, not supersede, immanent causation as unconditioned in the universe—for as a whole it is subject to no extrinsic and transeunt conditions—by Causality in the Unconditioned. And the supplementary concept is not introduced at some higher stage—that of life or of consciousness or of reflective thought in man ; it is present throughout at all stages. We do not assert that at some given level there is not causation, but Causality. We urge rather : No instance of causation, subject to limitations of time and space, save as the expression of Causality *sub specie aeternitatis*.

Hence there can be no antagonism. There is not even the alternative, " this " or " that." The alternative is, "*this* without that," or "*this* with *that* also "; more comprehensively, the world without God or the world just as it is but none the less dependent on God. A *de facto* nisus towards deity which we find running upwards along a special line of advance in the ascending levels, is fully accepted on the evidence. But this valid concept, under causation, is supplemented by the completing concept—no less valid at the bar of philosophy—of Nisus in Causality manifested in all natural events.

In foregoing lectures emphasis has been laid again and again, perhaps with wearisome reiteration, on such expressions as " within the system," " within the organism," " within the mind." There is nothing in these expressions to preclude acknowledgment also of that which exists or subsists beyond us —acknowledgment of a physical world, of other minds, and of God. The stress is on primary acquaintance with signs which have reference to that which, as signified, lies beyond us. We acknowledge God as above and beyond. But unless we also intuitively enjoy His Activity within us, feeling that we are in a measure one with Him in Substance, we can have no immediate knowledge of Causality or of God as the Source of our own existence and of emergent evolution.

APPENDIX

EVOLUTIONARY NATURALISM

Among the new tendencies in science which Professor Roy Wood Sellars enumerates in his *Evolutionary Naturalism* (1922) as "declaring themselves within the last two decades" is "the admission of creative synthesis in nature with accompanying critical points and new properties." And he says: "The extent to which this recognition of evolutionary synthesis has come to the front of late is surprising" (pp. 296-297).

I may perhaps be allowed to enter a reminder that the title of a chapter in my *Introduction to Comparative Psychology* (1894) was "Selective Synthesis in Evolution." I there urged that such selective synthesis is illustrated alike in inorganic, organic, and mental evolution; that there is again and again "an apparent breach of continuity, by which I mean, not a gap or hiatus in the ascending line of development, but a point of new departure"; that, for example, "there does not appear to be a gradual and insensible change from the physical properties of the elements to the physical properties of the compound, but at the critical moment of the constitution of the compound there seems to be a new departure"; and so on. Synthesis, with new properties at critical turning-points, was the burden of my evolutionary contention.

I no longer use the expression "selective synthesis" because Lewes's "emergence" (1875) is, I think, less

APPENDIX

ambiguous. To label the underlying concept I have therefore substituted "emergent evolution." If "evolutionary naturalism" be regarded as preferable I raise no protest. What needs emphasis is that, however it be named, as a frankly naturalistic interpretation it must stand or fall. In Mr. Alexander's phrase it must be accepted "with natural piety." On these terms I sought to treat it in the chapter to which I have alluded. But there and elsewhere I said that an activity which is selective and synthetic is disclosed throughout the operations of nature. That, in the sense intended, I should now more clearly distinguish as a separate issue. The two issues are (1) as to the validity of the naturalistic interpretation; and (2) as to the validity of the supplementary concept of Activity in terms of which the course of evolutionary advance may be explained philosophically. On the first issue Mr. Sellars and I, with perhaps some difference in detail, are in substantial agreement. With regard to the second we differ. He sees no need, and feels no call, for explanation save in the accredited meaning of this word as it is used in the universe of scientific discourse. He recognises no activity other than that which can be naturalistically interpreted subject to the canons of critical realism.

I am not sure how far I am at one with Mr. Sellars in this matter of critical realism. I am not sure whether my *acknowledgment* of a physical world does, or does not, seriously differ from his realistic *affirmation*. But I think that in our several conclusions there is at any rate much in common, though perhaps Mr. Sellars may not endorse the stress I lay on vision. He distinguishes the content of perception from the external existent itself which he speaks of as the object of perception. He urges that "we can no longer believe that we can literally inspect or intuit the very external existent itself." He does not "doubt the existence of physical things co-real with the percipient"; he does doubt whether such things can ever form part of the content of perception; for "reflection has discovered that the objective content with which we at first clothe these acknowledged realities is intra-organic" (p. 27). In other words he claims that the content of perception is interpretative of an entity affirmed as the object of this content. But to "affirm" is not to "intuit" this object (p. 48).

It may be noted that in one passage Mr. Sellars speaks of "realistic affirmations," and in another passage (on the same page 27, cf. pp. 32-145) he speaks of "these acknowledged realities." I venture to suppose therefore that his affirmation and my acknowledgment are so far equivalent. It may also be noted that, while distinguishing the content of perception from its object, he speaks of objective content. He also says, with the emphasis of italics: "Our basic principle will be that an entity is *made an object* by the knower, that it is not an object in its own right. It is, however, an existent of its own peculiar kind in its own right. Being known, that is being an *object*, happens to entities and does not affect them, for it is a function of the knower" (p. 23). I have sought to avoid such ambiguity—not I think of thought but of expression—as I find in Mr. Sellars's exposition, by earmarking the word "objective" to qualify the *-ed*-aspect of that which Mr. Sellars calls "content," reserving the word "thing" for that the existence of which in its own right I acknowledge. But even so the trouble is that what I thus seek to distinguish as a thing is, so far as known at all, an object of acknowledgment, or objective to acknowledging. Hence it may be said that the distinction of thing and object cannot be sustained. What can one say in reply? My answer may sound paradoxical. It is, in brief, that the thing is never an object *of perception*; it is an object *of contemplation* (cf. § VII.). In the perceptual experience of a cow or a rabbit there are this, that, and the other objects of perception; but in "such an animal" (cf. § XVII.) there

APPENDIX

are no objects of contemplation. At the level of perception there is neither acknowledgment nor affirmation. Unless one is careful to distinguish the content of contemplation, within which the acknowledged physical existent has place, from the content of perception within which it has no place, we are not in a position to take further steps towards the solution of the problems of epistemology on evolutionary lines. Then we can see in what manner the object of contemplation, under acknowledgment or affirmation, is interpretative of the object of naïve perception on a lower plane of mental development.

How far Mr. Sellars would accept some such position I do not know. I state it in order to clear the ground; not in a spirit of antagonism to his views. Indeed, my present aim is to lay stress on lines along which some measure of agreement may be reached rather than on those along which there must still remain some divergence. In the matter of acknowledgment or affirmation or knowledge-claim we have much in common. Furthermore, with differences of expression, we are, if I mistake not, at one in sundry consequent conclusions ; (1) that all objective content of knowledge, perceptual or contemplative, is within the person concerned—is intra-organic as he puts it—or, in other words, that " all knowledge arises and exists only in the consciousness of individuals " (p. 303) ; (2) that we have no " penetrative intuition of physical reality " (pp. 50-52), or, as I phrase it in view of current English discussion. we have no direct apprehension of the external world as existent in its own right ; (3) that what is perceived is not the physical existent itself, but " a mental substitute for the thing to which the organism is reacting " (p. 61) (I take " mental " to be here equivalent to " contentual ") ; (4) that the objective world, at any rate for visual experience, is one of reference from this mental substitute, one of psychic signs referred to acknowledged physical centres, one in which colour for example is "indicative of physical conditions" (p. 189)—in short that, as such, it is *made* objective "by the selective activity of the percipient organism" (p. 44); (5) that "no datum [selective construct of the perceptual order] is *like* its external cause" (p. 193), but is a psychic sign thereof which determines the course of behaviour. To these may be added (6) that where we part company with some new realists is in their transference to the physical world, as part of its intrinsic nature, of much that belongs to the perceptual content as objectively meaningful for behaviour (cf. p. 48); and (7)—though on this head Mr. Sellars says little—that where we part company with many modern phenomenalists is in the acknowledgment or affirmation of a physical world towards which their attitude is, I take it, agnostic in that they hold that no such acknowledgment is necessary for adequate interpretation of the given facts since a phenomenalist treatment is all that is required for purposes of science (cf. Russell, A.M., p. 98).

It may be that I exaggerate points of agreement and slur over matters on which we differ. Let me therefore be content to express a hope that there is not much in the critical epistemology that Mr. Sellars advocates which is subversive of that which I advocated some ten years before the twentieth century opened—not as a novel view, but as one that needed due emphasis—namely that, subject to the acknowledgment, or as I then said assumption, of a physical order, our perceptual world must be interpreted in terms of mental "symbolism" (*Animal Life and Intelligence*, p. 315. *Mind*, N.S. Vol. I., pp. 75-76).

It seems, then, that in our outlook on evolutionary naturalism, we are in the main not far apart; in accepting a physical system under acknowledgment or affirmation we have at any rate much in common; in sundry criticisms of new realism there is more of harmony than of discord. But in the acknowledgment or affirmation of Activity we part company. That which he accepts as the activity which we must " postulate " though we do not " intuit " (pp. 233-234) under physical affirmation embraces, I think, a good deal more than some of the members of the English school of philosophical criticism would allow to pass. So even here it is perhaps in regard to what is implied, as I think, by the activity he does accept that there is divergence of view.

There remains the concept of correlation. In so far as this is the antithesis of any form of animism, or, more generally, of the thesis the supporters of which affirm " solidary " intersection of two disparate orders of being, we are both on the same side of the fence. We are at one in believing that mind and consciousness in due course appear in that advance of events of which evolutionary naturalism seeks to give an interpretation. Some form of " double-knowledge theory " (p. 307) is pretty generally accepted. For Mr. Sellars, however, there is correlation of mind with consciousness. Mind is to be regarded as " a physical category." " We should mean by it the nervous processes which find expression in intelligent conduct " (p. 300).

Whether this rather drastic transference of mind from the psychical to the physical " attribute " under what Mr. Sellars speaks of as " psycho-functional correlation " (p. 308) will win its way to wide acceptance, and whether it will further his " purpose to achieve an adequate idea of mind which will harmonise the conclusions of behaviourism with those of the more traditional psychology " (p. 315) must remain open to question. A resolute effort is needed to re-orient one's old-fashioned notions; and I doubt whether Mr. Sellars himself has always been successful in helping one to do so. If mind be neural process, to such process the adjective mental is properly applicable. On this understanding ought Mr. Sellars to speak of the " mental content of perception " (p. 76) ? Ought he to say that " mental

L.M.E.

contents are intuited; the brain is not" (p. 54)? Are such statements as the following free from ambiguity? "Relating is something adventitious which supervenes upon the things by reason of the interest and capacity of the human mind. The mind brings them together ideally or mentally, not physically" (p. 200). And so on. No doubt it may be said that such expressions are elliptical and must be re-read subject to psycho-functional correlation. So be it. At all events, notwithstanding the inversion of current modes of expression, the salient feature still is that correlation is the basis of interpretation where neural processes and conscious content are under discussion.

But Mr. Sellars is not prepared to affirm or acknowledge such unrestricted correlation as Spinoza advocated. His contention is that "the psychical is of the very texture of the functioning brain," subject I suppose to psycho-functional correlation. If, then, the psychical be novel, "we have on our hands only the general question of the origin of the novel." "Frankly it seems to me," he says, "that there is novelty of an undeniable sort at every level of reality, but that here only are we on the inside so to speak" (p. 319).

Here we agree. But can it confidently be asserted that only at a certain level of neural functioning or even that only in organic functioning does correlation obtain? If this question be regarded as too speculative, let us ask: How far down "on the inside so to speak" does correlation extend in us? There is at any rate something to be said for the view that no limits can be set to its downward extension; that not only receptor-patterns but all the physico-chemical changes they involve have psychical correlates which if not directly still indirectly contribute to conscious "awareness"; that just as physical novelty involves the continuance of lower levels of physical existence, so does psychical novelty involve a continuance of lower levels of psychical existence. I am not prepared to admit that such a view " builds too exclusively upon mental contents and on introspective psychology." Nay, rather I regard it as an acknowledgment which on broad philosophical grounds is contributory to a constructive theory of the world supplementary to its interpretation in terms of evolutionary naturalism.

Such a constructive theory is openly and avowedly a philosophical creed which purports to be supplementary to this or that policy of naturalistic interpretation. In credal terms certain acknowledgments are accepted in an attitude of belief. Of course, in like attitude they may be rejected; or they may be relegated to the suspense account of strictly agnostic doubt, poised between the " yes " of acceptance and the " no " of rejection, as beyond the reach of positive evidence for or against them. In such credal terms I believe in a physical world at the base of the evolutionary pyramid and involved at all higher levels; I believe that throughout the pyramid there are correlated attributes and that there is one emergent process of psycho-physical evolution; and I believe that this process is a spatio-temporal manifestation of immanent Activity, the ultimate Source of those phenomena which are interpreted under evolutionary naturalism.

INDEX

Acceleration, in general theory of relativity, 262.
Acknowledgment, 24, 27, 33, 59, 111, 116, 141, 176, 222, 303.
Activity, 13, 61, 112, 192, 205, 208, 289, 303, 309.
Advenience, of physical influence, 51, 213.
Affirmation, 303.
Againness, place of in memory, 121.
   implies conscious revival, 145.
Alexander, S.—
   Emergent scheme, 9.
   space-time, 18.
   deity, 25.
   mind, 25, 29.
   nisus, 11, 30.
   God, 34.
   the non-mental, 40.
   relation, 67, 69.
   mark of past, 147.
   status of beauty, 225.
   colour as non-mental, 231.
Apprehension, 46, 51, 103, 105, 176, 196, 225, 231, 233, 235, 243, 265, 267, 273, 305.

Basis, of reference, 95, 114.
Beauty, realistic treatment of, 224.
Bergson, Henri—
   Science and metaphysics, 116.
   Disparate orders of being, 149.
   Doctrine of images, 152 ff.
   Pure and concrete perception, 157.
   Survival of past images, 159.
   recollection and memory-images, 162.

Berkeley, G.—
   idea and attribute, 39.
   relation involves act of mind, 68.
   esse est percipi, 78.
   consideration, 84.
   visual language, 238.
   causation and Causality, 292.
Bifurcation of nature, 233 ff.
Bradley, F. H., infinite regress, 75.
Brain, evolved on distance-receptors, 212.
Broad, C. D.—
   causal probability, 280.
   causal activity, 289.
Browning, R., *Abt Vogler* quoted, 4.

Carr H. Wildon—
   personal memory-images, 151.
   relatedness for neo-idealism, 181.
Causality, distinguished from causation, 89, 274, 290.
Cause, concept of, 275.
   in exact science, 276.
   as precedent to effect, 278.
   in historical treatment, 283.
   ground and conditions, 285.
   immanent and transeunt, 286.
   proportionality, 287.
Classical transformation, 257.
Colour, as non-mental, 225, 231.
   as projicient, 227.
Colour-signs, 236.
Clifford, W. K.—
   the eject, 198.
   4-dimensional scheme, 253.
   on the concept of cause, 276.

INDEX

Conatus, Spinoza's use of word, 132.
Conscious *of* and conscious *in*, 40, 149.
Consciousness, some criteria of, Apprehension or projicience, 49, 51.
 reference, 94, 199.
 felt againness, 108, 126, 135.
 felt coming and going, 146.
Construct, of object, 55.
 geometrical, 244.
 space-time frame, 253.
Contact-pattern, 48, 218 ff.
Container, space and time as, 249-252.
Contemplation, 43, 304.
Correlation, 25, 62, 140, 193, 199, 201, 307.
Creed and policy, 174.
Critical realism, 303.

Dependence and involution, 15-18, 60, 130.
Descartes, René, Causation and Causality, 290.
Dewey, John, stages of thinking, 173.
Distance-receptors, 46, 55-58, 211.

Effective relatedness, 20, 71.
Effluent event, 210.
Einstein, A., 257, 262.
Eject, 198.
Ejicience, 199 ff.
Emergent and resultant (Lewis), 2.
 Emergents unpredictable, 5, 65, 281.
Enjoyment, 27, 120, 168.
Evolution, the word used in two senses, 111.
Evolutionary naturalism, 302.
External relations, 76 ff.
Extrinsic and intrinsic, 19, 64, 69, 184.

Finding and seeking, 108.
Force, 21, 133, 149, 263, 277.
Frames of reference, 258.

God—
 as directive Activity, 33, 61.
 as Nisus, 34, 36, 301.
 as Efficient, 89.
 as Eternal, 63, 116, 141, 172.
 as Causality, 291, 301.

Heteropathic laws, 2.
Hume, David—
 phenomenalism of, 58.
 causation and Causality, 293.
Huxley, T. H.—
 personal touch with, v.
 Neurosis and psychosis, 144.
 Evolution and Ethics, 206.
Hypostatisation, 66, 149.

Images, under our hypothesis, 153.
 on Bergson's doctrine, 154 ff.
Imputed mind, 197.
Infinite regress, escape from, 75.
Influent event, 210.
Installing oneself within a system, 190, 221, 246.
Internal relations, 76 ff.
Intervenient organic events, 52, 213.
Intrinsic and extrinsic, 19, 64, 69, 184.
Involution and Dependence, 15 ff., 60, 130.

Kant, I., causation and Causality, 295.

Laird, John, beauty as a quality, 224.
Leibniz, G. W.—
 intellectus ipse, 18.
 Actus purus, 295.
 causation and Causality, 294.
Lewes, G. H., emergents and resultants, 2.
Local time, 53, 170, 255, 283.
Locke, John—
 on relation, 67.
 primary qualities, 186.
 power as Causality, 294.
Loose-endedness, attitude towards, 179.

INDEX

Lorentzian transformation, 260.

Mach, Ernst, the concept of cause, 276.
Meaning, perceptual, 43, 97.
Measurement, primarily based on contact, 218.
Mechanism, an interpretation in terms of resultants, 8.
Memory, tentative scheme of, 119.
  as disparate order of being, 149.
Mill, J. S., heteropathic laws, 2.
  on cause, 280.
Mind, different senses in which the word is used, 29, 37.
  is mind emergent? 37, 105, 136.
  as a physical category, 307.
Minding and the minded, 35.
  both included under mind, 41.
  both within the person, 50.
Mnemic causation, 283.
Moore, G. E., reference to use of "direct apprehension," 46.

New realism, 56, 77, 99, 106, 170, 196, 225, 267-8, 271, 306.
Nisus, 11, 30, 34, 36, 301.
Non-mental, the, 40, 52.
  colour as, 225, 231.
  image as, 240.
Nunn, T. Percy, on new realism, 56, 182, 268.

Object, as ingredient (Whitehead), 44.
  ambiguity of word, 98.
Objective, as minded, 40.
  clothing, 49, 304.
  world, 47, 195, 217, 233, 304.

Patterns, not only spatial but qualitative, 153.
Phenomenalism, 53.
  Bergson's variant of, 154.
Perception, 43, 152, 304.
  Pure and concrete (Bergson), 157.
Place, assigned and located, 53, 228.

Poincaré, H., Stress on relations, 183.
Policy and creed, 174, 270.
Presentation, 41, 100.
Primitive mind and primitive psychical system, 110.
Probability in respect of resultants and emergents, 281.
Projection, in third division of space, 49.
  applied to time, 251.
Projicience, 49, 105, 196, 213, 238, 243, 261, 265.
Properties as extrinsic, 19, 64, 185, 187.
  as acquired characters, 191, 226.
Psychic additions (Whitehead), 233.
  signs, 236.
Psycho-functional correlation, 307.

Qualities, as intrinsic, 19, 64.
  primary and constitutive, 186.

Reality, relatedness a mark of, 177.
  intrinsic and extrinsic, 188.
  levels of, 203.
Receptor-event, 210.
Receptor-patterns, 45.
Recognition, contemplative and perceptual, 122.
  characteristic of mind, 135.
Record under contact, 219.
  visual and optical, 244, 267.
Referable, the, distinguished from reference in being, 95, 114.
Reference, conceptual, 91.
  perceptual, 95.
  to source, 99.
  follows line of behaviour, 107.
  place in memory scheme, 119.
Reflection of images (M. Bergson), 155.
Registration, in memory scheme, 119.
  as pervasive at all levels, 132.

INDEX

Relatedness, extrinsic and intrinsic, 19, 69.
  effective and non-effective, 20, 71.
Relations indivisible, 74, 218.
  not terms, 75.
  external and internal, 76 ff.
  sense and direction, 80 ff.
Relativity, and relatedness, 243.
  principle of, 244.
  special theory, 259.
  general theory, 262.
Renewal of experience, 125, 127, 137, 138.
Re-presentation, 42.
Resultant and emergent (Lewes), 2.
  Resultants give continuity, 5.
  basis of mechanism, 8.
Retention, primary, 128.
  secondary, 128.
  tertiary, 138.
  a pervasive feature, 133.
  and *conatus*, 132.
Reverence, emergent character of, 4.
Revival, a factor in reference, 96.
  characteristic of life, 135.
Russell, Bertrand—
  public and private sensations, 57.
  prejudice and theory, 59.
  words and relations, 75.
  sense of relation, 80 ff.
  referent and *relatum*, 95.
  place of sense-datum, 210, 251.
  concept of cause, 276.
  mnemic causation, 283.

Seeking and finding, 108.
Selective synthesis, 302.
Sellars, R. W., *Evolutionary Naturalism*, 302.
Semicircular canals, afford meaning in terms of rotation, 247.
Sense-datum, 42, 210, 251.
Sherrington, Sir Charles—
  distance-receptors, 46.
  and the brain, 49, 55, 212.
  projicience, 49.
Shinn, Miss Milicent, the idea of vision, 54.

Significance, conceptual, 44, 96, 163.
Solidarity, 149, 307.
Solipsism, escape from, 195 ff.
Space-time, 9, 18.
  frame, 250.
Spatial frames, 243.
Spinoza, B.—
  unrestricted correlation, 26.
  attributes not causally related, 28, 202, 236.
  conatus, 132.
  God, 172.
  causation and Causality, 291.
Storage of memories, 168 ff.
Stout, G. F.—
  use of word "presentation," 100.
  original reference to source, 102 ff.
  primary and secondary retention, 128.
Stuff and substance, 69, 192.
  of mind, 194, 232.
Subjectivity, 161.
Substance as gotogetherness, 192.
  as implying Activity, 209.
Superposition, under contact, 219.

Tensor transformation, 264.
Term, restricted use of word, 72 ff.
Three-entity situations, 84.
Time, flow of, 24, 147, 252.
Transformation, Classical, 257.
  Lorentzian, 260.
  tensor, 264.

Virtual images (Bergson), 154.
Vision, 46, 54, 210 ff.
Vitalism, 12.

Whitehead, A. N.—
  object as ingredient, 44.
  bifurcation of nature and psychic additions, 233.
  local time, 283.
Wrinch, Miss Dorothy, on terms, 74.
Wundt, W., creative resultants, 4.

GEN. THEO. SEMINARY
LIBRARY
NEW YORK

GENERAL THEOLOGICAL SEMINARY
NEW YORK